THE SHAPE OF CHRISTOLOGY

THE SHAPE OF CHRISTOLOGY

STUDIES IN THE DOCTRINE OF THE PERSON OF CHRIST

John McIntyre

SECOND EDITION

T&T CLARK
EDINBURGH

T&T CLARK LTD
59 GEORGE STREET
EDINBURGH EH2 2LQ
SCOTLAND

First edition published by SCM Press Ltd, 1966
Second edition published by T&T Clark Ltd, 1998

ISBN 0 567 08646 1

British Library Cataloguing-in-Publication Data
A catalogue record for this book is available from the British Library

Typeset by Waverley Typesetters, Galashiels
Printed and bound in Great Britain by Bell & Bain Ltd, Glasgow

CONTENTS

Preface   vii

Preface to the Second Edition   ix

PART I
CHRISTOLOGICAL METHOD

1. What is Given in Christology?   3
2. The Method of Christology   25
3. Models in Christology   49

PART II
CHALCEDON-BASED MODELS

4. The Two-Nature Model   83
5. The Psychological Model   115
6. The Revelation Model   145

PART III
PROCESS CHRISTOLOGY

7. David R. Griffin   177
8. John B. Cobb, Jr   195
9. Norman Pittenger   225

PART IV
NEO-CHALCEDONIAN CHRISTOLOGY

10. John Macquarrie   259
11. Gerald O'Collins, SJ   283
12. What, then, of Chalcedon?   307

Index of Names and Subjects   337

PREFACE

It was a wise Providence which inspired Dr Warfield to insert in the terms of the Annie Kinkead Warfield Lectureship an instruction that 'every Lecturer shall publish the Lectures within twelve months after their delivery'. Indeed, the proverbial slip 'twixt the cup and the lip is as nothing compared with that between lectures and publication. So the Warfield Lecturer cannot but be grateful that even though grace abounds, the law nevertheless compels. The text published here formed the substantial basis of the Lectures as actually delivered in February 1965.

The invitation to deliver the Annie Kinkead Warfield Lectures is in itself honour sufficient, but the event surpasses even the expectation. I should like, therefore, to place on record my very sincere appreciation of the generous welcome extended to me by President and Mrs G. I. McCord and by Professor G. S. Hendry of Princeton Theological Seminary, and of the warmth of the hospitality shown to me by Professor and Mrs James Barr in their own home. It would be ungracious of me not to mention also the stimulus provided by the attendance and attention of the audience in the Miller Chapel, and by the questions of the students in discussion thereafter.

New College
University of Edinburgh
Whitsuntide 1965

PREFACE TO THE SECOND EDITION

When the opportunity was offered to me to 'update' the original text of *The Shape of Christology* (1966), the question arose as to which direction I should follow, for a number of movements in theology had emerged since then to influence christological definition, such as feminism and liberation theology, narrative theology and theologies sensitive to post-modernist themes. In the end I decided to follow through the Chalcedonian interest which dominated the 1966 volume and had far from spent itself in the modern period, and which therefore represented un-finished business.

The first main extension, then, was towards the christologies inspired metaphysically by, and dependent upon, process philosophy. These, while they set themselves steadfastly against Chalcedon, remained deeply under its spell in two respects. First, it was in reaction to what they considered the philosophical inadequacies of the metaphysics associated with Chalcedon that they turned to process philosophy to make good these defects. To that extent they remained within its magnetic field, even if at the negative pole, but were positively influenced by it even to the point of employing some of its concepts. Secondly, that influence was in evidence in another way, for some of these process christologies, as they might be called, sought a kind of validation in showing their conformity with, or at least their non-violation of, the main thrust of Chalcedon.

In order to prove, then, that Chalcedon was not a spent force even in the 1990s, I thought it would be instructive to explore the christological thinking of two of the most eminent writers in the field – Canon John Macquarrie and Professor Gerald

O'Collins, SJ. They had themselves lived intellectually through the theological vicissitudes of the intervening decades, and had emerged loyal to Chalcedon as in a special way related to the core of the Christian faith concerning Jesus Christ. Thereafter, it remained to assess the reasons for the lasting validity of the Chalcedonian Definition, and to look afresh at the roles it continues to play in our thinking about the person of Jesus Christ.

Advent 1997

PART I

CHRISTOLOGICAL METHOD

1

WHAT IS GIVEN IN CHRISTOLOGY?

If we were asked to give in a summary form *the* distinguishing characteristic of Protestant theology in our time, many of us would reply that it is its christocentric quality which claims this title. And the evidence would be convincing. It could be shown that not since the days of Marcion has there been such an exclusive emphasis upon the absolute significance of Jesus Christ, not indeed in the whole history of Christian doctrine has there been any attempt such as we have seen in our day to locate revelation only in the person of Jesus Christ and to deny its occurrence elsewhere in God's creation. Ours is the period of theology which invented the phrase 'Christ, the centre of history' and interpreted historical process as a span between his first and his second comings, so that all events contained therein derived their significance from this twofold reference. It is an emphasis which has appeared also in the more strictly biblical disciplines – in the contentions that Christ stands between the Old Testament and the New, as the person to whom the one points forward and the other points back; or that Christ is the unity of the Old and New Testaments; or again that the two Testaments are 'all about Christ' and that typological exegesis is the only proper method for the right presentation of the biblical message.

TWO FORMS OF CHRISTOCENTRICISM

In the doctrinal field, christocentricism has come to have two meanings. First, it may be applied to a process in which doctrines

3

are presented, not *seriatim* like pegs on a line only externally related to one another, but by being severally related to the doctrine of the person of Jesus Christ. For example, the doctrine of creation, which on the *seriatim* method of doctrinal presentation would come at the beginning of systematics and thereafter be forgotten about, on a christocentric presentation is at once related to God's redemptive purpose in Christ; creation is in order to redemption; the first creation is fulfilled in the new creation. The covenant with Israel is the prototype and promise of the covenant which will be fulfilled in the broken bread and the wine poured forth. If the fulfilment cannot be understood apart from the promise, *a fortiori* the promise is empty without the fulfilment. So, too, with eschatology; it is no longer taken solely as the final stage in the economy of redemption, the ultimate consummation in the end-time of the whole process: it has been integrated with christology and now it stands at the centre of the interpretation of Christ, and it adds a new dimension to the scale of the understanding of the person of Christ. Christology, in other words, becomes the medium of theological integration and its intensional complexity.

Christocentricism has, however, taken a second form in modern theology, namely, that of providing a basic interpretative structure for the explication of other areas of doctrinal material. In the two natures and one person of the Chalcedonian Christ is discerned an analogical formula which can be employed in areas of theology that are not immediately recognisable as christological. For example, it is not uncommon to interpret the unity of divine and human in the Church or in the Bible or in the sacraments, in a manner determined by the co-existence of human and divine in Jesus Christ. Of course, this application has to be strictly analogical and not univocal, or at once heresies would arise in the interpretative process. But the mention of heresy – and heresy is never very far away when the Chalcedonian definition is under consideration – draws our attention to a further noteworthy feature of the christocentricism of modern theology, namely, that it provides a working criterion of theological truth. In other words, christocentricism is not merely a medium of theological expression in our time; it is a norm of theological validity. It has been largely pressed into this office, as we shall see later, because of the failure of so many of the norms which have operated with such cogency in the past. Such norms as the Holy Scriptures themselves, the confessions of our churches (the classical creeds or the *Westminster Confession*) or even 'the inner testimony of the Holy Spirit', have all, for one reason or another, proved unable to operate as a single un-ambiguous criterion by which a point of doctrine could be settled with utter finality.

NEW FUNCTIONS OF CHRISTOLOGY

It is by this time clear, then, that christology has come to exercise in theology a range of functions for some of which it was not originally designed: in this range we find exegetical, expository and hermeneutical as well as normative and critical elements. At this point two sets of questions inevitably arise. First, to what extent can the old christology forged in the controversies of the fourth and fifth centuries and re-expressed in the sixteenth, sustain the weight of responsibility placed upon it in this new and varied context? In other words, have the many changes both within theology and in the cultures within which Christian theology has been from time to time formulated in any way affected the adequacy of the classical christology to the tasks which it has been set? Secondly, to what extent have these new tasks altered the character of the classical christology itself? Has it remained a constant in the variety of functions to which it has been adapted? It will be my main contention that classical christology has come under severe strain in these new settings in which it has of late found itself and that a crisis has begun to develop which can only be resolved by a radical reassessment of the basic *shape* of this central doctrine of the Christian faith as expressed today. These questions which I have been raising are so closely related to the basic structures of christology that no attempt to answer them can easily escape the more radical analysis.

THE GIVEN

The *shape* of any discipline may be regarded as a function of at least three variables: the given upon which the discipline operates; the models which it employs in the systematisation, organisation, exposition, analysis, interpretation and, in some cases, even the defence, of this given; and, thirdly, the method followed in operating these models. All three of these variables coalesce in the determination of the shape of christology, as they do of any other discipline; and our first task is to examine the first of these variables, namely, the given. Perhaps it may be of value, partly to throw light upon the christological usage, partly to point out the contrast between the christological and the ordinary usage, to bring out the different elements involved in the ordinary notion of the given. What we are not prepared for, perhaps, is the variety of content which the ordinary usage has, and which is a partial explanation of the complexity of the christological uses. The various meanings of the given are as follows.

THE GIVEN AS IMMEDIATE DELIVERANCE

First, the given may mean exactly what it says: it is that which is given directly to the percipient, or the knower. Here several points are being made. For example, the method of knowing is direct intuition of one kind or another. The given is the immediate deliverance of some external situation, which is immediately intuited. The percipient or the knower is not thought of as himself contributing anything to the given; indeed, any such contribution would at once introduce the possibility of falsification or misrepresentation. It would certainly reduce the purity of the given. In this sense, then, the given has a kind of intrinsic self-evidence; it carries its authority with it; it is thought to impose itself on the human mind from the outside. It is contrasted with interpretation, which is a conceptualisation of its simplicity. The given also has or is thought to have the quality of immunity to being doubted. In itself, it is unquestionable in a manner denied to the conclusions which we draw from it or the interpretations we impose upon it. It is regarded, consequently, as having a degree of universality which is denied to the latter additions to it; it is acknowledged by all who care to inspect the situation which it constitutes. The given, in this form, becomes a court of appeal, something to be cited in order to clinch an argument, something compelling, something immediately inspectible and readily accessible.

THE GIVEN AS LOGICAL POINT OF DEPARTURE

Secondly, a more precise form of the first meaning of the given is to be derived from Euclidean geometry. There the given is the premises from which the conclusion is to be logically deduced. In proceeding to the conclusion we do not add anything by way of private interpretation to what is already stated in the given, or implicit in it. The latter qualification has to be made, because the entire axioms and postulates of Euclidean geometry are not enunciated every time the given of any theorem or proposition to be proved is stated. But they are, as it were, contained within the given as conditioning its very statement. In proceeding deductively to the conclusion, the *QED* which every schoolboy knows, we are moving within the framework of an aprioristic conceptual system. While recognising that there are other, and contradictory, accounts of what is involved in deductive reasoning, I am not at the moment concerned with them; for there are enough people who take the presently expounded account of the given to justify our nominating it as one of the accepted accounts of what is meant by this complex term. A distinction is here being drawn which will be seen to be of importance in the christological context between the given as the basis of interpretations which may variously be imposed upon it (our first sense) and the given as the starting-point of a demonstration within a conceptual system (our second sense), a demonstration which follows by strict logical steps from the given as the premises. On the first sense, the given contains only what is immediately inspectible; on the second, it is rather like an iceberg with its major fraction submerged, and accessible only by dint of deep, submarine probing.

THE GIVEN AS THE PROBLEMATICAL

Thirdly, there is a view of the given, first expounded to me by my old teacher, Professor N. Kemp Smith, which regards it not as the crystal clear premise of an argument or deduction which can be drawn from it, but as a situation which in itself is essentially problematical. In terms of our first sense of the given it may be immediately inspectible – as an event in the sense-perceptible world, as a sensory experience more closely related to our bodies, as an emotional disturbance, or as a reading on an instrument. It may be open to public and universal examination, and it may force itself upon us with a certain undeniable objectivity. But for Kemp Smith none of these qualities of the given would constitute its *differentia*, which would be its capacity to present itself to us as a situation which was not self-explanatory, or self-authenticating – as a situation which was essentially a problem requiring some solution. The given would have this quality primarily because it was not immediately to be explained in terms of the information that we already had at our disposal; in fact, it might seem at some points to contradict established knowledge and to call it in question.

Understanding the given in this way, Kemp Smith saw it as the springboard of all genuine advance in knowledge – ranging from the simplest visual problem created by the appearance of the station to move as we sit apparently at rest in the train, to the complex enigmas created for the scientist by the odd behaviour of the denizens of the microscopic world. So far from lulling us into any sense of security by its self-assurance and precision of definition, the given creates a world of difficulties for us; it may even occasion despair and deep confusion of mind; it is not a blinding light or the final clarity. But it *is* creative – creative of that process which is only finally successful when the problem of the given is solved in a wider context of comprehensibility. One point is particularly noteworthy, namely, that a certain amount of perceptiveness is required in order to know when the given is problematical. It must be *seen* to be contradicting established principles and laws before it acquires the character of the problematical. It has to be seen to have a certain oddness before it sets genuine problems, which once set leave no peace short of their solution. Men had been observing apples falling from the beginning of time, on one occasion at least to their sorrow, but it was the perceptiveness of Newton which discerned the problem within the given and which finally compelled the problem to yield its solution, or at least its adequate description, if solution is no longer the permissible word in this connection. In a very real sense then, it is the problematical quality of the given which constitutes it as the given, because it singles it out from what has been called 'the manifold of sense', or 'the big, buzzing, blooming confusion', for precise and particular observation, analysis, description and solution.

A further respect in which this third sense of the given differs from the previous two is that whereas on their rendering the given remains unaltered throughout the subsequent process of interpretation or deduction, in a very real way the sheet-anchor of the whole process, on this rendering the given does alter character as the problem it sets is gradually solved; it acquires depth, richness of context, fuller meaning, as we would say. In a rather interesting way the authoritative quality which attached to the given in sense one above reappears in sense three in a normative quality which it now evinces: *it* is the problem which any solutions must solve. If any aspect of the given has been misrepresented, distorted or omitted, then the solution is to be discounted. If, therefore, the given is the starting-point of the enquiry, it is also the point of final return, for any explanation of the given stands or falls by what it makes of the problems set by the given.

THE GIVEN AS THE EXTERNALLY ORIGINATED

Fourthly, there is another way of looking at the given – much less romantic and highfalutin; one which regards the given as an abstract, something rather artificially excerpted from a very complex totality, and quite falsely regarded as capable of self-existence. Clearly there is implied here, as indeed in all three previous senses, an epistemological theory, namely, that what we know is an amalgam of external stimulus and categorical conceptualisation. The given is thus equated with the content of consciousness attributable to external stimulus; but in the nature of the case it is not able to have any existence apart from the total cognitive situation, or if it does have such an existence, it has it in a totally different form; there can be no such thing as an unsensed sensum, or an unperceived perception. Sense four may be distinguished from sense one by the fact that while in sense one the given, as in sense four, comes from beyond the knowing or experiencing subject, in sense one the given has independence of existence, ultimacy and authority, whereas in sense four it has none of these attributes. This difference is largely due to the fact that sense one reflects a naive realistic epistemological theory which is often rather innocently carried over into theological epistemology, as we shall see, with rather unfortunate consequences.

THE GIVEN AS PRIVATELY APPREHENDED

Fifthly, the instability of the given as defined in sense four induces me to propose a modification of this sense, according to which the given would be the total situation, what is imposed upon the knowing or perceiving mind from the outside plus the categorical conceptualisation or any other interpretation present at the start. This sense is a much less sophisticated form of the term than that presented by Kemp Smith. As I have said, it does not carry any of the elaborate qualities assigned to the given in senses one and two; but it does have the merit of drawing attention to one or two important considerations. For example, as against sense one, it recognises that what is given for one person may differ from what is given for another, even though there is sufficient material common to the two 'givens' to justify their being taken for the same situation. It does also draw attention to the fact that the given from which we start in any discipline is an extremely complex situation which is a combination of private and public, subjective and objective, externally imposed and personally interpreted circumstances. Even in an apparently abstract, aprioristic discipline, where the axioms and postulates, the theorems and the propositions have apparently highly rational and objective character, they nevertheless reflect quite private and personal systems of preference and selection.

THE GIVEN AS THE SUBJECT-MATTER OF A DISCIPLINE

So, sixthly, we might say that the given of any discipline is its subject-matter – what it is all about. This sense would include sense five but relate it to a discipline – making it the content of the discipline as well as its starting-point, making it the central subject of the discipline as well as its initiating circumstances. In this sense are gathered up most of the other things which we have been saying about the given; for the subject-matter of any discipline is basically something imposed upon us and not of our own arbitrary devising; it is, too, the premises from which all our investigations flow; with its problems and enigmas it stimulates and sustains our curiosity and concern; and it forms the contextual framework within which the whole discipline operates.

ATTITUDES TO THE GIVEN

Certain points may now be summarised from the review of the use of the idea of the given in certain intellectual disciplines. To begin with, we can see that the term applies to a considerable variety of content, some interpreters preferring to limit it to a fairly narrow, sophisticated minimum, others regarding it as a fairly comprehensive if somewhat unsystematised starting-point of the discipline. One of the major tasks, therefore, confronting any discipline is to define the range and content of its given. Another important point emerging from this preliminary discussion is that correlative to the interpretation of the given is a certain attitude on the part of the practitioner. Very often the given specifies the attitude to be taken up to it, but it is also permissible, as we shall see, to adopt a variety of attitudes to the given even where it is interpreted in one single way. The cases of a one-one correlation between the given and the appropriate attitude are fairly obvious. Where the given is interpreted as self-authenticating, then its presentation to the observer is compulsive; his proper attitude is receptivity and acknowledgement. If, on the other hand, the given comes in the form of the problematical, then a blind acceptance of its self-presentation would yield only confusion. The correct attitude here is to question, to analyse, to probe, to wonder. Where the given is the clearly enunciated premises of a deduction to be drawn from them, then the application of strict logical thinking to this process is what the situation demands.

We are, therefore, in fact now taking a further step and saying that the given not only determines the appropriate attitude to adopt towards it; it also prescribes the method we must follow in its explication. It should be added that such prescription may take the form of permitting several possibilities, while at the same time eliminating certain others. There is not always a necessary correlation between one interpretation of the given and one certain attitude.

The given, moreover, may be used to serve a variety of ends, and it will be such ends which determine which of the methods permitted by the given is employed in the event. For example, let us take as our given a system of visual sense-data which would be identified at Sotheby's, London, as a painting by the late Albert Namatjira, a member of the Arunta tribe in Australia. This given, in the context for which it was designed, becomes the subject of aesthetic pleasure, and this attitude will determine the method we shall follow in further examining and describing it. But this same given may happen to be in the room where the Aristotelian Society is having its meetings, and the picture, now treated strictly as a collection of visual sense-data, features as such as an illustration of the term 'sense-data' in a series of arguments. In this context, it is entertained in a rather different attitude; and the method of dealing with it is vastly different from that of aesthetic appreciation. It is the method of analysis and investigation, of perceptual consideration and even of pure sensing. Again, because Namatjira is reputed to have made his own pigments by an expert use of some of the soils in central Australia, the colours in the picture may serve a geological or an agricultural purpose. The paints throughout may be submitted to chemical analysis and the colours in this context may be of great significance. The geological end determines quite clearly the method which the analyst follows in treating the samples of soil appearing in the picture. A psychiatrist, whose interest lies in a correlation between mental attitudes and artistic production, may detect in Namatjira's depiction of the loneliness of 'the dead heart of Australia' something of the social, religious and cultural vacuum which the advent of Western culture and Christianity has created for the native peoples of Australia. Finally, a photographer who has come to despair over the inability of the various commercial companies to produce a complete spectrum of reliable colour-reproductions – the companies that are good with the greens turn out a red that looks orange – might well see in Namatjira's colour system the faithfulness of total reproduction which still seems to baffle the efforts of modern photographic science.

To summarise the conclusions to be drawn from this illustration, we may say that the term, the given, may apply to a variety of content even in respect of the same situation; that the same single given appearing in a variety of contexts or subserving a variety of ends may allow of a variety of attitudes to be adopted to it; and finally, there is a close, though not always a one–one, correlation between the view taken of the given and the method employed in exploring it, and a uniformly close correlation between the attitude taken to the given and the method employed in exploring it.

THE GIVEN IN CHRISTOLOGY

In turning now to the given of christology, we may at once anticipate certain complicating circumstances which will prevent us from simply 'reading off' the characteristics of an immediately and directly intuitable situation. First, there is the combined force of the considerations which we have just presented, namely, that the very notion of the given is itself non-simple. It is no refutation of this point to argue that the theological image converts the non-simplicity of the secular content into transparent clarity, for in fact there is a carry-over, as we shall see, of the non-simplicity into the theological reference. Secondly, when we look specifically at the theological situation, we find that there are several candidates for the office of the given and that as a result one of the main tasks is to judge among their several claims or alternatively to discover how indeed they may be reconciled with one another. I can conceive of no more urgent task in contemporary theology, for the recognition of the claim of any situation to be the given at once invests it with an authority, an ultimacy, and a status which compels the obeisance of the other members of the theological firmament. Indeed I am inclined to think that most of our theological disagreements are ultimately disagreements about the given. Thirdly, it is noteworthy that there is a problem not only concerning the candidates for the office of the given, but also as to what the content of the given is, once one of the candidates has his/its claims recognised. This question is not simply a repetition of the second, because people who agree, say, that Christ is the given of christology, might radically disagree over the content to be assigned to this given. Fourthly, we shall expect the discussion of the given of christology to be incomplete without some examination of the methods to be followed according to the different conceptions of the given.

SCRIPTURE AS THE GIVEN

Perhaps the most obvious candidate for the office of the given in christology is Holy Scripture, particularly the New Testament. There is no doubt that in the classical formative periods of christology, it was the Scriptures which constituted the given – not simply for the orthodox whose formulae triumphed, but also for the heretics who contended to the last that orthodoxy was a misrepresentation of the given of Scripture. It is also true that in modern christological controversies it is common practice to quote Scripture as a final court of appeal as if it constituted a given common to all sides of the controversies. There is, there-fore, an almost immediately convincing case for affirming that Scripture is the given of christology, given in the sense of being literally and authoritatively definitive of all that is affirmed within christology; and that we ought forthwith to desist from further search. But the matter is not so easy as that – for a number of reasons.

First, it is doubtful whether anyone operates with the *whole* of Scripture as his given, so that this form of the given as authoritative would be valid only for someone who was a completely consistent fundamentalist. As soon as we allow any principle of selection to operate, and there are few people who do not, then we have departed from allegiance to the total givenness and the single prescriptiveness of Scripture. On this ground, it is not to be assumed that Scripture may not turn out to be the given in some other sense already defined.

Secondly, it has always been an essential part of the Reformed view of Scripture that its true meaning is only rightly discerned through the *testimonium internum spiritus sancti*. Whatever else this fairly complex doctrine may mean, it does at least imply that the meaning of Scripture cannot be simply 'read off', as one would rightly expect it to be were one dealing with an immediately intuitable and authoritative given. Thirdly, it is very doubtful whether any one of us can now read Scripture except through the medium of the numerous interpretative symbols which the Church has constructed to ensure our right understanding of Scripture. The function of the confessions formulated by the Reformers has not always been fully appreciated in this connection. The confessions have been, of course, correctly regarded as short summaries of the faith to be used as a basis for instructing the young and confuting heretics or unbelievers. But they also had initially a further purpose, namely, that of providing the interpretative structure for the right understanding of Scripture. It is here that our present lack of confessional clarity is proving to be most harmful, in that it deprives our contemporaries, and particularly those who have to teach the young, of the adequate means of catechetical interpretation of Scripture. If, then, we wish to persist with the view that the Scripture is the given, then we have in honesty also to acknowledge that it is a given which comes to us in an extremely confused mixture of credal, confessional and modern theological additions.

Fourthly, the researches of New Testament scholars have shown that the Scriptures bear many signs themselves of being interpretative, and that it is possible by judicious and careful comparison and criticism to uncover some passages among those immediately delivered by Scripture that are more original than others. Another way of stating this same matter takes a theological form: Scripture is not the given itself; it is the witness to the given. We shall later examine the claims of this something standing behind Scripture to be the given of christology, but at the moment we may simply note that in a sense Scripture is not self-contained or self-complete, and that in fact on its own confession it derives its authority from beyond itself. It cannot therefore be the given in the sense that it is ultimate or self-authenticating.

Fifthly, such a conclusion, however, does leave open the possibility that Scripture may still be the given of christology in that it constitutes both its starting-point and its finishing-point: it prescribes the problems and defines the issues with which a fully articulated and integrated christology must finally deal. Such is the position for which I intend finally to argue but in the meantime it is necessary to examine the claims of other candidates.

MINIMAL HISTORICAL CORE AS THE GIVEN OF CHRISTOLOGY

Dissatisfaction with the view that Scripture is the given of christology has led to departures in two directions. The first, following the acknowledgement that Scripture is itself an interpretation of certain prior historical events, leads to the contention that the given for christology is those basic un-interpreted events which would be accepted by an agnostic scientific historian as having happened. Christology is then presented as an elaboration of these basic data agreed upon by everyone: the agnostic differs from the Christian in his refusal to make what he believes to be an otiose interpreta-tion. *Entia non multiplicanda praeter necessitatem.* Christians differ from one another in the range they give to their inter-pretations.

This view has a certain a priori attractiveness and strength in that it resembles the epistemological theory which regards sense-data as the given of the perceptual situation, in which they are elaborated into physical objects. But the attractiveness ends there. For it inherits all the fallacies of that epistemological theory, and particularly its failure to realise that such apparently simple entities as sense-data or uninterpreted historical events are arrived at only after a great deal of very sophisticated conceptual thought. They never exist for anyone at any time as the simply given in any of our previously nominated senses. In fact, in order to exist at all they have to be embodied in situations in which interpretation has already taken place. In the case of christology, it is impossible even to describe the so-called uninterpreted given, the single common observable for unbeliever and believer alike; for any description involves immediate interpretation of one kind or another. This so-called given of christology has to be rejected as an abstraction, or a will-o'-the-wisp, one which nevertheless was pursued by many exponents of the historical Jesus school. But many who have no longer any sympathy with that school retain the idea that some such abstraction constitutes the basic core of the factuality or the historicity of Jesus' life and death, a core which might somehow be reached through the removal of successive layers of interpretation and elaboration. If, in fact, it did prove possible conceptually to reach some such minimal historical core, it would be quite wrong to characterise it as the given in any sense.

THE GIVEN AS GOD'S SELF-REVELATION IN JESUS CHRIST

A further departure from dissatisfaction with the view that Scripture itself is the given of christology is made in the direction of saying that the given is God's self-revelation in Jesus Christ. The Bible points beyond itself to the self-revelation of God, which thus imposes itself upon the believer. It requires no authority outside of itself to establish its credentials; it bears the marks of its own authenticity, and so commends itself to the believer that he is left without occasion for question or doubt. To be exposed to this reality to which the Bible witnesses is to be convinced by it. This self-revelation is the ultimate; it is normative of all else that is to be said about God. It demands a single attitude from us of obedience and worship; in this context anything else would be blasphemy or unbelief. It is immediately intuited and does not involve any interpretative process on the human side. That precisely is the reason for the prominence which such a view is given today in most conservative groups in modern theology – that it rejects the whole natural theological movement according to which God may be known by some process of argument from the created world, or from man's moral nature. God is known only in Jesus Christ and only because he comes to us from the other side of the infinite gulf that separates the Creator from the creature. The emphasis is a sound one and one which had to be made, but it is difficult to resist the question of whether it constitutes a finally valid answer to the question of the given of christology. In other words, it may be a perfectly valid answer to a question, but not to *this* question. Let me try to indicate what I mean.

The contention that in christology we have to deal with a subject-matter which is not the finest and ultimate flowering of human inventiveness is a perfectly permissible way of saying that at the core of christology there is an event, there is a person who comes from right outside of the human situation as we know it. This intrusion, this intervention cannot be reduced to some psychological compensation or to a hallucinatory status. Thus stated, this view can be clearly seen to be an anti-statement, a rejection of that form of liberalism which was prepared to have 'religion without revelation'. But its virtues as an anti-statement do not serve it well where positive issues are to be solved. What is contained in this given which is God's self-revelation? The short answer, one might say the conventional answer, is: God himself; but the unsatisfactoriness of this solution may be based on the following considerations. To begin with, it is obvious that the short answer at once raises the further questions of the nature, attributes and characteristics both of the person in whom the revelation is taking place and of the person who is there revealed. When these questions are in their turn answered, then many of the traditional biblico-theological, or credal or doctrinal formulae are produced. In present-day conservative theology, it is the Chalcedonian christological pattern which is presented as the form of the divine revelatory event. Now if it really is intended from the start that the given of christology is the traditional Chalcedonian picture of Jesus Christ and of the God who is his father, then perhaps this fact ought to be stated from the start, and not introduced half-way through the discussion under the guise of revelation to reinforce a position or an interpretation which can historically be shown to have other sources.

We shall later be returning to a fuller examination of the place of the idea of revelation in christology but at the moment we may make these further brief comments. The idea of revelation does not of itself add any *content* to the given of christology. It is an account of how we come by this given, or more correctly, of how this given comes to us. But of itself it may permit quite a wide range of doctrinal variation. For example, Barth and Brunner both use the idea extensively in their christological assertions, yet they also differ quite extensively. A defence of the position we have been examining might be made by pointing out that in the revelatory process the believer is directed beyond or through the medium of revelation to that which is being revealed. It is then a case of immediate knowledge of an independently existing and specifically characterised reality. Without considering whether it is right to regard Christ as a medium beyond or through whom we must pass in knowing God through revelation, we can say that this claim to have direct knowledge of totally revealed reality is not borne out by the history of the Christian Church or of Christian theology. Such history is in fact more suggestive of a situation in which there is a mixture of the given from without and of interpretation from the human side; or of a reality who would not be known were he not to present himself to us, but in our knowledge of whom we betray human aberrations and misunderstandings.

What has to be noticed, then, even at this early stage in our discussion, is that the term 'revelation' may serve a variety of purposes: it may be used to describe what God was doing. When the Word was made flesh – he was making himself known; it may refer to *what* is known, a content, a subject-matter generally acknowledged by believers; it may, finally, apply to what the individual knows, something specially revealed to him. All these senses are perhaps operative most of the time but the consequence is not utmost clarity.

THE GIVEN OF CHRISTOLOGY AS THE HERE-AND-NOW CHRIST

It is possible, however, particularly if we have strong existentialist sympathies, to give yet another account of the given of christology, namely, it is the self-presentation of Christ to me, or to the Church, in the here-and-now. Such a view would criticise the three previous views for laying too much emphasis upon the place which past events occupy in the given of christology – by seeking it either in old records, in a minimal historical core in past events, or in some past self-revelation of God. The given of christology takes place in the encounter which we have with Christ in the reality of the existential situation, the point where we hear the Word preached concerning the crucified and risen One and we respond in faith and obedience, and where we pass from unauthentic to authentic existence. Christology is then the analysis and explication of that immediately given situation, the delineation of its basic constituents and the elaboration of its implications. This view may be expressed within a very wide range of variants, from the extreme existentialist forms which are thought by their critics to reduce christology to a type of self-examination or contorted introversion, to those which express the situation in terms of the Word of God and see the given of christology as a here-and-now address of God to the believer. In grouping these several views together, we are not insensitive to the radical differences that separate them. But they are single in their emphasis upon the contemporaneity of the given with which we have to deal in christology, and it is an emphasis which we shall be obliged to retain in our final summary. In the hands of some of its exponents, however, this view has been either irresponsible in its disparaging of the historical elements in the Christian faith or at best equivocal in its assessment of the place to be assigned to the historical or the documentary within the given of christology. That disparagement and that equivocation must be corrected in our own final summary.

THE COMPLEXITY OF THE GIVEN OF CHRISTOLOGY

What then are we to say about the given of christology? To begin with, I should want to suggest that we ought not to feel compelled to choose any single one of the four views outlined above, to the exclusion of the others, but look rather to a conclusion which somehow integrates them all. Thus, while the given of christology is a self-presentation of Christ in the immediacy of contemporary existence, and while this self-presentation is effected with singleness of purpose, namely, for the salvation of a human soul, it nevertheless will be exposed on analysis to be extremely complex in structure. If we define christology as rational reflection upon the person, nature and claims of him with whom we have to do when we make the confession, 'I believe in the Lord Jesus Christ', then in the process of such analysis the simple given reveals itself to be an amazing complexity. Here are some of the constituents of this complexity. There are the documents of the Holy Scriptures, which are still the ultimate source from which we derive all knowledge of Jesus Christ, and which continue to sustain such knowledge and the reflection we impose upon them. To deny the Scriptures a place within the given or the historicity of the events recorded within them is to forget the rock whence we were hewn. Another constituent element within the given for many of us now must be the biblical criticism which is so constantly with us in all our Christian thinking. There are, too, passages which will for ever be coloured for me because of something which Calvin, or Luther, or Barth, or Bultmann, or Vischer, or Ebeling, has written about them; and the given of christology is for me informed by that kind of statement of theirs. The creeds of the Church, and the continuing living witness of the Church are now built into the very fabric of the given from which we start. In the Reformed Church, we somewhat pride ourselves on cutting away the tangle of tradition, forgetting both that tradition may be a genuine medium of interpretative insight and that by now we have created our own rather rigid traditions which have a greater rigidity for all our pretending that they do not exist. We must include within the complexity of this given also our own response. Christology happens only within a believing community, and the given upon which it rests is something which happens only to believers. This response, in obedience and love, in faith and worship, is therefore a constituent element of the initially given; and its presence there is an index to the existence of other constituents which might well be omitted or neglected.

There is, then, a prima facie singleness, simplicity and immediacy in the given which is a construct of a variety of constituent elements. There is, too, a compulsiveness and authority attaching to the *totality* of the given which requires of us the appropriate response of faith, obedience and love. To stop to argue in the face of such authority and compulsiveness; to ask whether it is not in fact an illusion, a deception of the senses, noises in the head taken for the voices of the angels – to do any of these things is to deny the Christ who comes to us in such immediacy and directness. But the moment we depart from the immediacy of this faithful, obedient and loving response, in order to analyse the constituent elements within the whole, certain consequences must be carefully watched. For example, we must not commit the pretence of carrying over into our theological analysis all the attitudes and responses appropriate to the specifically religious situation: theology is necessarily dependent upon faith, but it is not simply an extrapolation of faith. It has to be allowed the freedom to stand back, to criticise, to wonder, to question.

A still graver danger to watch is that of investing any one of the constituent elements of the given which yields itself to us in separation from the others in the process of analysis – the danger of investing any one of these with the ultimacy, the authority, the compulsiveness of the totality. The Chalcedonian christology may be a constituent in the given situation in which Christ here and now makes his offer of salvation to me or imposes some demand upon me; but it would be wrong to extricate this christology from this situation, to hypostatise it and assign to it the compulsive authority, the ultimate validity of Christ himself. The I–Thou philosophy of Martin Buber may elucidate and sharpen my understanding of Christ's address to me, but this fact does not justify the elaboration of this philosophy into a self-existent, autonomous system with final authority. So we may proceed, *mutatis mutandis*, with Heidegger's existentialism, Whitehead's philosophy of organism, or Collingwood's historical categories. In a sense, the history of theological controversy is the story of the way in which opponents have vied with one another in a passionate earnestness to find in the constituent elements of *their* given, the definition, validity and ultimacy which are the attributes proper only to Christ himself. By that way we reach the point where to question a man's theological convictions is taken by him and implied by us to question his faith. We are today very close to the point of identifying faith with theology, and there is no greater source of bitterness in controversy.

2

THE METHOD OF CHRISTOLOGY

What I have been calling the shape of christology is determined by three constituent elements – the given, the method followed in the study and exposition of this given, and finally, the models which are the media of description, analysis and examination of the given. Our immediate concern now is with the *method* of christology. Perhaps the proper starting-point is to indicate what exactly we intend by the term, and what we wish to comprehend within it. Such definition is all the more important at a time when most disciplines are becoming explicit and self-conscious about their methods.

ASPECTS OF METHOD

METHOD AS ATTITUDE TO THE SUBJECT-MATTER OF A DISCIPLINE

At a first glance, all that may be intended by the term 'method' may be the way the given of the discipline is handled, the attitude adopted by its practitioners. For example, if the given lies in the field of one of the natural sciences, then a certain enquiring, experimental, searching attitude is demanded, an unwillingness to rest short of the final explanation, a desire to question old, established positions. If the given lies in the field of the literary arts, then a certain feeling for the substance of the material is necessary, a degree of empathy, of penetration into the mind and feelings of the author; or in the visual arts, into the aesthetic objects, the painting or the sculpture. So too in the religious field, the case might run, it is only the worshipper who can handle the material of faith. The sceptic by the nature of the case is cut off from the very realities with which he wishes to deal. Indeed much has been made, in recent theology, of this notion that in order to study theology, we must have a properly faithful attitude, even a prayerful attitude. In Martin Buber's words, 'God is not to be expressed but addressed.' Certainly, then, the attitude of the practitioner is one element in the way he handles his material.

METHOD AS LOGIC

Secondly, the logic employed must be a further very important element in the method associated with any discipline. A certain mystique has been building up around the notion of logic. At one time philosophers thought, and indeed some still do, that there is a single logic to cover all forms of human thought, namely, the Aristotelian; and that all forms of human argumentation and inference are subject to the laws of valid inference enunciated in the so-called traditional formal logic. Even when other forms of inference were recognised, the *universality* of the forms of inference and the laws governing them, was never departed from. The result was that exercises in literary criticism, experimental physics, poetry, mathematics, theology and ethics, to name but a varied few of many possible areas of human endeavour, were expected to conform to the same laws of thought, the same principles of valid inference, and were judged accordingly. R. G. Collingwood in his *The Idea of History* (Oxford University Press, London, 1946, p. 209) gives an interesting example of such methodological empire-building:

> And just as in the seventeenth and eighteenth centuries there were materialists who argued from the success of physics in its own sphere that all reality was physical, so among ourselves the success of history has led some people to suggest that its methods are applicable to all the problems of knowledge, in other words, that all reality is historical.

Collingwood adds at once, 'This I believe to be an error.'

When the notion of logic, however, was extended to include not only laws of inference but kinds of statement, and the principles governing their permissibility, the way was open for a more radical criticism of some disciplines, and even for a demolition of some of their central concepts and subject-matter, in a way which was impossible under the older interpretation of logic as governing the laws of thought. It is an old story now of how A. J. Ayer and the logical positivists reduced metaphysics and theology, not to mention ethics and aesthetics, to the status of non-sense; an old story, even, how the idea of language-games opened up new possibilities of understanding these forms of alleged non-sense, and led the way to the conception of different logics for different disciplines. Theology has not been slow to seize the occasion of this respite to establish with considerable address and precision the claim to a specific way of thinking and arguing peculiar to its own subject-matter. How far this process may legitimately be carried in the exposition of theological method is a question which we propose to examine shortly; but for the moment the point stands that an essential constituent of any method is the logic followed in developing the discipline, the kinds of statement that are permissible, as well as the laws of inference that may be appealed to in validating an argument within the discipline.

METHODIC SHORT-CUTS AND 'PECULIAR LOGIC'

It may be worth while to observe in this connection that the logic that governs arguments within a discipline is not always explicitly stated. In fact such arguments are full of what we might call logical short-cuts, series of steps within the longer process of inference which are simply omitted because they have become self-evident for the practitioners of a discipline. The process is readily observed in an orderly system such as Euclidean geometry, where conclusions reached by elaborate propositional proof in the earlier theorems are embodied as constituent parts of later demonstrations, and have, by that time, become virtually self-evident. It requires an almost unnatural process of thought to prove that opposite angles of intersecting straight lines are equal. The process is not so easily observed in less orderly disciplines, but without it no discipline could make any progress whatsoever. Two comments may briefly be made on this process. The first is that revolutions tend to take place in any discipline when these long-unexamined processes of submerged argumentation are unearthed and shown to be false. The second comment is that the existence of this kind of short-cut argumentation is part-explanation of what is, to some extent at least, a delusion, namely, that every discipline has its own quite peculiar logic. In many cases, these short-cuts as I have been calling them, when set out in long-hand, can be seen to conform to ordinary sorts of logic, the simple traditional logic or one of the inductive logics. The basic process is in no way different from the variety of short-cuts which the experts have developed. Theology is as guilty of this type of short-cut as any other discipline; but it is emphatically not alone in this condition. Its presence in any discipline compels exponents to be extremely careful in the elaboration of the steps of their arguments for the benefit of the layman.

TACIT ASSUMPTIONS AS A PART OF METHOD

There are, however, certain other rather vaguer considerations which might immediately be thought to be part of method, but which are certainly relevant to the way in which any practitioner handles the material of his discipline. Primary among these must be the tacit assumptions embodied in the premises from which he starts, assumptions of which he may not be even barely conscious, assumptions, on the other hand, which may be long-established starting-points which he has never seen fit to question. Those assumptions both limit the kinds of answer which he may give to his problems, and determine the questions that can be raised. In some cases they may even so prescribe the character of reality itself that entities which fall outside the limits defined have to be rejected as illusory or hallucinatory.

One of the most important of these assumptions is the conception of the evidence that is to be regarded as valid or relevant or permissible within the discipline – the evidence, that is, that is thought good enough to establish the conclusions to which the whole discipline is directed. The question of evidence is one of those most hotly debated by Christians with non-Christians. Are the Gospel narratives permissible as historical evidence, or are they presented with so much prejudice and acknowledged selection that they are to be disregarded in any accurate assessment of primitive Christianity? Or again, is the world of inner experience, the world of religious experience, so influenced by the subconscious, or even socio-economic pressures, that it cannot be allowed as a reliable guide to anything but the state of the human psyche at any given moment? But the question of evidence is by no means confined to debates of Christians with non-Christians. It appears as the central question in many legal cases. It is never very far away from the sphere of international politics, whether the issue be underground nuclear testing in Siberia or trade relations with Cuba or Cyprus. In most political arguments, the controversy is really centred around the question of evidence – whether a certain political judgement is borne out by the evidence or contradicted by it; whether the conclusions expressed do in fact follow from the evidence agreed to by both sides; and so on.

In philosophical discussions for thirty years now at least, the question of the nature of evidence has been fully examined under the name of verification. In what ways are different kinds of propositions to be verified? Is one way applicable to all, or does the character of the discipline determine exclusively the form of verification to be applied to its subject-matter? It would be wrong to suggest that the problem of evidence is coterminous with that of verification. Some ways of verification may not entail the production of what would normally be called evidence. For example, *reductio ad absurdum* forms of verification may require nothing that is positively evidence; the closest approximation to it is a state of affairs which negates the absurd consequence. Yet as we proceed to think out the problems raised for theology by the controversy over verification, it may be of value to remember that the question about verification may be most readily handled as a case of pertinent and permissible evidence rather than as a case of a peculiar type of inference.

METHOD RELATED TO THE RANGE OF CONCLUSION

Another aspect of method which deserves mention is the range of conclusion which the discipline expects to reach; or if it may be stated in yet more general terms, the general conception of what the discipline is about, or what it is up to. This conception is by no means a fixed quantity. At one time, as has been so fully pointed out by E. L. Mascall (*Christian Theology and Natural Science*, Longmans, London, 1956, pp. 47ff) and I. T. Ramsey (*Models and Mystery*, Oxford University Press, London, 1964, *passim*), science was conceived of as presenting a pictorially accurate account of the true nature of reality, the models employed in scientific theories being more adequate photographs of entities which the human senses because of their insensitivity could not perceive. The exact relation of scientific theory to reality may still be a subject of intense debate, but however the participants may disagree in other directions, in this they are at one, in rejecting the photograph theory of scientific description. Particularly in physics is it the case that the ultimate conception of what the science is about is effectively transforming the method of the science itself. Psychology, in previous centuries, may have regarded itself as the science of mind, the science which exposes the nature of the self; yet, as research proceeds, the science has come to accept less ultimate, less ambitious aims, contenting itself with an analysis of the processes that take place within the mind, with the motives that condition behaviour and with the drives and instincts that maintain life itself, rather than with photographic descriptions of mind itself or the pure Ego or some such ultimate reality. Ian Ramsey (op. cit., pp. 28f) has in a characteristically forthright way uttered this warning to those psychologists who forget that they too are not directly describing reality through their models:

> Let not psychology repeat the errors of a Kelvin: let not psychology sponsor picturing models and then repeat the pseudo-puzzles and tall stories which characterized physics in an earlier day. By all means let psychology have its mathematical models; but more than ever let psychology realize that its topic is a person who will never – logically never – be transparent to any or all models, still less covered completely by picturing models.

One might be forgiven for wondering whether the same kind of change is not making itself evident in theology too. The history of theology abounds in words designed to describe with great precision, and, it may be added, with near-omniscience, the nature and attributes of God. But it is significant that in modern theology there is a certain reluctance to indulge in this kind of comprehensive account of the divine reality. Even Karl Barth, who might leap to mind as a notable exception to this general statement and be regarded, with considerable justification, as a person who has left little yet to be said about God, is nevertheless well safeguarded against possible criticism in this respect. He has fully reinstated the paradox of the hiddenness and the revealedness of God, so that our human descriptions in the nature of the case fail to penetrate God's hiddenness; whereas the very notion of revelation itself always carries the possibility of human misinterpretation, for the risen Christ may still be taken to be a gardener, even by one who loved him. The final element, then, for the purposes of our present discussion, constituting and determining the method of any discipline is this general idea of what it is up to, its conception of the kind of statement it thinks to be feasible within the limitations it has set itself, and its assessment of the kind of conclusion to which it may legitimately move, following upon the premises it has accepted.

THE ALLEGED UNIQUENESS OF CHRISTOLOGICAL METHOD

When, then, we come to consider the method of christology, we shall expect to find a certain complexity of content within its structure; but we shall not perhaps be altogether prepared for the very strong claims that will be made for the complete *uniqueness* of this method. The chief claim for such uniqueness is the fact that the subject of this discipline is completely unique. He is very God of very God, of one substance with God himself. Even though he shares our human nature, being of one substance with us as touching our humanity; nevertheless it is a human nature without sin, though bearing our sinfulness, and totally obedient to God's will, though suffering the penalty of human disobedience. Consequently, the point at which he is most completely one with us is the point also of dissimilarity. Otherwise redemption would be frustrated. While it has often been argued that the method of christology is consequently unique, the case is one which must be carefully stated in face of the fact that in the course of christological study we find ourselves employing a whole range of varying methods, no one of which is by itself unique. It may turn out that the uniqueness of christological method lies in the unique way in which the several methods combine in christology. That possibility we shall examine later.

For the moment, I want to set forth at least some of the methods we find ourselves employing in christology and of the consequences which follow from such employment; and this evidence must compel us to be more cautious than is usually the case in our expression of the uniqueness of christological method. It shall be my contention that the so-called christological method is in fact a complex of several distinct methods.

LITERARY-CRITICAL METHODS AS PART OF CHRISTOLOGY

First of all, given the truth of the statement that the people of Israel were the people of the Book, and that this description is rightfully extended to the Christian Church; given too the central place which the biblical Scriptures play in all theological systems and doctrinal formulations; it is an immediate consequence that a necessary first element in christological method is literary-critical method. Every theological student knows that there are hard-and-fast grammatical and syntactical rules governing the construction of Hebrew and Greek sentences; that these rules are of the same kind as, if not also at times even identical with, the rules that hold in secular literature; and that the penalties for breaking these laws are as unpleasant and inescapable as they are in secular literature. (A call to the ministry has never yet been accepted, though frequently offered, as an excuse for a certain unconcern about the minutiae of Hebrew and Greek grammar and syntax.)

When we move away from this obvious situation in two directions, however, the basic point is often forgotten. On the one hand, at the level of the actual words used in the Bible, a great myth has been building up in our time that biblical words behave in ways peculiar to themselves. Thus, they are thought to gather to themselves whole constellations of meanings, which are immediately to be evoked on every occasion on which these significant words occur; they are not allowed to occur in humility and simplicity, but only and ever with their full ceremonial dress. As soon as we recognise the socio-contextual character of human language, we become aware that the meaning of words for speaker and listener, for writer and reader, is largely dependent upon the setting in which they occur and the purpose they were designed to serve. Agreed that many settings recur, and even where they change there must be sufficient unity of purpose in the use of the words to justify their recurrence; nevertheless, words are not carefully assembled packages with listed contents, which can pass from speaker to hearer without loss of value, or even with sure promise of identification. While, therefore, biblical words occur at times in settings different from those in which, say, scientific words occur, still they behave in these settings as other words do in theirs and, further, they are to be found in ordinary settings even within the Bible itself. There lies

the danger of the theological word-book approach to the
biblical records: it induces us to think of the Bible as atoms of
essential biblical concepts in some loose conjunction, instead of
as a vehicle of communication by a person or persons to others,
all within specific social and political as well as economic,
geographical and cultural contexts.

Dogmatic checks on criticism

On the other hand, it has been felt at various times in the modern
period of biblical criticism that some kind of dogmatic check
ought to be put upon such criticism. Few of us would still adhere
to the view that all forms of textual or literary criticism are
inappropriately applied to the biblical material; but some thing
of that attitude has lingered on in the minds of many who are a
little uncertain about where the line is to be drawn beyond which
criticism may not pass. For some, this line has to be drawn before
the virgin-birth stories are shown, on purely literary-critical
grounds, to be untenable. For others, the abandonment of such
stories would cause no difficulty, but they on the other hand
would hold out strongly for the resurrection stories in spite of
the difficulties created by the comparison of the different
accounts, and reject any attempt to discredit them on critical
grounds for fear of endangering the truth of the resurrection
itself. Whether we are completely aware of the fact or honest
enough to acknowledge it, most of us have never quite faced the
problem of how far we are willing to allow criticism to go. Yet in
one sense, we must be prepared to give it its head, believing that
since our faith comes ultimately to us through the Scriptures, it
stands or falls with them. This is not to say that all forms of
criticism are equally permissible; some may be patently anti-
theistic or naturalistic, and so be totally inappropriate to the
biblical material. It is to insist, however, that literary and textual
criticism must be retained as an integral part of christological
method. Christology must constantly be returning to the original
account we have of its subject-matter. It must be constantly

re-examining the terms in which the Bible first described Jesus. It must be reassessing the stories which the primitive Church recorded about him. For that re-examination and reassessment there can be no substitute, and to it there can be no end.

HISTORICAL METHOD IN CHRISTOLOGY

Closely connected with the literary-critical method, and to some extent containing it within itself, historical method must be regarded as the second major constituent element in christological method. Cullmann once wrote (*Christ and Time*, ET, SCM Press, London, 1951, p. 23): 'All Christian theology in its innermost essence is biblical history.' If we were to take this remark seriously, we should begin to realise that theological method has a great deal more in common with historical method than with the method of the natural sciences. This latter assimilation is one – I think unfortunate – consequence of an over-emphasis upon the claim that theology is a science. It certainly is not a natural science and one wonders whether it is any more of a science than is history. At any rate, I wish for the present to explore the element of historical method engrossed in christological method.

At the start there is the obvious similarity between Christian theology and historical study that they are both ultimately concerned with records, with their authenticity, and with the veracity and reliability of their authors. It cannot be stressed too strongly that the records hold this key position in theology in view of tendencies in two directions to reduce their importance. On the one hand, as a consequence of the introduction into contemporary theology of historical scepticism – which was so obvious a feature of the *Concluding Unscientific Postscript* of Kierkegaard and which has appeared in Barth's writings as well as Bultmann's, for they have this common ancestor – there has resulted a quite drastic reduction of the minimum of acknowledged historical fact required to substantiate the Christian faith. The reality of this tendency towards historical scepticism has resulted in post-Bultmannian attempts to dehistoricise as well as to demythologise the faith.

The second tendency towards a reduction of the significance of the records comes from a quite different quarter, in fact from a point of extreme evangelicalism. It is the tendency so to empha-sise the reality of the present experience of Jesus Christ that the authenticity of the records becomes an irrelevant question. In a discussion with David Frost on BBC television, Dr Billy Graham came very close to admitting that if modern criticism should disprove the truth of the Bible, his faith, now so deeply personal a relationship with a really present Christ, would be unaltered. One cannot but admire the depth of such personal conviction, but one may be forgiven for wondering how long this kind of personal relationship with Christ could be sustained without the reinforcing structure of the biblical literature and its narratives about Christ. My own guess is that without that structure this sort of personal experience would very soon become a rather formless, if not also joyless, mysticism. Of course, in the state-ment to which I have referred I do not believe that Dr Graham was really presenting his own true position. The man who is so often heard to say, 'The Bible says . . .' can be in no doubt about the part which the Scriptures play in the creation and sustaining of his faith. To hold a historical faith is to have a faith which stands or falls with the records.

It is for that very reason that christological method, like historical method, has to be concerned with the detail of historical authenticity and the assessment of evidence; in fact, the reliability of the records is part of the case for the Christian faith. It is not sufficient to say that the Scriptures are completely trustworthy in all matters of faith, life and doctrine, because what has been left unsaid carries strong negative implications. This view leaves open the possibility that in historical detail the Scriptures may prove to be unreliable, and that consequence is disturbing. The teaching about faith, life and doctrine comes in the Scriptures, in a hard shell of historical record; and if the shell is damaged, the contents at once become suspect. This is not to say that all the biblical narratives are factually accurate, nor is it to say that the order of events as recorded in the Scriptures is precise in every case. But it is to say that we must be prepared to submit the narratives and the recorded series of events to the most open-minded scrutiny of which we are capable. We must, too, be always ready for the possibility that it is not the recital of chronological data that is necessarily closest to fact; a slightly dis-ordered gossipy narrative may take us closer to the heart of what happened, and it is with 'what happened' that we are concerned in historical method rather than with a bald, unvarnished statement of fact.

MEDIATION IN CHRISTOLOGY

It is for this very reason that R. G. Collingwood in his *The Idea of History* insists that it is knowledge of the past rather than chronological recording which is the true task of the historian. This knowledge is an imaginative process in which the historian re-enacts the thought of agents in the historical past. It is a process in which he reconstructs the motivational patterns that underlay the overt behaviour of figures of the past. It is a process of rational integration of isolated items of evidence, so that they find their place within an explanatory system without being rationalised away. The historian's task is, so to speak, to know *now* what happened *then* through records that exist in the present but have their meaning, their substance, their reality in the past. To use his language, the records are the media of historical immediacy. They create the context in and through which the past is re-lived in the present. Admittedly Collingwood's account of history and of historical knowledge carries overtones of idealistic philosophy; it evinces, too, a degree of subjectivism which he may never manage to avoid. But it has so many close connections with christological method that we may be well rewarded for finding in it an ally in the exposition of christo-logical method. For christology, the records mediate a figure of the past, so that he becomes a reality in the present. This mediation is an endemic feature of the christological situation;

to try to escape from it results only in the creation of a mental or spiritual substitute for the real Christ. The development of christological reflection is a progressive determination of the factual detail of the person and work of Jesus Christ, of the penetration into depth of the narrative accounts of the Scriptures. At the centre of every christological statement is a historical statement endeavouring to make its escape. When the historical statement fails to appear, we may well ask ourselves whether we really have been dealing with a christological statement.

THE UNIQUE HISTORICAL PERSON, JESUS CHRIST

It would be wrong to conclude this brief comparison of christological method with historical method without mentioning the point of similarity of which most is made in popular accounts of the matter, namely, that as historical research has to do with the unique and the unrepeatable in human affairs, christological study deals with him who is absolutely unique, the God–man who differentiates himself so completely from all else in human history. J. V. Langmead Casserley (*The Christian in Philosophy*, Faber & Faber, London, 1948) described the unique event, or person, with which theology, along with history, metaphysics, poetry and drama, has to deal, as the singular; and thereby drew attention to the logical oddness of this category, which was neither logical universal nor logical particular, which was not a member of a class-universal, but something logically different from both. The point was well-made, and it was a comfort to theologians to know that their logical troubles were shared by historians, metaphysicians and others. But all the problems were not solved, because a uniqueness attaches to the event of the incarnation which is different from that attaching to 'first to climb Everest', and we obscure *this* uniqueness if we assimilate it to those other forms of the singular. Nevertheless, there is a uniqueness in the field of the historical which is foreign to the natural sciences; and it is on this ground that we would take historical method as the more reliable clue to theological method than any other.

GEOGRAPHICAL ELEMENTS IN CHRISTOLOGICAL METHOD

Once the part which historical method plays within christology is established, certain immediate consequences follow. The subject of christology, the God–man, Jesus Christ, lived in a certain part of the world and in a certain society. It is inevitable, therefore, that geographical and sociological considerations will affect the judgements which we pass upon the historical events in the Gospel narrative. It is rather significant that when theology was more outspokenly insistent than it is now upon the humanity of Christ, intense interest was taken in the geography of the Holy Land. The *mise-en-scène* of the incarnation was of great importance, for this was a human life, lived upon earth and in the midst of a nation in the eastern Mediterranean area. Geographical details were of relevance both to the form which the life took and the character it bore. But once a degree of scepticism concerning the historical detail of the incarnation began to be expressed, as we have seen, under the influence of Kierkegaardian existentialism; once the deity of Christ was reaffirmed in classical Chalcedonian terms; there came, it might appear almost automatically, a lessening of interest in the geographical circumstances of the incarnation.

Sociological analysis also has a contribution to make both in laying bare the main features of the society in which Christ lived, and in assessing the characteristics of the Christian community which grew out of the fact of the incarnation and within which the records were produced to present the story of this fact in all the freshness of its original impact. Once again we are in danger of so emphasising the divine character of the Church that we neglect its human sociological features. There is a docetism in the doctrine of the Church no less than in christology. So long as it is affirmed that the Church is the body of Christ in the world, so long will there be a place for sociological method in the understanding of how that Church has developed and of how it formed the records which are the basis of all christological formulation. In short, then, the fact of the incarnation compels us to acknowledge that part at least of christological method must be devoted to the examination of the geographical and the sociological aspects of the situation in which it took place; and that the method of such study must bear close affinity to the kind of investigation that we give to such subjects in more secular connections. To say otherwise is to endanger what Barth calls the 'earthly' character of the incarnation.

LITURGICAL METHOD AND CHRISTOLOGY

If we pursue a little further the idea that sociological considerations are pertinent to christological method, we very soon discover that one of the chief functions, indeed the highest function, of this community created by the incarnation is to worship God. When the christological subject-matter is approached, it has to be borne in mind that we are dealing with a person towards whom the proper attitude is not one of scientific curiosity, or detached inquisitiveness, but ultimately one of worship and adoration, trust and obedience. Clearly when handling the christological material, it will be unnatural, strained and somewhat unrealistic for us to try to maintain a reverent attitude of adoration and faithful obedience. We may have to suspend for a time the commission under which we stand as the bondsmen of Christ to go at once into all the world and preach the Gospel, or tend the hungry, the suffering and the underprivileged brethren for whom he died. We may simply have to do so in order to understand more fully what his nature is who commissions us. But we have to recognise that the kind of thinking that we do when such suspension takes place is second-order thinking, and that the primary relationship to Christ is that of obedience, trust, adoration and, supremely, love.

This liturgical element – I use the term in its all-inclusive sense of 'relating to worship', and not solely in reference to *orders* of worship – conditions the form of christological method at a number of specifiable points. For example, to begin with, we shall not be satisfied with any christological analysis which eliminates from its conception of who he is all valid basis for an attitude of worship to him. It is on this very score that humanistic interpretations of the person of Jesus Christ fail: they present to us someone who cannot sustain human *worship*; admiration, perhaps, even a sense of wonder at the courage he had in the face of danger and death, but never worship. That is given only to God. The questions with which the liturgical interest will always tax any christological analysis will, therefore, be: 'How easily does the analysis integrate with a living situation in which the believer trusts, loves and obeys Jesus Christ?' 'To what degree is the analysis organically united with the worship of Christ, so that it may finally come to inform, deepen and enrich the worship of Christ?' This is the final test of any christology, whether it can become part of that offering of himself to the Father which Christ makes at the centre of all truly Christian worship.

We shall expect next that something of this liturgical interest will manifest itself in the records which we have noted as forming a central part of the christological subject-matter. It will appear in the very purpose of the documents themselves, for they were designed not to be read as literature, nor even as history, but in order that men and women, through them, should come to be saved in knowing and being known of the Christ of whom they tell us. As has already been observed, it is not implied that because of this overriding purpose the documents bear no literary characteristics, or that they will be any the less historical. Indeed without the literary form and without at least a measure of historical accuracy, they would not serve the liturgical purpose.

The liturgical interest expresses itself in yet other ways. Some excerpts may be taken directly from the records and embodied in a modern act of worship: Eph 1.3ff, for example – 'Blessed be the God and Father of our Lord Jesus Christ, who hath blessed us with all spiritual blessings in heavenly places in Christ', or Rom 16.25–27, or 2 Cor 1.3ff, may all be the very words we use in order to worship God here and now. We have, too, the whole continuing practice whereby a text is made the basis of a sermon, so that a word spoken to someone two thousand years ago or even more may be at this very moment the means by which Christ speaks again to his people. This re-emergence of Christ contemporaneously with the preached word demonstrates to us that the documents of Scripture are not themselves the totality of our subject-matter, and also that christological method is not one simple approach to a completely uniform body of material. At the same time, the liturgical interest may be so dominant in the mind of the authors of the original documents, that the clue to their structure is to be found in the liturgical purpose they serve. Archbishop Carrington, for example, has adopted the thesis that the shape of the Christian year has been imposed upon the Gospel according to St Mark, and that its literary form is meaningless without this clue. The Gospel according to St John obviously bears the marks of much editing, but it is important to remember that this editing is not simply for the purpose of producing a document with a distinctive literary polish, particularly when compared with, for example, the Gospel according to St Mark, but rather in order to enable readers to enter into the right relation to him who is the way, the truth and the life.

ETHICS AND CHRISTOLOGY

My general contention, then, has been that christological method is a complex of different methods, the historical, the literary-critical, the sociological and the liturgical. There is one other component in this method which I should still like to add to those already named: the ethical method. Perhaps it is not inappropriate after so many years to quote P. T. Forsyth (*The Person and Place of Jesus Christ*, Hodder & Stoughton, London, 1911, pp. 222f):

The modern moralization of religion thus prescribes a new manner of enquiry on such a central subject as the person of Jesus Christ. . . . Now concerning the union of the two natures in Jesus Christ the old dogma thought in a far too natural and non-moral way. Its categories were too elemental and physical. It conceived it as an act of might, of immediate divine power, an act which united the two natures *into* a person rather than *through* that person. . . . There can be no unity of spirits like God and man except in a moral way, by personal action which is moral in its method as well as in its aim.

The moralisation of religion which P. T. Forsyth seems to take so much for granted in this passage has not proceeded with the steady progress which he anticipated. For example, what I might call the subordination of ethics to dogmatics has impeded somewhat the penetration of the ethical categories into the whole range of dogmatic thought; in fact, in this subordination, ethics becomes the derivative discipline, introduced almost too late in the process to exert any controlling influence. More seriously for christology, the reduction of the size of the historical picture of Jesus Christ, which has been a feature not solely of Bultmannian christology but largely of all christologies influenced by Kierkegaardian historical scepticism, has led to a proportional diminution of the conception of the strictly ethical aspects of the person of Christ. This process, in conservative circles at least, has contained an element of reaction against the almost exclusively ethical and non-dogmatic account of Christ which was given by liberal theology. Christ the great moral teacher or Christ the embodiment of perfect morality has been replaced by Christ, the Word made flesh or Christ the supreme revelation of the very being of God himself. It is important, then, to recognise the danger which Forsyth saw in previous christologies – that the introduction of the classical christological categories might lead to the possibility of non-moral ways of understanding Christ's nature, and to insist that ethical method must find a place as part of christological method.

We are inclined, perhaps, to attach too much importance to the moralising of theological categories, as if it were a modern phenomenon. R. V. Sellers writes (*The Council of Chalcedon*, SPCK, London, 1953, p. 164):

> (The Antiochenes) are supremely interested in man the moral being, and in particular concentrate on his power of self-determination. But it is important to notice that the conception of man as a free spirit is never considered in isolation, but always against the background of the thought of God's purpose for him. They may be called anthropologists, but their anthropology is intimately associated with their ethical and soteriological ideas. Whatever then, be the errors which the Antiochenes otherwise commit, e.g. that they affirm a Duad of Sons, at least in their conception of the humanity of Christ they stood firmly in the tradition of the scriptures themselves in contending for the genuineness of the humanity of Christ.

So, too, before we reject Theodore of Mopsuestia's idea that the union of God and man in Jesus Christ is only rightly understood as a moral union, such as that of man and wife, we must remember not only that he is here speaking analogically, but also that in a matter such as this an ethical category is probably more appropriate than a purely metaphysical one.

CHRISTOLOGICAL METHOD COMPOSED OF A VARIETY OF CONTRIBUTORY METHODS

I wish now to draw together the main conclusions that seem to be emerging from this general discussion of the constituent elements in christological method, or of what I have at times spoken of as the several methods which taken together constitute the christological method.

Perhaps the first immediately noteworthy point is that it is very difficult, if not impossible, to maintain that there is a peculiar and proper christological method different and distinct from those constituent methods which I have named. The positive form of this assertion is that christological method is a peculiar and specific complex of these constituent methods, and as such is not reproduced in any other disciplines – in spite of the fact that most of these methods appear in other disciplines. The enumeration of these constituent methods enables us to see how easily any one of them may usurp authority and at once present a radically distorted or gravely diminished account of the christological subject-matter. At one time or another in the history of doctrine or culture, this is exactly what has happened – when sociologists have presented the fact of Christ in terms of Judaic social, economic and political pressures; when literary-critics or form-critics reduced the documents of the Christian Scriptures to a fragment of their proper size; when scientific historians sought in these documents for the evidence of uncommitted and detached bystanders; when liberals drew a picture of the perfect man or offered an account of the fully-adjusted personality; or even when the liturgist constructed christology solely in relation to the worship of the Christian Church, hoping to save it from the humiliation of bitter controversy. This complexity of method accounts not only for the differences in approach between Christians and non-Christians, but also for the quite radical differences that occur between Christians. Some have one overriding interest, and others another, with the result that we have a variation as wide as that between Dibelius in his *Jesus* and Brunner in his *The Mediator*, or between B. Barton's *The Man Nobody Knew* and Bornkamm's *Jesus of Nazareth*.

The complexity of method which is said to characterise christology may be illustrated also from the complexity of the different items which to begin with we discovered in any method. The first of these which we mentioned (above, pp. 25f) was that of attitude. At once we notice that while Christ is the subject of Christian worship and devotion and consequently requires of us constant obedience and trust, nevertheless there must be a place within christology for a more questioning attitude. It must be possible to stand back, as it were, and critically review the documents, the literary forms, the narratives, the hymns, the confessions of faith, in order to determine their authenticity and their veracity. It will be necessary also to compare the ethical aspects of Jesus' teaching with that of moral teachers of other times, in order to bring out its essentially distinctive character; but that process of comparison will entail a considerable suspension of the urgency of his moral imperatives. In other words it will involve something of the attitude of the moral philosopher. And so we begin to observe that elements of the attitudes proper to the different methods constitutive of christological method are embodied in the attitude adopted in christology. The same is true of the logic employed in christology. It should by now be clear that there is not one peculiar christological logic, but that according to the kind of problem we are trying to solve, or the sort of aspect of the christological situation we are seeking to describe, or even defend, the logic we employ will in fact vary somewhat.

When we go on to such things as the tacit assumptions accepted in any method, the evidence and types of verification that are permissible, or even to the conclusions anticipated from the use of the method, it appears at a first glance that we have moved into areas where special 'religious' considerations might be expected to overrule all others. For example, when the application of the standards of evidence acceptable in historical study seem to be destroying the historical foundation of the Christian Gospel by disproving the historicity of the events of Christ's life, it might seem necessary to invoke some non-historical sanctions to restrain the historical method. Or if psychological analysts seem to be proving that Jesus was a schizophrenic or a paranoic, then the theological claims concerning his deity might seem to have to be invoked to secure the integrity of his personality. Or even when the moral philosopher is approaching a decision in favour of the ethics of Plato as against that of Jesus, a rejection of justification by works or an exposition of the greater importance of the death of Jesus than that of Socrates might be suddenly summoned up to redress the balance on the Christian side.

Two replies must, I feel, be made to extreme measures. On the one hand, we have to face the fact that any one of these possible, as we believe, misinterpretations of the person of Jesus Christ may be correct. It is a logical possibility that Jesus may have been a schizophrenic, that he may have taught an ethic which was less adequate than Plato's, or indeed that he may not have existed at all. The existence of this logical possibility is part of the fact that he entered human history and exposed himself to the ambiguities both of history and of historical interpretation. It is against the background of this logical possibility that faith is to be characterised as faith and never as sight. The atheist construes the logical possibility as reality, while the fanatic is in danger, at the other end of the scale, of converting faith into sight and claiming incontrovertible certainty on all points.

On the other hand it would be wrong to leave the impression that the ultimate decision between the possibility of the truth of these propositions being contradictory of Christianity and the authenticity of Christian faith lies with a peradventure of faith, even when this peradventure is reinforced with a high doctrine of the Holy Spirit. Such is a burden more heavy than human faith and decision can rightly be called upon to endure. There is an alternative: namely, that within and among the several methods which, we have argued, are constitutive of christological method there operates a system of checks and balances so that the final construction is one which is in agreement with the substance of the faith. The existence of such a system is not in itself a reason why the atheist ought to use it, for he would no more wish to do so than a tone-deaf person might choose to argue about the cadences in a piece of music. Nor does the existence of the system eliminate all occasion of disagreement among Christian theologians, for they will still argue about the adjustment of the checks and balances. The important point is, however, that they will argue within the system and expect to convince their fellows by drawing upon evidence from within it and employing inferences that are valid within it. What they ought not try to do is to escape from the system into a christological method which claims to stand above and apart from all the others we mentioned and to have veridical knowledge on all the questions at issue. Some theologians may try to do so, but they will go out by the front door only to re-enter by the back door; for they too must in the end speak of documents and history, of ethics and psychology, of liturgy and logic. At that point they have returned to the fold, and we are perhaps just a little relieved that they have found it necessary to do so. They might have been right!

3

MODELS IN CHRISTOLOGY

One feature of Christian worship which even the most callous familiarity cannot fail to observe is the sheer variety of titles ascribed to Jesus Christ. They range from the list which is part of the Old Testament Advent lesson, Isa 9.6: 'And his name shall be called Wonderful, Counsellor, The mighty God, The everlasting Father, The Prince of Peace' to the great climax of phrases contained in the Nicaeo-Constantinopolitan Creed: 'And in one Lord Jesus Christ, the only-begotten Son of God, Begotten of his Father before all worlds, God of God, Light of Light, Very God of Very God, Begotten not made, Being of one substance with the Father, By whom all things were made: Who for us men and for our salvation came down from heaven, And was incarnate by the Holy Ghost of the Virgin Mary. And was made man.' Within the limits of this wide range there lie the names which occur within the Gospels themselves, where Jesus is described, or rather describes himself, as the way, the truth, the life, the shepherd, the vine, ransom, and so on; as well as the many titles which later theology has employed – leader, hero and religious genius.

Clearly, the use of such a variety of titles creates problems for biblical students, who must decide, for example, which of the New Testament terms are going to have precedence over others; how far contemporary Jewish usage or previous Old Testament usage or even classical usage is to be allowed to predetermine the interpretation of New Testament terms; and whether there are irreconcilable differences of emphasis when the terminology favoured by one evangelist is compared with that of another. In approaching the question of the place of models in christology, obviously we shall be obliged to keep these biblical problems in mind; but the issues that confront us here are slightly different. It is clear, for example, that we cannot rest content with a view which simply adds these different titles together, as if they were all obviously compatible descriptions of an immediately observable entity or person. They are drawn from vastly different contexts; they carry a seemingly endless variety of implications and refer to a wide range of situations. It is therefore necessary to evolve some account of how they are uniformly affirmed of the same subject without contradiction and without ultimate confusion. Some consideration will have to be given to the purposes which are served by the variety of titles applied to Jesus Christ. They are not simply proper names for him nor are they only denotative; they are in some sense descriptive of who he is and of the part he plays in the will of God for the salvation of mankind. In short, we shall have to ask what these titles are. The quick answer to that question is that titles of the sort we have been mentioning are the models with which the christological method operates in dealing with its given, its subject-matter. Our present task then is to indicate what the term 'model' means in this application; to specify the various sources and functions of models, and particularly of christological models; and to indicate the part which they play in defining the character of theological language.

IAN T. RAMSEY'S VIEWS ON MODELS

Ian T. Ramsey has drawn together (in *Models and Mystery* (Whidden Lectures), 1964) a number of views on models, and contributed on his own side a very illuminating analysis of their nature and function particularly in relation to theology. We may best begin by reviewing what he has to say.

Basic to his whole position is a distinction between 'picturing models' and 'disclosure models' or, as Professor Max Black would call them, 'analogue models'. The former featured prominently in the scientific theory of Lord Kelvin's day. The models which science employed were thought to be replicas or copy-pictures of whatever it was they were modelling. Models serve a rather different purpose in modern science: they form 'a collection of distinctive, reliable, and easily specifiable techniques for talking about a reality which is ultimately mysterious' (op. cit., p. 4). There are, as it were, three elements in the situation: first, the phenomena which have constituted a problem for the scientist and defy either explanation or description in terms of known laws, principles or hypotheses; secondly, the model which displays some structural similarity to the phenomena; and thirdly, a theory or deductive system of a very complex nature associated with the phenomena, from which certain fundamental notions are selected in the model for simplified treatment. Professor Ramsey speaks of the relation of the model to the phenomena in a variety of ways in addition to that of isomorphism already mentioned. For example, the models 'chime in with and echo' the phenomena (op. cit., p. 13); and as a consequence of this relation, they are together associated in a disclosure, a disclosure about some mystery in the universe. While the idea that models are descriptive is rejected (op. cit., p. 20), it is equally strongly affirmed that the disclosure of which the model is a medium entails both a deeper understanding of the reality disclosed and a degree of ontological commitment to it. In other words, the model is not a figment of the imagination nor is it a precise picture, but it does enable us to be articulate about some aspect of the universe.

There is a sufficiently far-reaching parallel, Professor Ramsey thinks, between models in science and models in theology to justify description of the latter in terms of the former. To begin with, the phenomena which constituted the events of the life, death and resurrection of Jesus Christ were so complex and involved, and the minds of Christ's followers were still so far removed from precise theological definition, that models were called in to give immediate interpretation to the phenomena. They provide a basis for conversation concerning the phenomena and for the further proclamation of them without anticipating the precision of later dogmatic formulae. Again, where the phenomena are particularly complex, the models may single out specific aspects of them and so enable an understanding of them which would otherwise prove impossible. So, too, religious models, drawn from the universe or man's experience of it, must so chime in with the religious phenomena which they model as to create a disclosure situation, yielding insight and understanding. While it is not possible to verify a religious model by means of any deductive inferences which we may draw from them, a practical test is not altogether wanting, in that it may be shown to incorporate a wide range of relevant phenomena and meet a variety of practical needs. This test is called 'empirical fit' by Professor Ramsey. It is an aspect of models which we shall endeavour to demonstrate is of immense contemporary importance.

Later on (op. cit., chapter 3) Professor Ramsey draws on a more literary interpretation of models when he compares them with metaphors, but secures roughly the same result as that yielded by his investigation of scientific models. Metaphor involves the juxtaposition and consequent interpenetration of two contexts in such a way as to produce fresh disclosure which includes both within itself. Alternatively, metaphor is 'a tangential meeting of two diverse contexts' (op. cit., p. 52) in such a way that discourse concerning one is facilitated and enriched through the application to it of the terms of discourse of the other. Once again, the metaphor yields deeper insight into a mystery which would otherwise elude our grasp; the metaphor is the medium of disclosure of a reality which, or who, claims our commitment. There is then no doubt about the objective reference of the metaphor, but it is not the objective reference of precise description. There is a 'logical gap between the model and what the insight reveals, between the model and the situation in which it is fulfilled' (op. cit., p. 59). It is the existence of this gap which prevents the metaphor from being descriptive or pictorial. It is the combination of the metaphor and the original in a single insight which secures for the metaphor a role in the understanding of objective reality. Once again the relation between metaphor and religious language is shown by Professor Ramsey to be of prime importance. It is possible to see much of the language of theology as metaphorical, and to hold that the various metaphors which theology employs continue to yield 'cosmic disclosures', in short to be the literary media of divine revelation. They point to the mystery which even in disclosure retains its mysteriousness.

I have stated Professor Ramsey's views at such considerable length for two reasons. The first and obvious one is that it is a remarkably penetrating and imaginative account of the nature and function of models in theological discourse. The second is that this book, of an importance far beyond its size, has served to direct my own thoughts on the subject in ways which Professor Ramsey did not intend and which are not necessarily extensions of his thought but which would make little sense without his account before us.

There would appear to be several basic problems relating to models – their nature, their logical status and their function particularly in theology and christology; and I propose to begin by examining the variety of functions which they perform. It is hoped that we shall thereby drive a road through to some clearer conception of their nature and status in the christological context.

THE FUNCTION OF MODELS

MODELS AS MEDIA OF DISCLOSURE

With Professor Ramsey's account in front of us it is impossible not to start off with the function of *disclosure*. Perhaps it is absolutely right to lay the emphasis primarily on this function of the models, namely, that they exist to serve God himself, to be the media by which he is to be known, worshipped and obeyed. Far too often the question of models is seen as a logical question, of how human language can penetrate to the heart of the divine mystery, of how a linguistic extrapolation is achieved so that, with human grammar and syntax, we are able to speak of God himself.

But they are, on the contrary, moments in the divine self-disclosure, part of the way in which he addresses himself to us, and declares his purpose for our lives. This fact must override all that we say about models; and we must constantly remind ourselves of it particularly when we are in danger of being immersed in the logical details to which we are now required to direct ourselves.

Take, for example, the way in which the disclosure might be said to take place. When Professor Ramsey is talking of scientific models, he says that there is a certain isomorphism between the phenomena in the ordinary world and the models, which when the one is applied to the other yields a disclosure of some reality beyond them both. It is necessary to cash the values of this abstract account of the matter to see clearly what it implies.

Let us consider, for example, the situation in which Christ's authority inspired the centurion to believe that Christ would cure his sick servant (Lk 7.1ff). The actual phenomena in this case would be the outward bearing of Christ, some word the centurion had heard, or the inward peace which shone from the face of Christ. The model would be the centurion's own exercise of authority. 'For I also am a man set under authority, having under me soldiers; and I say to one, Go, and he goeth; and to another, Come, and he cometh; and to my servant, Do this, and he doeth it' (v. 8). A certain isomorphic relationship between Christ's behaviour and his position yielded the disclosure, which took an interesting form. For the centurion did not say, as if concluding an argument, 'And so I observe that you hold a position of very high authority and are able to command whatsoever you wish, confident that it will be executed.' Instead, he stated the practical consequence which Christ's possession of that authority entailed for the present situation. 'Say in a word, and my servant shall be healed' (v. 7b). The Gospels abound in examples. In Jn 10.1ff, Jesus speaks of a good shepherd who goes before his sheep, and whom they follow; the good shepherd whose voice they know; the one who will finally give his life for his sheep. To check progress to this point, we may say that there are three elements in the model-situation; the phenomena in the everyday world, the model, and the subject of disclosure, to which we are directed through the association of model and phenomena. The most significant example of all is perhaps the occasion of the institution of the sacrament of the Lord's Supper. At Lk 22.19, 20 we read:

> And Jesus took bread, and gave thanks, and brake it, and gave unto them saying, This is my body which is given for you: this do in remembrance of me.
> Likewise also the cup after supper, saying, This cup is the new testament in my blood, which is shed for you.

These verses, when looked at in terms of the logic of models, are of great interest, chiefly for two reasons. First we do not have one but a series of models in both cases. We begin on each occasion with phenomena, in v. 19, the giving of bread, and in v. 20, the offering of the cup of wine. Model one, in v. 19, is the breaking of the body of Christ; and model two is the vicarious sacrifice involved in the breaking of the body of Christ, and the ultimate disclosure, the soteriological purpose served by these events. In v. 20, a third model is inserted with the words, 'the new testament', the initiation by God of a new relation to fulfil the promise contained in the old covenant that God had made with Israel. But the final disclosure is the same, God's purpose of salvation for those who receive the sacrament. If we follow the account of the institution of the sacrament of the Lord's supper as recorded by St Paul in 1 Cor 11.23ff, we find the recurrence of an aspect of the model situation which we noticed in the account of the healing of the centurion's servant (Lk 7.1ff), namely, the practical act. The end-term of the series of models and of the final disclosure enshrined in the celebration of the sacrament is not simply disclosure of a truth, even the highest soteriological truth, but the eating and the drinking, the receiving of the Body and Blood of Jesus Christ. The second point of interest about the models used in the institution of the sacrament is that they converge on the same disclosure, or more precisely, on the disclosure of the same reality, the single purpose of God. It might be called a 'hinge disclosure' because both series of models depend upon it for their validity and indeed for their meaning, and because however free and open the series may be at the phenomena end, it has to be firm and fixed at the disclosure end.

When Professor Ramsey moves to the comparison of models and metaphors, he retains the triadic structure which we have mentioned above. A metaphor occurs when two contexts are allowed to interpenetrate so that terms applicable within the range of the one are given a reference within the other. As before, this juxtaposition of contexts, this interpenetration generates a disclosure. It does so by *pointing* the understanding in the direction in which the disclosure is to be gained. When we examine the record of the institution of the sacrament of the Lord's Supper in the light of models as metaphors, we observe once again the importance of the fact that the models as metaphors point in the same direction and to the same subject. What is true in the immediately obvious way of the sacramental models must be equally true of the others. Linguistic and literary as well as logical chaos would result if the models pointed in many different directions, to many different subjects. It is for this reason of great importance to hold that the parables of the Kingdom (Mt 13.24ff) in spite of the diversity of the models – a man sowing good seed in his field (vv. 24ff), a grain of mustard seed (vv. 31ff), and leaven in meal (vv. 33ff) point to a single reality. It is this uniform reference which saves them from being a kaleidoscopic series of prettily poetic pictures.

Theological and scientific models compared

It might be argued that theological models resemble metaphors more closely than they do the scientific models. When Jesus says, 'I am the door of the sheep' (Jn 10.7), he would appear to be using a metaphor, rather than a scientific model. Or again, 'I am the true vine, and my Father is the husbandman' (Jn 15.1), savours more of literary device than scientific inference. The case is, however, far from complete against the employment of the scientific approach to models. Professor Ramsey is careful to point out (op. cit., p. 16) that there are great differences between scientific models and theological models. For example, the scientific model is made the basis of precise deductions which subsequently become the subject of extensive experimentation for purposes of verification or falsification. The deductions result in conclusions relating to definite modes and quantities, and there can be no comparable element in the conclusions which theological models yield. Nor, we may now add, would it be right to regard theological models simply as hypotheses which stand or fall with the conclusions we deduce from them. They have an independence of existence and status which forbids such arbitrariness in our attitude to them. In other words, we cannot apply the concept of scientific model to the analysis of theological language without taking pains to illustrate the ways in which the two kinds of models differ from one another.

The question might well be asked whether models in theology are in any aspects different from literary metaphors. A provisional answer may be given at this stage. It is that while ontological reference is present in both there is a greater degree of ontological commitment to the former than to the latter. In a sentence embodying a metaphor, the commitment is to the subject compared with the metaphorical entity or concept. In a sentence embodying a theological model, the model is itself part of the subject of commitment, and in some cases even prescribes the form of the commitment. For example, the model of shepherd as applied to Christ entails the commitment of trust, whereas if we talk of him who will be the judge of the quick and the dead, the commitment is one of humble submission to his judgement. From the fact, then, that theological models are not simply equivalent to scientific or literary models, we might be tempted half-humorously to say that we are employing models as models in the theological reference. Whether we have not in fact come rather close to interpreting theological models as analogies is a point to which we shall return. For my own part, I should be inclined to say that the theory of models succeeds in reinstating the doctrine of analogy in modern theological logic and in saving it from being a purely scholastic form of doctrine, and that analogy is to be interpreted in terms of a theory of models and not vice versa.

Are models descriptive?

We have been saying that one of the functions of models is to disclose reality, and that where several models are used in series, they are 'hinged' to a single reality. The question which I wish now to examine is whether we can legitimately ascribe the function of *description* to models.

Professor Ramsey rejects what he calls the 'deceptive attractions of descriptive language' (op. cit., p. 68) and it is very clear that his objection is to pictorial representations, which are thought to reflect reality with the accuracy of a mirror. Clearly he is not saying that when using model-language we are out of all relation to reality, or that the reality which is disclosed by the successful models is an undifferentiated blur. He does say, on the contrary, that models enable us 'to come to a reliable . . . understanding of the phenomena' and 'to be reliably articulate about (the universe)' (op. cit., pp. 13ff). The distinction between 'articulate' and 'describe' is one to which Professor Ramsey wishes to adhere very closely. Even although the former means 'to express clearly', he would interpret it rather as the delineation of relations within a mystery which might otherwise remain inexpressible. However, if we break with the equation of description with pictorial representation, then it becomes possible to include articulation within the meaning of description, and to say that articulation by means of models is the form which description takes when we are dealing with certain parts or aspects of reality. In fact, Professor Ramsey seems almost to prepare the way for this position when he allows (op. cit., pp. 13–14) that 'the model arises in a moment of insight when the universe discloses itself in the points where the phenomena and the model meet'. The model is authenticated by reality. This admission is not a way of saying that there is a one-one correspondence between the model and reality. But it is to say that in employing created models we are describing reality in the only way that is possible to us.

When once again we give cash-value to our models, the position becomes clearer. When Jesus says, 'I am the shepherd', or 'I am the door', clearly he is not using language which is pictorially representative. Jesus did not go about Palestine leading sheep from place to place; nor did he protect the entrance to a house and keep people out or, swinging back, allow them to enter. At the same time, he was not, in using these models, failing to describe his own nature and function; nor did he imply that his nature was inexpressible, or his function indescribable. He was in fact describing his own nature and saying that he could be trusted as a leader through all the vicissitudes of life, and that he so loved his people that he would give his life for them. He was saying that it was his purpose to open the way for men to come to the father, and he invited men and women to enter God's presence through knowing him. When he said, 'This is my body which is broken for you', he was obviously not there and then breaking his own body; nor was he simply employing a metaphor which pointed beyond itself to an ineffable reality. He was speaking of his own death, and he was, by using this model, describing it as a sacrifice. So, too, when he says, 'This is my blood which is shed for the remission of the sins of many', he describes, by means of the model of the cup blessed and poured forth, the nature and meaning of his death. In other words, it is almost as if the model is compounded partly of an element which does not carry the ultimate reference to the reality disclosed, and partly of an element which has the direct reference to the reality and constitutes part of the disclosure. This latter element seems to be constituted of the area common to the two contexts whose intersection creates the metaphor situation.

MODELS AND ANALOGY

I should like to make two comments on the position we have now reached. The first is that we have returned again to the case for relating models to analogy – not, as we said, to a scholastic and quasi-mathematical form, but to one which does greater justice to the idiosyncrasies of human language as it is used, more justice that is to literary forms than to logical structures. Susan Stebbing (*A Modern Introduction to Logic*, Methuen, London, 1933) quotes a distinction drawn by J. M. Keynes between what he calls positive analogy and negative analogy. Given two entities S and N which resemble each other in definable respects which may be enumerated, thus, $p_1, p_2, p_3 \ldots p_n$ and differ from each other in further definable respects, thus, $r_1, r_2, r_3 \ldots r_n$; we denote the former the positive analogy and the latter the negative analogy. Clearly every analogy we employ consists of a balance of the one against the other. Or we may change the figure (or the analogy!) and say that between them they constitute a spectrum; and when the negative analogy far exceeds the positive we begin to approach the fanciful in literary description, or typological exegesis, or sermon illustration; and when the positive analogy far exceeds the negative, we are approximating to flat description. Proper analogy occurs in the middle range of the spectrum.

If I may digress for a moment: the balance of the negative to the positive analogy in ordinary conversational–analogical argument or illustration is one of the greatest sources both of misunderstanding and of the popular conversational sport of one-upmanship. When we ourselves employ any analogy, we do so because of the positive content which illustrates our point or our theme; but our opponents, with churlish malevolence, at once seize upon the negative analogy and demonstrate its plain absurdity. The one-upmanship reply at that point is: 'Of course, it is only an analogy', which reply is calculated to give you sufficient time to abandon that particular analogy and look for another more satisfactory.

Where, however, there is a heavy balance in favour of the negative analogy over the positive, it is not unusual for the speaker or the writer to quote several analogies one after another, so that collectively, by throwing light upon one another and enriching one another, they may establish the clearly significant positive analogy. In this process, the analogies, as it were, refine and define one another; they provide the means for determining their own accuracy; and among them, they yield the very disclosure of which Professor Ramsey spoke. But in doing so they describe through their progressively clarified positive analogy the reality to which they refer.

In christology generally and in the biblical statements about Jesus Christ, we have both kinds of analogy – those which carry a fairly even balance between the negative and the positive analogy and those which show a preponderance of negative over positive analogy and which are offered, therefore, in rapid series. Examples of the first I would find in the several ways in which the Bible and subsequent soteriology have spoken of the death of Christ – as victory over evil powers and principalities, as ransom, as penal substitution, as vicarious satisfaction, as moral example, and so on. Here there is not the intensive interpenetration of one model by the other which we get in the second form; indeed, the history of soteriology shows how effectively one theory of the death of Christ can be formulated to the exclusion of the others. The parable of the wicked husbandmen in Lk 20.9–19 would be another case of an analogy whose balance of positive to negative is so even that no supporting analogies are required for the further definition of its meaning or its reference. The rapid succession type of analogy occurs in the Gospels, in the instance we have mentioned of the parables of the kingdom. Perhaps the best modern example is Hymn 419 in the *Revised Church Hymnary*, where the name of Jesus is spoken of as, at one and the same time, sounding sweet in a believer's ear, soothing his sorrows, healing his wounds, driving away his fear, calming the troubled breast and finally, being 'manna to the hungry soul, and to the weary rest'. The culmination comes when Jesus is addressed as 'Shepherd, Husband, Friend'; 'Prophet, Priest and King'; 'Lord, Life, Way and End'. This plethora of models, of course, creates an almost infinite richness in the final description, as each helps the other in the process of greater definition.

What must be carefully emphasised, however, is that at no point is it quite possible to extract the positive analogy and to state it in a non-analogical way; or, if that view seems to be an overstatement, the end-product is such a two-dimensional, superficial account that it cannot compete with the analogies even as a description. It may have been some consideration of the sort which prompted the now famous line of Tillich that with the exception of the statement about Being Itself, all language about God is analogical. This difficulty, namely of transcending the model, the metaphor, or the analogy, prevents us from ever assuming that we have exhaustively described or defined the mystery of the Word made flesh. We never grasp it in the immediacy of non-analogical language.

MODELS AS MEDIA OF APPREHENSION

The second general comment I have to make on the idea that model language is to be regarded as nonetheless descriptive may be illustrated from a theory which the late Professor Kemp Smith used to hold about the ontological status of secondary qualities. He was not prepared to say with the naive realists that they were externally existent in reality, that the things of the world were blue or green, cold or hot, sweet or sour, and so on, in themselves. Nor would he agree with the subjective idealists that these secondary qualities were purely subjective ideas, existing only in our minds and in no way related to anything that might be termed an external world. Between these two extremes, he argued, lay a more accurate view, that secondary qualities were the terms in which we apprehended the external world and consequently described it. He did not deny that the secondary qualities had an existence in their own right; they were events in a spatio-temporal continuum, complex occurrences with biochemical and physiological as well as physical aspects. But when their position is considered within the knower–known relationship, they function as the media through which reality is known by sense-percipient people, the form in which they understand reality and the means by which they adjust themselves to it, and indeed live their lives within it. The status of models in christology, we are contending, is somewhat similar. These are the terms in which we apprehend the person of Jesus Christ, or rather it is in such terms that he apprehends us – as the shepherd who leads us, cares for us and finally dies for us; as the door, through whom in very fact we enter into the presence of God; or as the way, in which to walk is to live life to its fullness. When, therefore, we use the models, we are not simply connecting one set of symbols by comparison with another, as if the reality to which they applied had no control over them. We are in fact talking about Christ, and we are *describing* him in terms of the models. We are saying that he is like this and this and this; and we check the models by what we have come to know about him. At the end of the day, then, our models are controlled and indeed authenticated by the reality, Christ, whom we have come to know albeit through them.

I should like at this point to make certain comments. The illustration from Kemp Smith's epistemology is not applicable in all respects to the christological model. Once again, we are using models as models! No one but a naive realist in epistemology would want to say nowadays that if we were to probe scientifically into the microcosms of reality they would bear the qualities which reality reveals at the macrocosmic level. Colours, tastes, smells, heat, cold, pressure, sounds disappear among waves or vibrations or electrical charges or discharges; and scientists and even some philosophers may be forgiven for thinking the latter to be reality and the former illusion. What we must admit, however, is that reality may not 'in itself' have many of the characteristics which sense perception attributes to it. It would, I should say, be unthinkable that Christ 'in himself' should not possess in some measure at least some of the qualities which we attribute to him when we describe him in terms of the models, say, which we derive from the Bible. Not only would we want to hold that there does not exist the disparity between the models (partly in the positive analogy of their content and structure) and the character of Christ which distinguishes sense-data from waves and vibrations; but we shall insist that there can be no contradiction by the mystery still remaining within the person

of Jesus Christ and his nature as we understand it through the
models. Mystery surrounding Christ there must always be, but it
is not the sort of mystery which might turn out to be a denial of
what we know of Christ when we speak of him as shepherd, or
ransom or door.

Secondly, we are now coming very close to the point of
recognising that some of the language which we use of Christ
has finally transcended the status of model to become immediately descriptive of Christ. I feel a good deal of sympathy with
Tillich's view that Being Itself is ascribed to God non-analogically.
It is difficult to see how such a term could be employed analogically; it seems to have a divine set from the very start. But some of
the terms which we have come to apply to Christ, chiefly on the
basis of their scriptural origin, come into the same category; for
example, when we speak of him as life, truth, and Logos, it is
extremely difficult to cast these attributes in a negative–positive
form so common to analogical predication. There is an identity
of content between them and the very nature of Christ which
precludes the rough approximations of model-type assertions.
To say so is not to deny either that when Christ first used these
terms of himself or was so described by St John the Evangelist,
there was then an element of analogy in them; or that we may
use these terms today in reference to other realities than Christ.
What is meant is that now we know that Christ is the key to
what these terms signify, for he is each one, and that other applications are declensions from that absolute meaning, secondary
and derivative applications.

The position for which I am arguing, then, is this, that the
terms in which we understand Christ's character are the ways in
which in fact he exists. We reject the theory that the models are
simply ideal or mental representations of a reality which may
differ from them, as we reject the theory that like signposts they
point to a reality which bears no more than a directional relation
to them: the signpost with the name New York 50 miles tells you
nothing about the character, size, climate of the city except that
it lies so far in a certain direction. If we speak of Christ as a
shepherd it is because he has certain qualities which authenticate

the comparison, and it is of those qualities themselves that we are talking when we describe him as shepherd. Without such earthing of our language in the person of Jesus Christ, it is hard to see what such language is about.

THE NORMATIVE ROLE OF MODELS

A further characteristic or function of models in christology is that they may become *normative*; that is, they tend to be the criteria by which we judge the truth or falsity of the statements about Jesus Christ. Probably they have always fulfilled this function from the earliest days of Christian theology. When models such as the notion of the Messiah, or the Son of Man, with all their rich associations, ousted such notions as that of prophet or rabbi or magic-worker, a criterion – norms – had been set up to regulate and control the correct description of Jesus Christ and to condemn the inaccurate, which eventually became known as the heretical. The position became still more acute in the great period of the christological controversies when the models which the various parties adopted guided them in their own assertions and in their condemnation of one another. Traditionally, however, the Church has come to rely not upon models as the norms of its theology but upon creeds. Even at the time of the Reformation, when the doctrine and practice of the medieval Church was laid alongside the written word of God and tested by its faithfulness to that word; and when the written word of God as witnessed to by the *testimonium internum spiritus sancti* was acknowledged to be the supreme rule of faith; there very soon came a time when men formulated confessions to secure the right interpretation of Scripture and to prepare young people by catechesis to ensure a correct understanding by them of the open Bible placed in their hands.

It always seemed to me a curious anomaly of our celebration in 1960 of the quatercentenary of the Reformation that we should have made so much of the rediscovery of the Bible and so little of our desperate need for subordinate standards. It was right

that we should honour the former of these Reformation achievements; for the theology of at least the past two decades has been
more closely related to biblical foundation than probably any
since the days of the Reformation itself. These have been the
great decades of biblical theology, of the biblical doctrine of man,
of time, of baptism, and so on. But at the same time we are
becoming fully aware of what I can only call the intellectual
dishonesty of the Articles Declaratory and the Declaratory Acts,
which over the years have allowed ministers of the churches in
Scotland to withhold their confessional allegiance to those
elements in the *Westminster Confession of Faith* which do not
belong to the substance of the faith. I refuse to believe that one
may excerpt from the *Westminster Confession* the doctrine of
double predestination or the view of hell, and leave the other
doctrines of the documents unaffected. To remove double predestination is to propose a change in the understanding of the
character of God. To alter the character of Sunday from that
assumed in the Confession to something of a more liberal nature,
as has been suggested by the General Assembly of the Church of
Scotland in recent years, is to change also the pattern of life as
the Westminster divines conceived it. There is a grave vacuum in
Reformed theology which was originally filled by the classical
confessions, of which the *Scots Confession* was among the most
outstanding, and later by the *Westminster Confession*, and which
has been created by the inroads of continuing theological reform.
This vacuum cannot be readily filled by wide use of the primary
standard of doctrine and theology, namely the Scriptures; for
they all too clearly are interpreted this way or that, if one may
not be unduly cynical, according to doctrinal, confessional or
ecclesiastical preference.

It is at this very point that models have acquired a normative
importance which they have not hitherto had on their own.
Previously, they may have operated normatively, but they have
done so within the framework or under the cover of an accepted
subordinate standard – a creed, a confession or a rule of faith.
When L. S. Thornton uses A. N. Whitehead's category of
'organism' as the central interpretative principle for expounding

the person of Jesus Christ, he is not simply adopting a concept which is hermeneutically useful and intellectually contemporary. He has adopted a norm which permits him to make certain christological statements and prevents him from making others. A line is now drawn between the true and the false, the valid and the invalid. When the kenoticists adopted the notion of *kenosis*, they were not simply constructing a christology on the basis of a text in St Paul (Phil 2.5ff). They were adopting a model on the basis of which they accepted some traditional christological statements and departed from others. They made a great deal of those christological passages which emphasised the weakness, the hunger, the humanity of Christ, but minimised any which appeared to make too much of his retention upon earth of the full attributes of deity, those which he had before the incarnation and which he would recover thereafter. Nor need the model be normative solely for christology. Kenoticism can easily extend its model into the ethical field and interpret the christological norm as a behavioural norm. The revival of the Chalcedonian two-nature model in christology has been very rapidly followed by its penetration into other fields – the doctrine of the Church and the doctrine of the Bible, for example – and it has produced its own crop of charges of heresy against those positions from which it differed, as it did in the fifth century. We have heard of a Eutychean doctrine of the Church, or a Nestorian doctrine of the Scriptures; and the use of the adjectives derived from the names of christological heresies is its own evidence of the powerfully normative functions of models in modern christology and theology.

This normative function of models may explain two rather paradoxically incongruous aspects of this modern scene. The first is the emotive element which is not far-removed from many theological controversies. The *odium theologicum* has never been something to joke about: it has cast a shadow over a subject which should throughout have been irradiated solely by the grace and love of Almighty God. But it has inevitably arisen where, using their models as heresy-detectors, theologians have thought to discredit one another's views by aligning them with ancient falsehoods. There is an unfortunate custom intruding into the modern christological scene, of naming one's opponent, of identifying his views with those of some dishonoured heretic. Quite apart from the anachronism which often lies at the heart of such judgements, the effect upon the atmosphere in which theological discussion is conducted is disastrous. Truth, least of all theological truth, never came through hatred, least of all through the *odium theologicum*. The second aspect of the modern scene, which is connected with the normative character of models is the way in which, as a result of the collapse of the subordinate standards above-mentioned – the Thirty-nine Articles have suffered as badly in this respect as the *Westminster Confession* or the *Sermons* of Wesley – the different churches have come to acknowledge together the validity for them all of agreed models. Whereas, in the past, the subordinate standards operated radically to divide denominations, in the present situation models which surmount the old barriers create a basis for ecumenical unity. The point is often put in a different way, of course, when it is said that church differences are now horizontal rather than vertical, and that the same kinds of theological differences reproduce themselves almost exactly within the different denominations. This ecumenical influence of the models in their normative capacity may, in part, atone for the part they play in fostering the *odium theologicum* within denominations. The unfortunate aspect of the situation is that both consequences follow from a single cause.

THE INTEGRATIVE FUNCTION OF MODELS

Closely allied to the previous function of models in christology is one which I have called their *integrative* function. By their presence in christological formulation, they provide it with a unity which it did not have when theologians did not rely so heavily as they do today on models as controlling categories. At one time, the contents of theology were presented as if they constituted the several atomic items of a series, a longer version of the Apostles' Creed, with no internal coherence and no genuinely systematic structure. The fashion nowadays is the reverse: theology is highly integrated and carefully structured, and the medium of articulation is the theological model. This end is achieved in somewhat different ways perhaps in different areas of scholarship.

For example, in the field of biblical studies there has been a revival of interest in typological forms of exegesis. Sometimes typology has taken the straightforward action of discerning the lineaments of Christ in Old Testament situations, as when it is suggested that Jacob wrestled with Christ at Peniel (Gen 32.24ff), so that the imposition has been of New Testament concepts upon Old Testament situations, characters and events. Nor can we ever forget that it was not left to patristic, reformed or neo-orthodox expositors to invent the practice of typology. For Christians it is already embodied in Scripture, in St Paul's affirmation (1 Cor 10.4) that the spiritual Rock of which the Israelites drank in the wilderness and which had followed them in their journeying was Christ; and clearly in St Paul it was no newly created art. He was adopting an accepted form of Jewish exegesis. At other times, the typology operates in a directly opposite direction, and the Old Testament provides the *typos* for the exposition of New Testament situations and occurrences. A notable example of this kind of typology is given by John Marsh in his *The Fullness of Time* (Nisbet, London, 1952, pp. 44ff, 84ff) where the pattern of the Exodus is used as the basis for the exposition of the life and ministry of Jesus Christ. Again, it may be a concept such as that of covenant which spans the Old Testament and the New which provides the overall *typos* for the exposition of the central themes of both Testaments. In such a case it is difficult to determine the direction of the flow of interpretation. Another type which seems to span and include both the Old Testament and the New is that used so frequently in the sermons in the Acts of the Apostles, namely, promise and fulfilment. An interesting extension of the biblical type-form is to be seen in the way in which Barth uses the parable of the prodigal son and the notion of 'the far country' to describe the distance which God in Christ came to redeem mankind. These examples are chosen wildly and at random; for I am not so much concerned with the variety of typological exegesis and interpretation as with the fact that typology is an instance of the integrative function which models fulfil, more particularly in the field of biblical studies. Its employment in this field raises constantly the question of the point at which the type, applied to the text, begins to distort and misrepresent, and to violate the canons of historiography and of historicity which are implicit in the biblical narrative.

The unity of the Bible is itself a model

When we speak of the *integrative* function of the models employed in biblical typology, it is not always observed that the very notion of an integrative function is, in a sense, itself a model. To put the matter in another way: most typologies, whether ancient or modern, presuppose the *unity* of the Bible. But the very notion of unity is itself a model. Perhaps someone might be tempted to say that it is a purely formal model, but when the evidence is examined it would appear that it is the structure of the unity model which in most cases determines the form which the typology takes and the lengths to which it is prepared to go. I should like, therefore, to spend a little time in consideration of what the unity of the Bible is thought to be, for our conception of the unity of the Bible, or the form of the model of unity which we employ, prescribes to a very considerable degree the way in which we use not only the Old Testament but also the New when speaking of Jesus Christ.

The obvious first conception of unity which springs to mind is that associated with the old Protestant view of the Bible. It is a unity of system, a unity of propositions which all directly or allegorically or typologically refer to Jesus Christ; but recourse was had to allegory and type only after it had proved absolutely impossible to make the direct reference. The consequence was that texts from the Old Testament almost as readily as from the

New could be applied to Christ. It is as if Christ were contemporaneous with all parts of the Scriptures, whether before or after his birth. A sustained passage such as Isa 52.13–53.12 still constitutes a major problem for Old Testament scholars, if pressed to say of *whom* in fact the author was speaking when describing the servant of Yahweh – an actual known figure of the day, who had suffered greatly; the whole nation of Israel in their historical sufferings; the ideal Israel, as it would be were it truly to be God's servant and God's agent in the world; the loyal and faithful core of Israel, the minority who were to suffer for the nation; or indeed the Messiah that was yet to come. But on the view of the unity of the Bible now before us the passage is an accurate description of the person of Jesus Christ. It found concrete and final embodiment in him.

It has become customary nowadays to be explicit in rejection of the so-called proof-text method, the type of theology which resorts constantly to scriptural quotations in order to clinch a point in theological controversy. The determination of the relation between the quotation and what it is thought to prove can be an exceedingly complex exercise in hermeneutics. Not infrequently the text is designed to conceal some lacuna or *non sequitur* in the main argument. Often it is assumed that what the text is taken to prove is a paraphrase of the text itself. The presence of a textual reference, particularly when inserted within brackets, should be taken as a danger signal by anyone engaged in the serious reading of theology. The content of the text apart from the bracket is to be approached with the greatest caution, and the brackets themselves to be entered at walking speed. But if you succeed in discovering the relation between what a man puts within the brackets and what he says or writes outside of them you will have discovered the secret springs of his theology.

Unity of devotional purpose

Though it does not come in quite the correct logical order, I should like to mention as the next form which the model of unity may take, unity of devotional purpose. It comes at this point, however, only because it forms an interesting subsection to our notion of unity of system. For while perhaps a considerable number of us might reject the idea that the Bible is a system of propositions contemporary with Christ, as one of our theological principles, nevertheless, our devotional practice would imply a rather different position. When we join with the whole Church on Good Friday to listen to Isa 52.13–53.12; when we hear once again the story of Abraham and Isaac (Gen 22.3ff), and particularly the words of Abraham, 'My son, God will provide himself a lamb for a burnt offering'; or when we read the 23rd Psalm or Isa 9.6f; it is inevitable that we should at once be thinking of Christ in the terms of each of those passages. When the reference is not so clearly to the person of Christ, but more to some aspect of his character or some event in his life, we may still make the application even though we are well aware that the original author was speaking about someone in his own time and not about Christ, who may have lived as many as eight hundred years later. There is an extension of this process into the ethical field when we find that a command given in a context quite foreign to us, a command given even in a passage whose authenticity we might on textual critical grounds feel compelled to question, comes to us as a direct imperative of the word of God. Those are all everyday experiences for those who use the Bible as the basis for the daily devotional period. Their significance is that the Bible is clearly acknowledged by us to have a unity of devotional purpose not dissimilar to the kind of unity which we called systematic, and which many people would reject as part of their theological principles. To put the case quite bluntly, they reject fundamentalism as a theological formula only to accept it as a devotional presupposition. I sometimes wonder whether it is not in this area that we ought to be looking for the cause of the breakdown of the devotional disciplines of our time not only among the people of the Church but also among ministers. It would be too extreme to say that to fail to correlate devotional reflection with textual or theological criticism and analysis is to base one's devotions upon a lie and to be a hypocrite;

but doubt about the historicity of an incident, or the authenticity of a saying may prevent either from being the medium of the word of God to us in our need. It certainly would seem to be the case that it is the fundamental sense of the unity of devotional purpose of the Bible which sustains the more strictly theological conviction about its systematic propositional unity.

Unity of centre

To return to the theological analysis of the model of unity, we may mention as the third form – unity of centre. This model may be looked at in two ways. On the one hand we may think of the unity which is given to the circumference of a circle through the relation in which it stands to its centre. The Bible may then be thought of as the circumference of a circle with radii pointing inwards to Christ as its centre. On this view, the Bible is eccentric: it has a centre beyond itself. To understand the Bible we have to look in the direction in which it is pointing and, wherever we open it, we find that it points to the same person, Jesus Christ. We do not find that every radius points in the same direction, for the simple reason that every radius begins from a different point on the circumference. The starting points of Abraham and Moses, of Amos and Isaiah, of Peter and John, of Paul and James, were all different, but at the centre of the circle on the circumference of which they stood was Christ himself. Without him they would not have existed as a circle; with him at the centre they are bound to one another. On the other hand, we may think of Christ creating of the Bible a unity, by standing between them as the one to whom the Old Testament looks forward and the New Testament looks back. The former utters the promise of the One that is yet to come; the other declares the fulfilment of the promise, proclaiming that that One has come. Consequently, the relation of Christ to the Old Testament is different from that which he bears to the New. It is impossible then to adopt the position of those who hold to a unity of system and to relate all of Scripture uniformly to Christ. Instead, it is as if they were a gulf between the two, a gulf created by the incarnation. Prophecy looking towards Christ can never be used of him as if it knew that he had come. Expectation is misrepresented if it is merged with consummation. They stand separated but in their separation held together as the two ultimate parts of the context of the incarnation, its before and after.

Unity in the records of God's mighty acts

It would be wrong to omit from a review of this kind some reference to the model of unity which conceives of it as a record of God's mighty acts. This form is perhaps ultimately a combination of unity of centre and unity of system. It shares with the former the fact that it is eccentrically constituted; it is a record of acts done by God; it points beyond itself to the events which it records. On the other hand, it forms a very closely knit system of interrelationships, in which the divine purpose unfolds itself to the redemption of mankind. Operating with this model christologically, we see the incarnation as the supreme mighty act of God, the consummation of all else. With this model, the method of christology tends to be dogmatic-historical. But once again, the point emerges that the model defines and controls the method.

CRITERIA GOVERNING THE USE OF MODELS IN CHRISTOLOGY

At the start I mentioned that one of the most characteristic features of christology is the immense range of terms which the Church has employed to deploy its account of Jesus Christ. Of those that are drawn from the Old Testament some are applied directly to Jesus; while others, given a special significance in being applied to Jesus, in the process are deeply changed. Yet others are New Testament terms *simpliciter* and they derive their meaning strictly from within its limits. But the history of christology has yielded a whole new crop of fresh terms, their originals coming from philosophy, ethics, social or economic circumstances, or even biology. When we look at this immense range, we cannot easily escape the question of how these different models gain ascendancy and popularity the one over the other. Few criteria would seem to operate.

The first is that the model which correlates a higher proportion of the biblical material concerning Christ and of the Church's witness to Christ and obedience to him, than its fellows is the more likely to gain allegiance. To adopt Professor Ramsey's language: it is isomorphic with a greater number of biblical and church phenomenal situations than are competing models and consequently is the medium of disclosure over a wider area than they are. For example, the model of the *eschaton*, while referring primarily to the end-time in history, has in recent years been related not only to the whole incarnation, in terms of what we now call realised eschatology, but also to individual incidents and events within the incarnation itself. Some of Jesus' parables are seen to have an eschatological significance; baptism is linked with the *eschaton*; the Last Supper points forward both to the coming crucifixion and to the end of history. An isomorphic structure, paradigmatically instanced in the *eschaton* proper, links together a whole range of phenomena, and discloses the presence of him who is not *eschaton* but *eschatos*. The covenant model we have already seen plays the same correlating role, linking the death of Christ not only to the Old Testament and God's purposes of salvation there declared, but to the Last Supper and to every celebration of the sacrament of the Lord's Supper which takes place thereafter in the Church. Other comprehensive models of this standard come to mind – the kingdom of heaven or the Son of man in the Gospels, the model of stewardship in the letters of the apostle Paul, the Lamb of the book of the Revelation, and so on. Any one of these models correlates an immense variety of biblical material. By comparison, at the other extreme, we might quote the model of 'husband' which appears in John Newton's hymn, 'How sweet the name of Jesus sounds' (*Revised Church Hymnary*, Hymn 419). This model would have a much narrower range of relevance than some of the other models which appear in the same line, 'Shepherd, Friend, King', and so on.

The second criterion which seems to apply in the selection of models, almost one might say in their self-selection, for it is not always a procedure which is explicitly and consciously followed by the Church, is as follows. The model which sets the phenomena of Scripture and of the life of faith in the Church based upon Scripture within the deepest perspective tends to gain ascendancy. The model of the Logos which places Jesus Christ in the context of the ultimate nature of God, which locates him within the very being of God from the beginning; which sees the events of the incarnation as the final consummation of a process which had been taking place throughout the whole history of Israel; a model with such depth to it is superior to one such as rabbi, which pictures Christ only as a teacher, a creature of time, coming to be and passing away. The model of the Son of God gives the same depth of perspective as does that of the Logos, and it establishes itself over against some such notion as that of wonder-worker, which makes him a person only of his own age and of human stature. Probably the ultimate ground for our rejection of a purely human Jesus is the shallowness of the pre-sentation it offers to us, and the resultant sense of loss and dis-appointment that it creates within us. It has omitted an entire dimension. He takes a two-dimensional approach to a reality which has depth and mystery to it. Its picture is flat where the reality is perspectival.

The third criterion we might consider to be relevant when comparing christological models is that that model is preferable which throws light on those areas of our religious thought and action to which we should have felt it to be immediately relevant. The notion of the *eschaton* is concerned with the end of history, and with that anticipation of the end which took place in the incarnation and has yielded the notion of eschatology. But it has a relevance beyond the interpretation of history, the parables and even the sacraments, to the field of ethics. If Jesus Christ is the great contemporaneous *eschatos*, then we are living now as in the very end-time; we stand now under God's mercy and judgement; so that we dare not live our lives carelessly and thoughtlessly or sinfully. The Judge and Saviour awaits. Morality in these terms acquires an urgency and gravity which it would not have on other historical or metaphysical grounds. The Son of Man model, even although, and perhaps because, it is such an exceedingly difficult model to plot with accuracy, has fruitful and illuminating points of contact with the Christian doctrine of man: a model primarily applied to Jesus is a most useful basis of exposition of further aspects of the humanity which he bore. Stewardship, a model drawn from an agrarian economy, by a rather remarkable transvaluation, is an effective medium for demonstrating not only our obligations to God and our neighbour in respect of time spent, talents employed and possessions shared, but also the very grace of God towards us and our effective guardianship and propagation of the Gospel which is the story of his grace towards us. An effective model illumines areas to which it was not in the first place directed.

So, fourthly, the models which finally establish themselves in the Church's understanding of the Scriptures and in its proclamation of the Gospel, are those which mediate Christ, his love, his forgiveness, his power and his truth; which sustain faith and renew it with the very life of Christ; which lead to fresh commitment to him for work to be done in his name and for his kingdom's sake; and which issue in sincere obedience to Christ and to his will. The model which does not meet these empirical demands, however impeccably demonstrated its scriptural authenticity, however dogmatically respectable its sources, can never hope to survive as a genuine medium of insight into Christ's nature and of our obedient and loving response to him. In a word, the only genuine purpose of a christological model is to make possible the service and love of Christ, through a true understanding of him.

IMAGINATION AND MODELS

Since it seems to be the case that no compulsive character can readily be attached to the models unless they are thought of as *given* to the theologian; since, too, the model seems to be a vehicle of varied christological expression and not uniform or standardised; the question might well be asked, Whence do models derive? The answer that commends itself to my judgement is that the creation of models is part of the function which imagination fulfils in theological activity. Theology has been singularly slow to allow imagination a place within its sacred precincts; and one ought not to be surprised if as a result a good deal of theology has been correspondingly unimaginative. This suspicion of imagination has had several sources. For example, it has been associated with fantasy-thought, with the creation of illusions, hallucinations or compensatory systems. It has been a medium of escape from the harshness of reality. It has, alternatively, either added to reality or presented a false picture of reality. At no time is it recognised as a medium of truth. For that reason it has acquired a moral stigma. There is no more complete condemnation of any story than to declare that it is 'pure imagination'. The Scriptures have added their own toll of severe judgement on the term. 'For the imagination of man's heart is evil from his youth' (Gen 8.21d). There has been a fear, too, that if we allow imagination a place within the activity of theological construction we are giving formal recognition to the fact that man may discover truth for himself. That would be christological Pelagianism. Two replies may be made to this fear.

First, it is perfectly possible, if we wish, to safeguard the pneumatological proprieties, to say that in this process of imaginative construction man does receive the assistance and guidance of the Holy Spirit. The Holy Spirit would be thought of not as dictating a series of propositions which man could faithfully repeat, but as working creatively, as it were, from man's side. It is difficult, as we noticed before, to pursue any further description of the psychological process in which the Holy Spirit inspires the mind or will of man. *That* he does so is all that we are presently concerned to acknowledge, on this first reading of the situation.

The second and quite different reply to the fear that the acknowledgement of the presence of imagination in christological construction may concede too much to the ability of man to think for himself, is to say that a good deal of the time in theology that is exactly what man does – he thinks for himself. There is a passage in *The Doctrine of the Word of God* (p. 14) which comes surprisingly near to saying something similar:

> (Dogmatics) knows the light that is perfect in itself, that discovers all in a flash. But it knows it only in the prism of this act, which however radically or existentially it may be regarded, is a human act. . . . The creaturely form which God's revealing action comes to take in dogmatics is therefore not that of knowledge attained in a flash, which it would have to be to correspond to the divine gift, but a laborious advance from one partial human insight to another.

Barth here comes very close perhaps to wanting to have it both ways. Dogmatics 'knows the light that is perfect' – but the act of knowing is human and fallible. God's revealing act is the subject of dogmatics, but it is known in a process of advancing from one partial human insight to another. What Barth is saying, it seems to me, is simply this: God in his revelation – or as we would prefer to say, God in Jesus Christ – is the subject that dogmatics deals with; but it deals with this subject not by writing down a series of divinely communicated propositions, but by humanly and fallibly and painfully slowly thinking about them. Such thinking is a process involving perception and insight – both of which are, I should say, functions of imagination.

A good deal has been said in recent years about man having come of age, and I must confess that I cannot follow very much of it, for it seems to be a rather disguised way of saying that modern man is godless. It is the atheist's answer to 'Except ye become as little children'. But I can just see that in theology we have in a sense to be ready to stand on our feet, to recognise that our theology, our christology, is *human* thinking about God, *human* thinking about Christ. There is an element of deceit in pretending that these are not our thoughts but God's thoughts, blasphemy, perhaps, more than deceit. The danger then is that we become so convinced that our thoughts are God's thoughts that we make a fair shape at reproducing the wrath of God against those who have the effrontery to disagree with us.

Theology, christology, is none the worse for being humble – and none the less true for it, either.

It is for this reason that I should like to say a concluding word about christology, models and faith – two words in fact. On the one hand, if models are deliverances of imagination, we shall be a little reluctant to claim for them immediately the sanctions of faith. They do not come to us with the authority of Christ himself. They do not impose themselves upon us as the dazzling light of truth. They represent our partial insights, our slow advance from vantage-point to vantage-point. If we assign to them the sanctions of faith, very soon we find ourselves seeking to impose them upon our fellows; or we set up the machinery of the Inquisition or its Protestant forms of anathema, which are not without their painful examples. Faith has Christ as its subject and its goal and nothing less.

On the other hand, it must be insisted that unless the models serve faith at the end of the day, they will neither justify themselves intellectually nor will they even survive. There is a theological schizophrenia as well as other sorts. It is the state of mind in which we cling with a return-to-the-womb desperation to the simple form in which we first found and expressed our faith; and at the same time practise all the sophistries of christological hair-splitting, existentialist elaboration and systematic proliferation. Schizophrenia is not a stable state of mind; and the tragedy is that when it finally resolves itself, both of its constituent elements are destroyed. Christological models, therefore, which are not derived from faith, will finally if they be true models find their place and their home in faith's worship of and prayer to its Saviour and Master.

PART II
CHALCEDON-BASED MODELS

4

THE TWO-NATURE MODEL

It will have become clear by now that in a quite fundamental way the model is the controlling element in the development of any discipline. It determines how we shall handle the given from which the discipline takes its beginning. It dictates the method we follow in imposing form and structure upon the given. It regulates our discussions with one another upon the validity or invalidity of statements made within the given. I propose in the second part of our discussion to examine more closely three of the more important models which have in the past operated in the christological field, and more particularly to try to discover to what extent they continue to be models that we may rightly employ in the execution of our christological task.

JESUS CHRIST, HUMAN AND DIVINE: THE BIBLICAL WITNESS

Beginning with the two-nature model, I should like to indicate its main constituent features. The feature that is most obvious is, of course, the description of the person of Jesus Christ as both human and divine. We have become so accustomed to this sort of characterisation that we are unaware now that even by using this quite simple descriptive form we have firmed into hard usage something that was still fluid and malleable in the Scriptures themselves, and we have even given the description a twist which is not immediately recognisable as biblical.

The Scriptures obviously do not think of Jesus Christ in dualistic terms, which in honesty we must admit is one of the first impressions created by the use of the two-nature model. Jesus moves among men and walks and talks as a single person, even in situations which later theology has come to associate with one nature rather than with the other. When Luke says at 2.52 that 'Jesus increased in wisdom and stature, and in favour with God and man', he does not say that it was in respect of his human nature that he was developing from childhood to maturity nor does he even raise the question of how this growth could be related to a perfect divine nature. There was a single, not a dual, situation, with the boy Jesus becoming a man. When he worked his miracles, feeding the five thousand (Lk 9.14ff), healing the woman 'which had a spirit of infirmity eighteen years' (Lk 13.11ff), when he cured the blind man (Jn 9.1ff), no suggestion is made by the evangelists that these were particularly a demonstration of his divine powers or nature. Even in the great prayer of John 17, when Jesus makes his awareness of his oneness with the father unmistakably plain (Jn 17.5, 10, 21), there is not the slightest hint that one part of his person is speaking, or that what he is saying might not be entirely true of the whole of his person. When he faces the final agonies on Calvary, no excuse is offered for his weakness – for example, that it is in his human nature that he is brought low, while his divine nature still reigns in heaven. It was left to later apologetic to invent subtleties, one might even say deceptions, of this sort. After the resurrection, in spite of the quasi-incorporeal character of his manifestations, Jesus is presented as having a body; he still bears the wound marks in his side and hands, into which a doubting Thomas may thrust his hand and his fingers to obtain what we would call empirical evidence. But it is evidence not simply that the body of Christ has not been annihilated by death and that his human nature is raised from the dead, but also that, as we would say, the divine nature, that Word that was with God in the beginning, the Word that was made flesh, had been brought back from the dead. The implication is clear: the indicator to the presence of the human nature operates automatically as the marker for the divine nature, so completely are they regarded as elements in a single situation. The matter of one being present with the other is not even mentioned: it is taken for granted.

It would be wrong, however, to give the impression that the human–divine categorisation is an improper imposition which later theology made upon an originally basically simple biblical given. There must be some justification both in the words and the events recorded in Scripture to give the categorisation a prima facie plausibility It is to be found, as shown by the example we gave, in some of the things Jesus did, according to the narratives; for reflective men pondering over the events after the resurrection must have seen that even his moments of greatest human weakness were accompanied by a courage and glory which were more than human; that even when he worked his miracles, most of all when he was raised from the dead, the situations had a human side which was an inalienable aspect of them. So often it was human compassion that was the motive of the miracles; it was the presence of the human body which carried conviction about the reality of the resurrection. In other words, the distinction arose out of the given for anyone who pondered it in the Holy Spirit. One might then conclude that the distinction was implicit in the given which confronted the disciples and the evangelists, were it not that we must say that it was to some extent explicit in some of the ways men spoke of Jesus. The Son of God concept may be and has been taken as a recognition of the divine nature of Jesus; and the Son of Man concept, in addition to its apocalyptic associations, has been said to carry the human reference.

> But we must guard against ascribing also to the first Christians – much less to Jesus himself – the intention of using the Son of God designation to say something about the Son's identity of substance with the Father. The New Testament title does point to Christ's coming from the Father and his deity, but not in the sense of later discussions about 'substance' and 'natures'. (Oscar Cullmann, *The Christology of the New Testament*, ET, SCM Press, London, 1959, p. 270)

The birth narratives in Luke's Gospel, whether we decide on their ultimate historical authenticity or not, clearly indicate that from a very early date the Church acknowledged in Jesus a person who, for all his being born of Mary, has a mysterious, divine beginning described by saying that he was conceived by the Holy Ghost. The sustained witness to what we call the deity of Christ in the aforementioned Great Prayer of John 17 combines in that Gospel with countless testimonies to the genuine reality of the humanity of Christ. The basic material is all there in Scripture for the Church's subsequent definition of a firm distinction between the human nature of Jesus Christ and the divine; but Scripture prefers not to speak of the distinction in these terms. The change is not all gain, as may be seen from a comparison of the colourful biblical descriptions with the often sterile, logical structures of subsequent scholasticism.

In fact, had the point been put with any directness to, say, St John, whether he might not be persuaded to use the term divine, *theios*, rather than *theos* (God) of Christ, his reply would have been that the former is much too equivocal. It threatens to place Christ in some intermediate status lower than God and higher than man, a *tertium quid* with identity with neither. 'The Word was with God', says the Prologue to St John's Gospel, 'and the Word was God.' To quote Hoskyns and Davey (*The Fourth Gospel*, Faber & Faber, London, 1940, I, p. 136):

> Since the anarthrous *Theos* is personal, more is stated than that the Word is divine. The Word of God is no neuter thing, no mere power: He acts with personal consciousness and will.

The New Testament method, then, is not to fix the description of Jesus Christ by means of a sharp dualism, but rather to elaborate the various situations in which Christ gave himself *to* men and women, and for them, to tell over again all the wonderful things he said, and how he opened up the very heart of God to believers. One circumstance, therefore, that we shall have to mark very carefully in our consideration of the two-nature model is the extent to which it succeeds in conserving the unity of the person of Jesus Christ.

THE ARISTOTELIAN SOURCES OF THE
TWO-NATURE MODEL

In the actual execution of its task the two-nature model in most of its forms draws heavily on the logic of Aristotle's *Categoriae*, c.5. One of the relevant passages may be quoted at length (2a.11–19 translated by Walter and Martha Kneale, *The Development of Logic*, Oxford, 1962, p. 26, a book to which I should like publicly to acknowledge my debt), for it deals with the very important distinction between primary substance (*prōtē ousia*) and secondary substance (*deutera ousia*).

> Substance in the most literal and primary and common sense of the term is that which is neither predicated of a subject nor exists in a subject, as for example, the individual man or horse. These things are called secondary substances to which, as species, belong the things called substances in the primary sense and also the genera of these species. For example, the individual man belongs to the species man, and the genus of the species is animal. These, then, are called secondary substances as for example both man and animal.

It is important that we should endeavour to grasp what Aristotle is saying. The distinction he makes here becomes regulative, as we shall see, of the definition of orthodox theology some seven hundred years after he made it, and remained so, one might say, even until our time. Perhaps it is simplest to begin by breaking down this rather concentrated account into the form of an example, 'Tom Jones is human.' Here Tom Jones is the primary substance. Humanity is predicated of him, though admittedly the Greek structure would oblige us to say 'man' rather than 'humanity'. As we would put it, he is the subject of all the circumstances, characteristics, qualities and experiences that we would normally associate with being human, or occur within the range of being human. Tom Jones is cold; ambitious; friendly; married or industrious. He is the subject to whom we refer the different predicates we have mentioned in the sentence; the subject, not just in the grammatical sense, in which a subject is so-called in relation to the predicate of the sentence, but the actual subject who has these qualities, adopts certain attitudes or reaches certain decisions. So we can see why Aristotle has contended that primary substance in this sense 'is neither predicated of a subject nor exists in a subject'. We would not think of saying that Tom Jones could be predicated of anything or anyone else, or that he exists in anything or anyone else. He exists in his own right, very much Tom Jones. Secondary substance, on the other hand, is predicated of something else, and it must always exist in something else. Sometimes, the secondary substance is a very inclusive genus such as animal, or only a species such as man; but all secondary substances, either genera or species, belong to primary substances.

In parenthesis, it ought to be pointed out that Aristotle seems to move rather too readily from talk about predication to talk about belonging to a species or genus, but this assumption has been so widely commented upon that it is perhaps sufficient here only to draw attention to it. Further, he equates 'being predicated of a subject' (*kata tinos legesthai*) with 'being in something' (*en tini einai*) – a point to which we shall later return. His main contention is fairly clear.

At *Categoriae* 5 (2a.34ff, again following the translation of W. and M. Kneale, op. cit., p. 30) Aristotle writes:

> Everything except primary substances is either predicable of primary substances or present in them as subjects. . . . Animal is predicated of man, and therefore of individual man; for if there were no individual man of whom it could be predicated, it could not be predicated of man at all. . . . Everything is either predicated of primary substances or present in them; and if these last did not exist, it would be impossible for anything else to exist.

Aristotle is understood here to be affirming one form of his theory of universals. While Plato argued that universals exist *ante res* – the Forms pre-exist the particulars which embody them; and nominalists much later argued that universals exist *post res* – we derive them conceptually from the world of existent things which are qualified by various attributes; Aristotle's position was that universals exist *in rebus*, that is, only as realised in particular subjects. If the world of ordinary existence were to disappear, Plato would still have his ideal Forms, laid up in heaven in perfection, and the nominalists could still retain the concepts of real things in their minds; but for Aristotle with ordinary existence the universals would disappear also, 'for without primary substance, it would be impossible for anything else to exist'. Normally, also, that would be the direction of the argument: if there is no *prōtē ousia*, primary substance, there can be no secondary substance, *deutera ousia*.

NO *PHYSIS ANHYPOSTATOS*

ORIGINS OF THE THEOREM

These two principles which we have selected from the *Categoriae* of Aristotle became, in fact, the foundation of the two-nature model, subject to one qualification: namely, that for the distinction between *prōtē ousia* and *deutera ousia* was substituted that between *hypostasis* and *physis*. The theory of *universalia in rebus*, that the *deutera ousia* does not exist if there is no *prōtē ousia*, was employed in the form that there is no *physis* without a *hypostasis*, no *physis anhypostatos*. The ubiquity of this principle in post- and pre-Chalcedonian times is strongly emphasised by R. V. Sellers (in *The Council of Chalcedon*, SPCK, London, 1953, p. 318 n. 2 and p. 188), who discovers it in John Maxentius (*Dial c. Nestorian* i.6), and Ephraim of Antioch (in Photius, Biblioth. Cod. ccxxix. PG ciii.993C); and it could be added that it is implied in the christology of Hippolytus (*c. Noetum* 15) in so far as he anticipates the doctrine of *enhypostasia*. Timothy, Bishop of Alexandria, could write in *Refutation of the Synod of Chalcedon and the Tome of Leo*, Pt 6: 'There is no nature which has not its *hypostasis*, and there is no *hypostasis* which exists without its *prosōpon*'; and Philoxenus, in *Against Nestorius*: 'There is no nature (*k'yânâ*) without a person (*q'nômâ*) neither is a person without a nature' (both Timothy and Philoxenus are quoted by R. V. Sellers, op. cit., pp. 260 and 260, n. 4).

Our next sections will illustrate the determinative influence of this single principle of no *physis* without a *hypostasis* upon all shades of christological thought in the formative centuries of that discipline, as well as in modern times. For the moment it may be important to pause to notice what is happening. In the New Testament, as we saw, there is the acknowledgement, the confession of Jesus Christ as both human and divine, a distinction drawn in a variety of terms but nevertheless fundamental to the Church's understanding of Christ's person. This distinction is about to be expressed in a model whose basic structural features are drawn from the heart of Aristotle's logic. This fact has to be kept clearly before us because, in many of the christological controversies, biblical texts seem to be so constantly the subject of difference of opinion that one might be pardoned for thinking that these great controversies dealt only with matters of biblical exegesis. On the contrary, it could fairly be said that it was this 'no *physis anhypostatos*' principle which was the great divider and it is the clue to the variety of biblical exegesis. The quite astonishing further fact about this principle is that whereas it seems to us to have a fairly straightforward connotation, when applied to the christological material it permits of a whole range of christological interpretations. This range is our immediate next concern.

IN NESTORIANISM

In selecting a number of representative positions in illustration of how the 'no *physis anhypostatos*' principle was used in the classical period of controversy (fourth and fifth centuries), I do not wish to become involved in too much critical detail, discussing, for example, whether Nestorius was a Nestorian and so on. It will serve our purpose if we are able to show how this principle might be embodied in a specific model, even though there is doubt as to the authenticity of the writings or traditional interpretation of an author's thought.

Perhaps the most obvious implementation of the principle is to be found generally in what is known as the school of Antioch, and associated, when falling into heretical form, with the name of Nestorius. Given that Jesus Christ is to be regarded as both human and divine, and that there is 'no *physis* without a *hypostasis*', it would seem to follow that in Jesus Christ there are two *physeis* and two *hypostaseis*. This contention is reinforced both by Greek philosophical views about the difference between God who is impassible, incorruptible and eternal and man who is passible, corruptible and mortal, and by biblical accounts of the ways in which God surpasses man, for example, according to Isa 55.8f: 'For my thoughts are not your thoughts, neither are your ways my ways saith the Lord. For as the heavens are higher than the earth so are my ways higher than your ways, and my thoughts than your thoughts.' Both the whole creation narrative as it is written down in Genesis 1 and 2, and the imaginative expression of it in Second Isaiah, leave the reader with a lively sense of what a later theologian was to call 'the infinite qualitative difference between God and man'. Theodore of Mopsuestia had summed up the situation in the words,

> It is well known that the one who is eternal, and the one whose existence came into being later, are separated from each other, and the gulf between them unbridgeable. . . . What possible resemblance and relation can exist between two beings so widely separated from each other? (Quoted by R. V. Sellers, op. cit., p. 162)

Given this difference between the natures it was inevitable that to secure the integrity of both they should each have a *hypostasis*. God and man in Jesus Christ each had his own nature and person; otherwise, they would be lacking in reality. Language was used which seemed to confirm the consequent dualism. Theodoret writes (*Ep.* cli): 'In Christ we contemplate the manhood through the sufferings, and we apprehend the Godhead through the miracles.' Scripture is examined carefully with a view to assigning different texts to different natures.

Probably the main psychological spring for the Antiochene attitude was a fear of confusing the two natures of Jesus Christ. Classically the name of Nestorius has been associated with carrying this fear to extremes and thus creating a dualism of the person of Jesus Christ. All the charges brought against the Antioch school may not be entirely justified. For example, it is difficult to see why H. R. Mackintosh (*The Person of Jesus Christ*, T. & T. Clark, Edinburgh, 1912, p. 203) should say that they (Theodore and his group) could scarcely 'call Jesus more than a supremely inspired man', or that 'Jesus is man side by side with God.' Jesus is, for the Antioch school, and even for Nestorius, God–man. Whatever they say about 'the difference' it exists even for them within an ultimate unity. Nestorius says: 'Two perfect natures, both without confusion and without division, must be observed in our Lord Jesus Christ.' In other words, together with the 'no *physis anhypostatos*' principle, there is working the first constituent element in the two-nature model, drawn as we saw from the Bible itself, namely, the unity of the person of Jesus Christ. That it should be recognised by Nestorius who is classically associated with dualism, shows how necessary a part it is of the two-nature model.

IN EUTYCHEANISM

On the other hand, the traditional opponent of Nestorianism, namely Eutycheanism, takes the notion of the unity of Christ as the regulative element in the model, but is nevertheless obliged to offer its account of how the two natures are to be reconciled with this unity. Eutyches is historically regarded as making two emphases, which gained him the reputation of heretic. First, he rejected the idea set forth in the *Formulary of Reunion* that Jesus Christ is 'out of two natures hypostatically united', and argued for the formulae: 'out of the two natures before the union' and 'not two natures but one after the union'. It is nowhere explained clearly how Eutyches interpreted the transition from the two natures to one. He is not arguing for a transmutation of the human into the divine, nor does he countenance the swallowing up of the human by the divine. Secondly, he rejected the idea that Jesus Christ was *homoousios hēmin*. But he is, nevertheless, not a docetist in respect of the body of Christ: Christ had a *sōma anthropinon*, a human body. To his reply to his attackers, Eutyches lent a certain acidic quality by pointing out that there was no place in Scripture where the phrase 'two natures' occurred, and whereas the term *homoousios* had no scriptural basis either, it did at least have patristic authority. Later the monophysites gave the ultimately logical grounds upon which a position like that of Eutyches might rest. Timothy of Alexandria, after enunciating the 'no *physis anhypostatos*' principle, affirmed that if there are two natures, then there are two *prosōpa*; 'and if there are two *prosōpa*, there are also two Christs'.

Comparing this conclusion, which is the logical consequence of Eutychean thought, with Nestorianism, we may note certain interesting points. First, both views combine an acknowledgement of the unity of the person of Jesus Christ with compulsion to express a judgement on how the two natures are related to this unity. Each throws the emphasis on a different point, but seeks to embody the other emphasis in some way or other. Secondly, both fail to establish their position by an outright and convincing appeal to Scripture; at most, in support of their own position, they are able to cite the absence of scriptural evidence for the opposite theory. Thirdly, most important of all is the way in which the 'no *physis anhypostatos*' principle yields such contrary interpretations of the person of Jesus Christ. At this early stage, we may begin to register a suspicion that the models in theology may not altogether merit the claim to the normative function which they so widely perform in this discipline. To give the suspicion a further degree of substance, it would be necessary to discover on what extraneous grounds (granted the absence of clear scriptural direction) one form of the model is to be (or was, by the formulators of orthodoxy) preferred to any one of the others. Meantime, we may proceed to another expression of the two-nature model.

THE CHALCEDONIAN DEFINITION

This time it is what is thought to be the classical expression of it that we shall consider, the Chalcedonian Definition of the Faith.

> Therefore, following the holy fathers, we all unanimously teach that Jesus Christ is to be confessed to be one and the same Son, our Lord Jesus Christ, the same perfect in Godhead, the same perfect in manhood, and the same truly man, consisting of a rational soul and body, of one nature with the Father in respect of his Godhead, and of one nature with ourselves in respect of his manhood. . . . One and the same Christ, Son, Lord, Only-begotten, to be acknowledged in two natures (which exist in him) without confusion, without change, without division, without separation; the difference in nature being in no way removed as a result of the union, but rather the property of each nature being preserved and concurring in one person (*prosōpon*) and *hypostasis*.

It is now commonly acknowledged that this document is at its most explicit when it excludes the heresies. No Eutychean or Nestorian could find much comfort here. But when we try to advance beyond the negatives into a definition of the positive view which is offered, there is not much to guide us within the document itself. Clearly the unity which we took to be part of the two-nature model is here affirmed. It is *one and the same* Son who is the subject of our confession and acknowledgement; no suggestion here of a Duad of Sons, or of two Christs. Even when it is said that there are two natures with two series of properties, nevertheless these properties concur in a single person and a single *hypostasis*. This fact cannot be too often repeated, in reply to critics of Chalcedon who aver that it presents a dualistic view of Jesus Christ. In an almost literal sense, its first and its last words about Jesus Christ are that he is *one*.

As we have just seen, going on to look for the other features of the two-nature model, it is equally explicit that in Jesus Christ the two natures, human and divine, exist to their fullness. As eternal Son, he is consubstantial with the Father; here is the fullness of Godhead in no way diminished by reason of the incarnation. In his human nature, he is identical in essence with ourselves. The presence in him of deity in no way reduces his human nature to an illusion. It is possible in reference to Jesus to deploy two series of properties and to affirm them equally of the single person.

When we continue beyond that point and endeavour to identify the person to whom the two natures are attributed, it would almost certainly appear that it is the *hypostasis* of the divine nature of the Logos who is the subject of the incarnational situation. I must say 'almost certainly' because however closely you look at the text it is difficult to see what the document really intends. This much is clear: there is no question of there being a second *hypostasis* or person. In other words, there cannot be a human *hypostasis*. This interpretation of the situation is at this point reinforced by reference to Cyril, in whose writings it is somewhat clearer that the human nature of Jesus Christ is a *physis anhypostatos*. Whether Cyril tries to correct this patent violation of the principle of 'no *physis anhypostatos*', as H. R. Mackintosh suggests (*The Person of Jesus Christ*, p. 207), it has to be admitted that no attempt is made within the four corners of the Chalcedonian Definition to make any such correction. It is for this reason that popular criticisms are levelled at the Chalcedonian Definition: it offers an impersonal view of the human nature of Christ (*anhypostasia*). For us 'impersonal' means hard, callous, indifferent, even unloving; and it is a term with pejorative connotations, and in this context even damning implications. However, if we do apply it to Chalcedon – and there is no real evidence to suggest that we should – it is to be construed logically; or at most ontologically, as signifying that the human *physis* of Jesus Christ has no human *hypostasis*. It is assumed in the definition – a point that might be questioned – that this lack does not reduce the true humanity of Christ.

What must, I think, be said, however, is that so firmly is the 'no *physis anhypostatos*' principle rooted in the minds of all participants in the christological controversies of the fifth and sixth centuries that the vacuum which was created by the indecision of Chalcedon on the matter of a *hypostasis* for the human nature was one to be abhorred. It is a matter of consequent interest to discover how it was filled. Two possibilities existed and they were adopted. Curiously enough, they have both acquired importance for our modern handling of the two-nature model.

LEONTIUS OF BYZANTIUM

The first is traditionally associated with the name of Leontius of Byzantium (*c.* 485–543). That interpretation of the Chalcedonian Definition which denied that the human *physis* of Jesus Christ had a *hypostasis* came to be known as *anhypostasia*; and it was in contradistinction to that view that Leontius sought to solve the same problem with his theory of *enhypostasia*. We have already seen how the 'no *physis hypostatos*' principle had operated to give both Eutycheanism and Nestorianism; and how, also, the Chalcedonian position was in a rather unstable position because of its failure to conform to the principle. We have also seen how the original principle of 'no *physis anhypostatos*' derives very directly from the *Categoriae* of Aristotle, with a variation in specific nomenclature. Leontius, in giving the two-nature model his cash-values, draws more heavily upon the reserves of Aristotelian logic. He does so in two stages. First, he elaborates considerably upon what is involved in the term 'nature' (*physis*) (see R. V. Sellers, op. cit., p. 317). Following the Aristotelian conception of definition as *per genus et differentiam*, he holds that *physis* is to be defined in terms of genus, species and essential qualities and properties. These terms all apply to what we would call the universal, i.e. 'nature' is that which the particular entity shares with all the fellow-members of the genus. *Hypostasis*, on the other hand, carries the reference to the principle of self-existence, particular and individual existence, of the sort the single entity has over against the logical group. The individual instance is distinguished from the other members of the group by peculiar characteristics of its own, *idiōmata aphoristika*, some of which are separable accidents (*symbebēkota chōrista*) and others are lasting (*symbebēkota achōrista*). So far nothing that makes any great difference to the basic interpretation of the two-nature model has been contributed by Leontius. Secondly, he affirms, in line with the Chalcedonian Definition, that the human nature of Jesus Christ has no *hypostasis* of its own, but adds that it is not on that account *anhypostatos*. In fact, it is a *physis enhypostatos*, an enhypostatic nature; it finds its *hypostasis* in (*en*) the *hypostasis* of the Logos. Through the union with the divine nature, and as a result of not having a *hypostasis* of its own, the human nature is not absorbed. Its integrity is preserved through its sharing in the *hypostasis* of the Logos. The distinguishing characteristics of the particular man who Jesus was are then attributed to the divine *hypostasis* as well as the essential qualities of the species (man) to which he belongs. In this way he has secured a form of Chalcedonianism against the principle that it is impermissible, even impossible, to affirm a *physis* without a *hypostasis*.

This view was destined to have such a normative effect upon subsequent christology, both in the seventh century and in our own time, that it might be important to draw attention to three prima facie defects which it seems to have.

First, there is the criticism which Harnack made so long ago (*History of Dogma*, ET, Williams & Norgate, London, 1898, IV, pp. 233–4 n. 3), and it is echoed by H. R. Mackintosh (op. cit., p. 218), that 'A pious Apollinarian monk would probably have been able to say with regard to the *hypostēnai en tō Logō*: "Apollinaris says pretty much the same thing only in somewhat more intelligible words".' It is not unusual to substantiate this charge of Apollinarianism by pointing out, as does W. N. Pittenger (*The Word Incarnate*, Nisbet, London, 1959, pp. 100–3), that on enhypostatic terms, the human nature of Christ has consequently no strictly personal centre; there is no ego around which the human life may move and upon which its experiences can 'home'. So the question has to be raised whether we may rightly ascribe to Jesus Christ the fullness of humanity, or whether in fact E. L. Mascall is correct in saying (though the very phrase is a self-condemnation) that Christ's human nature is an abstraction (quoted by Pittenger, op. cit., p. 101). Clearly the enhypostatic theory is not Apollinarianism in the strict sense.

For, while Leontius affirms that the Logos takes human nature, Apollinaris speaks more specifically of the *flesh*. There are sentences like: 'He who was once "without flesh" is now revealed "in flesh" as God incarnate (*Theos ensarkos*); but he remains still one and the same person'; and again, 'in Jesus Christ there is a unification of flesh with Godhead into one person' (the quotations in this sentence appear in Sellers, op cit., respectively pp. 138 and 140). Leontius' position therefore only resembles that of Apollinaris in so far as both of them omit from Christ's person the human ego. Even if we were to come at the question from the side of the trichotomic anthropology which Apollinaris employs, and affirm that while Jesus Christ has a human body and mind, the human spirit is replaced by the Logos, we could find no clear parallel to anything in Leontius. It would perhaps also be a little premature to follow too closely Pittenger's interpretation of *hypostasis* as a centre of human experiences; for, as we shall see later, it is not immediately justifiable to translate what is a strictly logical concept into psychological terminology. What we could say, however, is that if the *hypostasis* is an essential part of what we associate with humanity (even if it is not strictly a part of human nature as *physis*), then in respect of his humanity, Christ is not completely one with us.

A second criticism, which might be raised against the *enhypostasia* of Leontius concerns the relation of the divine *hypostasis* to the human *physis*. In the Aristotelian paradigm of this relation, the *prōtē ousia* is the individual in which the *deutera ousia* is particularised or at least it is the subject of the particularised form of the *deutera ousia* or the universal. In other words, the *prōtē ousia* is not just a blank area in which we stick the stamps of the *deutera ousia* and are at liberty to choose whichever stamps we wish for the purpose. On the contrary, it is so closely and integrally related to and congruous with the *deutera ousia* that it is understandable and describable only in terms of the latter. When we substitute for the *prōtē ousia–deutera ousia* relation that of *hypostasis–physis*, then we see just how difficult it is to remove the human *hypostasis* in the belief that the divine *hypostasis* can function in its place. The particularity and individuality of the man Jesus would be removed. In fact, it would be impossible to differentiate the *man* Jesus from the man Peter or the man John unless, in some way, the human *hypostasis* were retained.

A third criticism of *enhypostasia*, and one which could be the most serious of all, follows. If the *hypostasis* is understood to be so linked to the *physis* humanity that the latter cannot exist except as particularised in the several *hypostaseis*, then the redemption of the whole man is placed in jeopardy. For there is another important christological principle which we have not so far stated, which runs: 'What Christ did not take, he did not redeem' (Gregory of Nazianzus, *Ep.* ci in Migne, PG 37, 181). If, therefore, the *hypostasis* forms part of what it means to be human, then surely man's redemption requires that the *hypostasis* in a man be redeemed as well as his *physis*. It was this principle, too, which was the final basis for the rejection of Apollinarianism: because Christ did not take the spirit of man, but only his body and mind, the spirit of man was placed beyond the range of Christ's redemptive power. At this same point, any doctrine involving *anhypostasia* would be open to criticisms of being a defective basis for soteriology. In a very real sense any christology stands or falls by the soteriology which it makes possible, or implies.

BARTH ON ENHYPOSTASIA

The enhypostatic christology has come to figure so centrally in Barthian theology that it may not be inappropriate to consider what Barth himself has said on the subject (*Church Dogmatics* IV/2, ET, T. & T. Clark, Edinburgh, 1958, pp. 49f). Drawing upon such writers as Hollaz, Polanus and Heidegger, Barth says that *hypostasis* meant the independent existence, the *propria subsistentia* of Christ's humanity. The human essence is adopted by the Logos and taken into unity with himself. Barth also feels that to say that it was a *homo*, a particular man, that was united with the Logos and not *humanitas* would allow a degree

of autonomy to the human nature which would endanger the
whole of christology. Barth does not explain the reason for his
rejection of such autonomy, but one might guess either that it
would imply Nestorianism, or that it would assign an unduly
high place to the creature alongside the redeemer in the incarnation. Man would be a co-redemptor. Barth is, however, aware
of something rather like the difficulties we have been mentioning
which the enhypostatic theory raises for the right presentation of
the human nature of Jesus Christ.

He writes:

> The objection has often been raised that (the enhypostatic
> theory) seems to involve at an important point a denial of Christ's
> true humanity, a concealed or even blatant Docetism, since it
> must obviously belong to the true humanity of Christ that he
> should have an independent existence as a man like us. (op. cit.,
> p. 49)

Barth seems to think that what the *anhypostasia*, presupposed in
the enhypostatic doctrine, denies is the autonomous existence of
the humanity of Christ. But it is more than doubtful not only
whether the *propria subsistentia* is rightly translated as 'independent existence', but also whether any christologian, even the
most extreme Nestorians, ever thought of the human nature as
autonomous. Accordingly Barth goes on in fact to mention what
the anhypostatic theory would deny, namely, that the *humanum*
exists in Jesus Christ in the form of an actual man. (One wonders
if Barth would accept *prosōpon* as a fair translation of the term,
and admit that there are then two *prosōpa* in Jesus Christ.) Barth
makes a final break with the logic out of which the whole
enhypostatic theory has been constructed when he says that Jesus
Christ is a real man only as the Son of God: for it is no longer
possible to see the original *prōte ousia–deutera ousia* distinction
on which that theory rests in the relation of a 'real man' to the
Son of God. Barth, I should say, is right in insisting upon the
fact that in Jesus Christ the *humanum* exists in the form of an
actual man (though how, having said so, he can still believe that
in Jesus it was not a *homo*, i.e. a particular man, but *humanitas*

that was united with the Logos, is difficult to understand). But if he still wishes to avoid both Nestorianism and docetism then he must revise his definition of the human *hypostasis* (as equivalent to 'independent existence') and of its relation to the human nature and the divine *hypostasis*.

EPHRAIM OF ANTIOCH

It has always been of interest to me both that the quite radical difficulties which have been mentioned above in connection with the enhypostatic interpretation of the Chalcedonian Definition have not inhibited the widespread development of this theory and that a possible modification of a theory which goes a long way to meeting some of the difficulties has not been presented in this setting. I am referring to Ephraim of Antioch, whose views have been preserved for us in the writings of Photius of Tyre, though I am concerned with one part only of his teaching and not with his ecclesiastical-political activities which were extremely varied. He maintains customary Chalcedonian positions; for example, that Jesus Christ is of one nature with the Father in respect of Godhead, and of one nature with men in respect of his humanity; that the two natures are not to be divided, for 'two natures does not mean two *hypostaseis*'. But what I would consider to be his originality emerges when he tries to explain the 'two natures in the union which is according to *hypostasis*' (quoted by R. V. Sellers, op. cit., p. 323, q.v. for an interesting account of Ephraim) by saying that while the two natures as such are not confused or compounded one with the other, the two *hypostaseis* are. Accordingly the *hypostasis* of Jesus Christ is a fusion of the human and the divine *hypostasis*: it is *synthetos hē hypostasis*. I am not interested to argue the authenticity of Photius' review of Ephraim's theories, or even the validity of Ephraim's other theological assertions. But it does seem that his theory of the *synthetos hē hypostasis*, the composite *hypostasis*, meets not a few of the difficulties created by the enhypostatic theory.

For example, first of all, by insisting upon the presence of the human *hypostasis* in the composite *hypostasis*, it secures the wholeness of the humanity which Jesus Christ took, and firmly avoids the docetic and Apollinarian tendencies of the enhypo-static theory. Jesus Christ is a real man, not simply *humanitas* or the *humanum*, so really man, in fact, that it was possible for someone to write a purely human account of his life and death. In view of the different ways in which subsequent writers, e.g. W. N. Pittenger, have come to use the two-nature model, this advance on *anhypostasia* and *enhypostasia* which doctrinally guarantees the integrity of the human nature of Jesus, is a genuine gain. On the strictly technical side it serves to protect Chalcedon from the common charge that it operates with an 'impersonal' view of the human nature of Jesus Christ.

Next, if we follow up the soteriological approach to Ephraim's theory, we could argue that it also secures the totality of the atonement of man. There is no hidden corner of his person, no aspect of his whole being which escapes the redemptive power of God. All has been taken, and all has been redeemed. Thirdly, it meets Barth's criticism that if we allow that the Logos took not only *humanitas* but also *homo*, then we affirm the autonomy and the independence of human nature. For, if the human nature has a *hypostasis* which is conjoined with that of the divine nature, there is an end of independent existence and autonomy. God brings the human nature and its *hypostasis* under his control as its creator and redeemer.

Fourthly, Ephraim's theory has the additional advantage that it answers to the way in which we speak about the events of the incarnation. If we were to ask, 'Who is the subject of the stories which the Gospels record? Who took the loaves and the fishes and with them miraculously multiplied fed the multitude? Who suffered and died on Calvary? Who, indeed, was raised from the dead?', there could be but a single answer, 'Jesus Christ', and not 'the Son of God, *simpliciter*'. The latter phrase, 'the Son of God', would appear as the subject in a sentence answering the question, 'Who was incarnate?' Answer: 'The Eternal Son of God.' But after the incarnation, it is the God–man who is subject of what subsequently happens. In the end, this fact explains why it is so artificial, if not entirely erroneous, to try to assign some of the experiences to one nature, and some to the other. The God–man may 'have access' to certain experiences because he is divine, and to others because he is human; but ultimately it is he himself, and not either of his natures, who has the experiences and is the subject of them.

DIFFICULTIES FOR CHALCEDONIAN CHRISTOLOGY

THE DOCTRINE OF SUBSTANCE

I should like now to look at some of the difficulties which might arise for someone who today seeks to express his christology in terms resembling those of the Chalcedonian Definition. Perhaps the first stumbling-block which he would encounter would be that of the doctrine of substance presupposed by all forms of the two-nature model, the ultimate distinction between a sub-stratum or *hypostasis* and the nature (with all its attributes and accidents) which inheres in it. Locke's views on substance (*An Essay Concerning Human Understanding*, Oxford University Press, London, 1934, p. 155), springing from his rejection of 'depraved Aristotelianism', may first be stated in his own words:

> If anyone will examine himself concerning his notion of pure substance in general, he will find he has no other idea of it at all, but only a supposition of he knows not what support of such qualities which are capable of producing simple ideas in us.

This 'something I know not what' which Locke was prepared to retain in its unknowable form because of the necessity to think of qualities as qualities of *something*, this self-existent sub-stance was rejected by Berkeley and Hume, the first because he judged the very conception of substance to be self-contradictory, the latter because for him there was no empirical evidence for a substratum either physical or spiritual. The reinforcement of the older empiricism by modern forms of positivism has made it difficult for anyone to introduce into the modern theological scene thought-structures which have such a decidedly Aristotelian substance–attribute character as the two-nature models. To have said so much might appear tantamount to having closed the case. Substantialism seems to be no longer a live option even for someone who still feels that there may be some defence left for metaphysics in general. Not quite, or, at least, not entirely.

It has always been a matter of great curiosity to me that ordinary people all of the time, and philosophers when they forget their calling and indeed their set attitudes, and are simply relaxing over a cup of coffee, should speak and act *as if* the substance–attribute distinction were an absolutely valid one. When the latter speak of the coffee being sweet and cold and having rather unpleasant grounds swilling about in it; when they give a brief description of the characteristics of the new no. 6 iron which they have purchased; then they do not refer to constellations of sense-data held together by some form of inherent attraction, or of nuclear sense-data which are *maxima sensibilia* occurring at a certain point in space-time. They seem to be, by their speech, as committed to the basic Aristotelian language structure as the Philosopher himself. In other words, ordinary language with its distinction between subject and predicate seems almost to imply, if it is going to have any sense at all, something very like the distinction between substance and attribute, or rather substances and attributes.

I obviously do not wish to press this point too far. I am *not* saying that it was a good thing that subject–predicate analysis of the proposition should have exercised such a prolonged influence upon Western logic; that it is possible to reduce all propositions to the subject–predicate form; or even that the subject of every sentence refers to a specifiable ontological existence. Too much argument has flowed under logical bridges for one to be quite so naive as that. All that I do want to say is that there are many sentences – far, far more than the debunkers of the concept of substance realise – which are 'about' something or other, something which has qualities of a certain sort, behaves in a certain way, and is related to other existents in specific ways. This something or other is the subject of the sentence even if it is not its grammatical subject. The proposition thus asserted would be a nonsense if it were not about something other than itself, something which had qualities, etc.

THE TERM NATURE: A SECOND DIFFICULTY FOR MODERN CHALCEDONIANISM

A second difficulty meets us when we contemplate the re-instatement of the two-nature model. It arises over the meaning of the term 'nature'. Let us look first at the human nature. The obvious starting-point is presented by the original form of the two-nature model. The human nature as such is what we would call the logical universal; and the definition of it would be *per genus et differentiam*, that is, by means of the genus to which the individual belongs and the differentiating properties of the species. It is not an easy matter to define human nature exhaustively in this way; certainly I have never seen it defined with the precision shown by Plato in his definition of an angler (*The Sophist*) or by Susan Stebbing in 'members of the university' (*Introduction to Logic*, p. 436). But clearly the kind of definition which is contemplated is in terms of man's belonging to, say, the genus creature, having differentiating properties such as rational, moral, religious, sociable and so on. It is inevitable that there should be a certain amount of reaction both against such a con-ception of humanity, as we shall see when discussing Jean-Paul Sartre, and against the idea that it was such a vague generalisation that Jesus assumed at the incarnation.

I have already indicated that it is one of the defects of a strictly anhypostatic theory of Christ's human nature that it lands in that impasse. If we are going to avoid the impasse, the only solution is to revise the logic of universals at the basis of the two-nature model. Cook Wilson, in discussing the nature of qualities, once said that they are 'this-suches', being neither universals, suches (because they were *particular* occurrences of one kind or another, a particular blue, a particular good, etc.) nor absolute particulars, this-es, because they were instances of some *general* quality which other things also possessed; they participated in both forms of being; they were *this* and *such*, or this-suches. It seems, surely, that the same is true of the human nature of Jesus Christ. It is general human nature (the universal) which he shares with us, but it is also a particular of the universal, because he had all his own peculiar human characteristics. What we must not allow ourselves to forget is that it is the soteriological interest that is predominant in the discussion of the human nature of Christ – not the logical or even the metaphysical. It is important to acknowledge the universality of Christ's human nature, so that all men may share in the benefits of his atonement; but it is equally important to do justice to the particularity of the human nature of Christ, in order to secure its reality.

JEAN-PAUL SARTRE AND HUMAN NATURE

Our discussion of the human nature of Christ would have a rather reactionary quality in a modern setting if we did not contemplate the strictures passed upon the very idea of human nature by Jean-Paul Sartre. While there would be very few English-speaking theologians who would follow the existentialism of Sartre, and he has had no one to play Bultmann to his Heidegger, nevertheless I find his thought a rather searching catalyst for some of the dissatisfaction which many people feel when confronted with Chalcedonian formalities. For example (and I confine myself to *Existentialisme est un Humanisme*, Nagel, Paris, 1947), take his affirmation that there is no such thing as human nature. Technically, the denial follows from his contention that when we are thinking of man we must say that existence precedes essence, and from his denial of God's existence. Practically, this rejection of the very idea of human nature is his protest *against* the philosophical conception of man as the *res cogitans*, or of man as an instance of some universal man, the ethical or the political man, *in favour of* man as he exists, who breaks into the world, who meets himself, man who protects himself towards the future, man who wills to act. It is an acknowledgement that man must accept responsibility for his own existence, both in himself and in conjunction with the whole of humanity. With such a protest before us, it would be difficult to revert to the rather lifeless and stylised conception of humanity offered in Aristotelian definitions. Besides, one would be rather insensitive not to observe that it is possible to state this protest as to the 'man' of religious thought, the man who provides evangelical fodder, the man at whom our sermons are beamed, the average member of the congregation, even the man who is the subject of salvation. Each one of these is a type, bloodless and universalised – indeed no man at all.

But perhaps the most interesting feature about Sartre's view of humanity is the way in which he succeeds in combining the individualism, which is a necessary corollary of a strong emphasis upon decision and choice, essentially very personal acts, *and* the universalism which saves his philosophy from being entirely subjectivist. In this respect Sartre would appear to correct what is a defect in Kierkegaard's theology – one to which Kierkegaard was driven, more than most Christian thinkers would be, because of his violent criticisms of the Church of his time. Sartre also, in seeking a medium for the expression of the universal in humanity in the context of personal individuality, seems to be under a pressure similar to that which dictated the efforts of the exponents of the two-nature model who combined a theory of first substance with that of the second substance. Sartre uncovers the transpersonal or the universal element in the human situation in a number of ways. He says that when man chooses himself (affirms his existence, we might say) he chooses at the same time all men. When we act, we do so in the light of some universal image which we entertain of what man ought to be. Our value-structures, our range of responsibility includes the whole of humanity. Here is the lie direct to any criticism that existentialism is a form of moral, economic or political escapism.

Sartre imparts further depth to the dimension of universality in his doctrine of man by maintaining that the other is indispensable to my existence, and that the decision which man makes for himself is made within a world of other persons, with liberties set over against mine, which I must honour. Further, if it is not permissible to speak of a human nature which is a universal essence, it is possible to speak of the universality of the human condition. 'It is in no way fortuitous that modern writers should speak more readily of the condition of man than of his nature' (Sartre, op cit., p. 68). 'His condition' is a phrase designed to cover the limitations under which man exists in any historical period, in any society, pagan, feudal or proletarian – to be in the world, to have to work, to be subject to death. In man's purposive behaviour, which can be understood by other men even though they belong to different epochs, Sartre finds yet another constituent of the universality of humanity. What Sartre has succeeded in doing for the modern understanding of the universalism which must be a part of our interpretation of human nature is that he has transferred it from the realm of logical universals to that of human society, human beings in relation to one another, human beings in decision. There can be no going back from that secure position.

Finally, Sartre puts his finger upon that aspect of existentialism which has always made it attractive to Christian theologians, namely, his deep suspicion of ready-made moral codes to cover every situation in which a decision is called for. It is not that he is anxious to dispense with all accepted standards and advocate immorality. What he does wish to emphasise is the necessity for human decisions in the face of human situations. In the face of such situations we have a sense of *délaissement* (abandonment). We do well to ponder the fact that such an experience may often be part of Christian existence. Christians are often called upon to act in situations in which there is no clear word from the Lord, and no clearly charted moral codes by which to pick their steps through economic or political obscurities. If the phrase 'being adult' has any significance – and I deplore some of its contemporary applications – it means at least this, that God asks us to make up our own minds and not to be always hoping that we shall receive a coded programme from the moralists or a dictatorial fiat from himself. While therefore this discussion of Sartre's view is an intrusion upon our main theme, the justification for it lies in its indication of the task that confronts us when we endeavour to give modern cash-value to the concept of human nature, one of the basic ingredients of the two-nature model.

KARL BARTH AND HUMAN NATURE

Having considered the terms in which Sartre deploys the notion of human nature or, more exactly, what it means to exist as a human being, we may with profit consider what a Christian theologian, namely, Karl Barth, has to say on this same subject, when he deals with the doctrine of creation (*Church Dogmatics* III/1, Part I, 1958, pp. 184f). He develops his view of humanity in his commentary upon Gen 1.26f:

> And God said, Let us make man in our image, after our likeness; and let them have dominion over the fish of the sea, and over the fowl of the air, and over the cattle, and over all the earth, and over every creeping thing that creepeth upon the earth. So God created man in his own image, in the image of God created he him; male and female created he them.

This commentary acquired importance in the study of the problem of women in the ministry in the Church of Scotland, in that it was embodied (one must say, rather uncritically) in the report made by that Church's Panel on Doctrine to the General Assembly in 1964. It came to have a quite unfortunate effect upon the subsequent discussion of that very vexed topic by Presbyteries. In brief, the case against women in the ministry was as badly stated as that for women in the ministry. It is not therefore altogether from academic reasons that one examines the source from which the trouble came. The stages in Barth's commentary are: first, he says that 'He created them male and female' is an immediate interpretation of the previous sentence, 'God created man'. Secondly, the notion of 'the image of God', the basis of man's creation, is not defined in terms of man's peculiar intellectual talents and possibilities or of his reason, but in terms rather of sexual differentiation. Thirdly, while admitting that sexual differentiation is 'common to man and beast', Barth thinks that in the case of man 'the differentiation of sex is the only differentiation'. Fourthly, the fact that man exists as either man or woman is affirmed to be the paradigm of everything that happens between God and man. Fifthly, the climactic statement is that the fact that man is created and exists as male and female will 'prove to be a copy and imitation of his Creator as such'. (The addition to this anthropology made by the Church of Scotland's Panel on Doctrine (*Reports to the General Assembly*, 1964, Blackwood & Constable, Edinburgh, p. 761) reads as follows: 'The basic unit of humanity is not the individual human being, male and female, but man-and-woman as one.' Mt 19.5, 'They twain shall be one flesh' is quoted by the authors in support of this view, no reference being made, oddly enough, to Gen 2.24c, the original of Christ's quotation.)

It would obviously be unfair to burden Barth with responsibility for all the statements of the Panel upon man-and-woman, but since their position is a logical *sequitur* of his theories, he must accept his share of responsibility. These theories of Barth cannot be accepted for the following reasons.

First, it seems to me that Barth's whole line of thought begins to go wrong at the very start, in his exegesis of Gen 1.27: 'God created man in his image . . . male and female created he them.' Instead of absolutising the sexual differentiation between man and woman, the author would seem to be doing precisely the reverse. He is saying, surely, that whether one is man or woman, one is still made in the image of God. In other words, sexual differentiation is irrelevant to man's or woman's being made in the image of God, or indeed of being an instance of the *humanum*. Surely, among other things, this is one of the points that St Paul is making at Gal 3.28: '. . . there is neither male nor female: for ye are all one in Christ.' It is – I should have thought, clearly – here affirmed that once one has been baptised into Christ, and lives in him, then in this context sexual differentiation has become irrelevant. One could almost make a case for saying that sex, particularly with a capital 'S', the exciting kind you might say, is in the Bible associated with the sinful period between the fall and redemption. Pre-fall man is really, as we would tend to see him nowadays, rather sexless. It is not till after the fall that he is aware of being naked. After redemption, when the image of God is remade in him he appears once again to transcend sex.

Secondly, we are led, consequently, to think that by taking the Genesis story as the norm for understanding both the *humanum* and all man–woman relationships, Barth has allowed the marital relation to dominate his description. This defect is all the more destructive of the validity of what he asserts consequently, because the Adam–Eve relationship is not so much marital as crypto-marital; one dare not say pre-marital for fear of mis-understanding. Barth is led to the rather doctrinaire statements both that the sex-relationship is 'the original form of . . . all intercourse between man and man' and that sexual differentiation is the paradigm of all that takes place between man and God. Neither of these statements is true; and the fact that Barth's doctrines led to such improbable conclusions might have deterred him from affirming them.

Thirdly, Barth says several other unsatisfactory things on this same page (op. cit., p. 186). For example, he fails to show clearly how the sex differentiation which man shares with beasts is nevertheless the basis of his differentiation from the beasts. Barth gives the curious reply that the only differentiation which man has is that of sex. It is difficult to resist the conclusion that Barth is here the victim of a simple logical muddle. He says in effect: 'Man (in general) = df. man/woman. Sex is the basis of differentiation of man from woman. Therefore, Sex is the basis of differentiation of man in general.' It is difficult to see how similar logic could not be applied to cattle, dogs, deer, etc. with the same non-compulsive conclusions. No attempt is made by Barth to show how the male–female relationship could possibly be a *copy* or an imitation of man's Creator. The main point which he is trying to make is that man is not man in isolation but in relation to his fellows: when he is I to a thou. In being so, he reflects the *societas* that exists in the Godhead, in the intra-trinitarian relationships of Father, Son and Holy Spirit. But this I–Thou relationship could consist of man and man, or of man and woman, even when not married or in love with one another. There is no need to construe it in sexual–marital terms. In fact I doubt if such nonsense need detain us.

The really serious implication of this sexual definition of humanity is the christological one. If humanity exists only in the man–woman form, and if this form is interpreted normatively in terms of the marital relationship, then the humanity of Jesus Christ is incomplete, and the full demands of the Chalcedonian Definition are not met: as touching his manhood, he will not be of one substance with men. It is no help to add, as some of Barth's apologists have attempted to do, that in the Church as his bride, our Lord fulfils this requirement. To advance this kind of defence is to do one or other of two equally unacceptable things. *Either*, it is to make the Church part of the human nature which Christ assumed at the incarnation and so part of the incarnation itself, and such a view goes far beyond even Roman Catholic theories about the Church as the extension of the incarnation. *Or*, it is to say that Christ at the incarnation did not have this female element in his human nature but acquired it when he created the Church. Such a view would be an admission that the humanity which Christ assumed at the incarnation was defective.

HUMAN NATURE AS THE HUMAN SITUATION

I wonder, therefore, whether if we were to try to deploy the content of the human nature of Jesus Christ, we would not, of all the devices laid before us, fall most readily into the kind of language which Sartre uses. When we speak of the Logos assuming human nature, we tend to deploy that phrase in this way. We speak of him entering into the human situation; taking to himself the sorrows, the broken relationships, the economic injustices, the political tragedies in which men find themselves; shouldering the burden of their sin, and taking from them the overpowering guilt of it all; and so making it his that he dies where they should have died the death that really was theirs. In taking human nature in this sense, he makes decisions; he senses the *délaissement* (abandonment), the utter loneliness of man forsaken by man, and the recovery assured to man who reaches that point of dereliction. In his own body, he has tracked the way back from that outer hell, so that men so placed shall know for evermore that one has stood there before them and by them. To meet him at this point of total abandonment, to realise, as St Anselm said, *quantum sit ponderis peccati*, is in that very moment to know the forgiveness that is offered them through Jesus Christ. In other words, what we should like to offer instead of a stylised definition of human nature is what I would call a situational deployment of that concept, which sets out what human nature means in terms of actions, decisions, conversations, addresses, parables acted and spoken, life and death, hell and resurrection. But at that point of deployment, we have, I feel, almost crossed a category barrier. At least, we are beginning to change models, to substitute for the two-nature model, the psychological model. To that we must now turn.

Before we do so, I want to make one concluding comment. It is that while we have been able to deploy one of the constituents of the two-nature model – the human nature – we seem to be rather at a loss to present a similar deployment of the other nature, the divine nature. We might cite briefly Tillich's 'ground of being' as a possible example of the reformulation of the divine nature; but we should be compelled to note that that reformulation is very much in the category of a stylised, logical form, or even formality. There is nothing quite comparable to Sartre's revision of what it means to be human, or even to Barth's. There may be, I believe, an explanation. It is that emphasis upon the doctrine of revelation has switched attention away from God to the revelation in which he is known. The revelation becomes all-important; and divine nature is deployed in terms of a 'life lived and a death died'. Because of this switch, we give notice that we intend to look also, therefore, at the model of revelation, for it is there that we should expect to learn of divine nature.

5

THE PSYCHOLOGICAL MODEL

When we turn from the two-nature model to what I have entitled the psychological model, it may at first appear that we have moved away from the logically concise to something which is definable only in the vaguest terms. But it must now be clear in recollection that in fact the two-nature model is a deceptively simple description which cloaks an amazing range of variation from Nestorianism to *enhypostasia*. For this reason it should not be unexpected if we encounter a variety of description under a single title. Since the phrase 'the psychological model' is of my own invention, it may prove helpful to indicate what it means. The psychological model is a comprehensive description of those interpretations of the person of Jesus Christ which both hold that it is *possible* to speak significantly of the motivation, feelings, purposes, cognition and in fact the mind of Jesus Christ; and go on to affirm that interpretation of this sort contributes insights in christology which are obtainable in no other way and for which there can be no substitutes. Discussions of the psychological model have therefore taken two forms. On the one hand, they have been concerned with the whole validity of the claim to penetrate the *psyche* of Jesus Christ and set down in meaningful terms what the thoughts and purposes of a God man could possibly be. Sometimes the argument has never gone beyond this point. On the other hand, when it has, the questions have immediately arisen of how far one may go on this tack and at what point a reverent agnosticism should begin to raise its head.

Probably, however, no time could be less opportune than the present for raising the matter of the psychological model. Günther Bornkamm has written (*Jesus of Nazareth*, ET, Hodder

& Stoughton, London, 1960, p. 52): 'The nature of the sources does not permit us to paint a biographical picture of the life of Jesus against the background of his people and age.' A few pages earlier (op. cit., p. 24) he had asked the question: 'Shall we regress and once again attempt a detailed description of the course of (Jesus') life biographically and psychologically?' His answer then had been: 'Certainly not. All such attempts are doomed to failure.' However, despite this shaky beginning, Bornkamm – to continue our original quotation – finally comes away strongly with the assertion: 'Nevertheless, what these sources do yield as regards the historical facts concerning the personality and career of Jesus is not negligible, and demands careful attention.' These quotations from Bornkamm state, then, the problem for the psychological model, namely, 'Has the recent history of textual, literary and historical criticism come to invalidate the psychological model altogether?' We are obliged first of all, therefore, to look at that problem. But Bornkamm does rather also suggest that whereas in the immediate past, the matter seemed almost to be closed at the point of agnosticism, now he wants to open a fresh door upon what he calls 'the personality and career of Jesus'. In other words, a change has come over the situation, and the psychological model requires a fresh examination.

RELIGIOUS AGNOSTIC ASSESSMENTS OF THE PSYCHOLOGICAL MODEL

It is inevitable therefore that we shall start with those considerations which produced the agnostic assessment of the psychological model. These have become so much a part of the modern New Testament critical scene that it may be superfluous even to mention them. I only do so because of their relevance to the question of the psychological model.

The general assumption with which we may begin is that since the New Testament is the product of the primitive Church, it is a post-resurrection document. Sometimes the corollary is stated that the New Testament tells us more about the mind of the primitive Church than it does about that of Jesus. What it says of Jesus it says in the context of the knowledge that Jesus is risen and that his messiahship has been confirmed. There can be, therefore, it is implied, no possibility now of entering into the pre-Calvary situation, of penetrating to the uncertainty and the dubiety which may have been in Jesus' mind as the course of his life unfolded itself. The way in which this attitude is included as the unquestioned premise of what purports to be an argument can be easily illustrated from Bultmann (*Theology of the New Testament* I, ET, SCM Press, London, 1952, p. 26):

> Some advance the following reasoning as an argument from history: The Church's belief in the messiahship of Jesus is comprehensible only if Jesus was conscious of being the Messiah and actually represents himself as such – at least to the 'disciples'. But is this argument valid? For it is just as possible that belief in the messiahship of Jesus arose with and out of belief in his resurrection. The scene of *Peter's Confession* (Mark 8.27–30) is no counter-evidence – on the contrary! For it is an Easter-story projected backwards into Jesus' lifetime, just like the story of the Transfiguration (Mark 9.2–8). The account of Jesus' baptism (Mark 1.9–11) is legend, certain though it is that the legend started from the historical fact of Jesus' baptism by John. It is told in the interest not of biography but of faith.

It is difficult to resist comment on this passage, because it illustrates so adequately the *inaequum certamen* upon which the psychological model is engaged. For example, in the first place Bultmann says that while an argument has been advanced to the effect that the messiahship of Jesus is comprehensible only if Jesus was conscious of being the Messiah, nevertheless 'it is just as possible' that belief in his messiahship had a quite different source, namely, belief in Jesus' resurrection. Bultmann does not really mean that the one argument is just as possible as the other. In fact, his whole ensuing discussion illustrates that since we are enclosed within the resurrection-faith, we are in no position to know anything of the messianic consciousness of Jesus. Any argument which involves knowledge of the pre-resurrection

mind of Jesus is based upon a false premise. It is quite unfair
therefore of Bultmann to introduce a theory which is in his
judgement the only theory with the understatement that 'it is
also possible'.

Secondly, the language of projection is introduced in this
passage of Bultmann as a flat statement, whereas in fact it is both
emotive and loaded. It is emotive because it entails an element of
value-judgement, indeed, of rejection. It is loaded because it
implies that whatever is projected is false. It is the language of
psychological delusion, of inventions to atone for deficiencies, of
fantasy to compensate for disappointments. The impression left
by the passage from Bultmann is that the incident of *Peter's
confession* is the attempt of the primitive Church to make a hero
out of an ordinary drab mortal, to make a Christ out of a Jesus. It
is certainly tantamount to a denial of any possibility of penetrating to the mind of Christ as it might have unfolded itself in his
encounters with his disciples. The word 'projection' is almost like
a signal to us to regard as inaccurate whatever follows.

Thirdly, it is rather interesting that Bultmann is not prepared
to sever the link with history as we would ordinarily understand
it. Of the account of Jesus' baptism by John, while using once
again the language of rejection to dismiss it as legend (somehow
'legend' is a dead-for-ever word: it has no hope of survival after
death as has the term 'myth' which goes through a series of
metempsychoses), he nevertheless acknowledges that the legend
did start from the historical fact of Jesus' baptism by John. The
legend was not wholly up in the air: it was earthed in something
that men saw and heard. In so far as the 'legend' might be quite
permissibly understood to make known to us what was in the
mind of Christ at the time of his baptism, the rejection of the
legend is effectively the rejection of any psychological inroad into
the christological situation. The historical fact of Jesus' baptism
by John was, on this reading, an event with an outside but lacking
entirely any inner structure of the kind assigned to it by the
evangelist.

Fourthly, the keystone in the arch of Bultmann's pattern
appears when he finally says that the purpose of telling the legend

is to serve 'not biography but faith'. There are several unresolved problems here – for example, whether faith is aware that what purports to be something very like biography (in so far as it tells stories about parts of one man's life) is in fact a legend; or whether there is any appropriateness in the fact that faith should be supported by projections (on the face of it rather a major concession to the critics of Christianity). What is not made plain and what concerns us here particularly is whether faith is successful in penetrating within the psychology of Jesus; and if it does, whether it is competent to make statements about such psychology. There is, too, the unsolved problem of the validity of faith's statements about the mind of Jesus. Granted that they are not biographical, that is, not testable by the criteria of ordinary historiography, is it permissible to say that they would be admitted in a court in which special pleading may be made for statements asserted on the basis of faith? In this examination of a short extract from Bultmann, we have encountered many of the difficulties presented for the psychological model by the New Testament critical school which interprets the Gospel records as reconstructions of the life of Jesus from a post-resurrection standpoint.

SCEPTICISM CONCERNING HISTORICAL KNOWLEDGE

A second very important influence has led to widespread suspicion of the psychological method, namely, the sceptical or even agnostic conception of the nature of historical knowledge. I doubt if any single consideration has affected the whole of modern religious epistemology, as well as New Testament criticism and also understanding of the nature of faith, quite so much as the theory that all historical knowledge has a built-in probability coefficient. It is an almost unexamined premise of most modern theology which unites thinkers who, as we shall see, differ from one another in many other ways. My own opinion is that it represents the influence of Kierkegaard upon modern thought and it persists even when theologians consider that they have rid themselves of the existentialist elements of his theology and philosophy. On this ground, therefore, one of the most momentous assertions in modern theology must be Kierkegaard's statement (*Unscientific Postscript*, ET, Oxford University Press, London, 1941, p. 25) that 'Nothing is more readily evident than that the greatest attainable certainty with respect to anything historical is merely an *approximation*.' If we wish to give the obverse side of the coin which produces existentialism, we have to add the further quotations, 'There can in all eternity be no direct transition from the historical to the eternal, whether the historical is contemporary or not' (ibid., p. 89); and 'The transition by which it is proposed to base an eternal truth upon historical testimony is a leap' (ibid., p. 86). In view of the tremendous importance of these theories in subsequent theology and christology, we may in passing indicate that there are two possible sources for this assessment of historical knowledge as approximate, or, as we would say, probable knowledge.

SOURCES OF HISTORICAL SCEPTICISM

The first source is strictly epistemological. If we divide all knowledge into truths of reason and truths of fact – as a long tradition in philosophy has done – then inevitably we shall tend to regard historical knowledge as concerned with the latter. If, further, we assign a coefficient of certainty to knowledge of truths of reason, then knowledge of truths of fact will tend to become a kind of second-class knowledge. This tendency has been arrested in our time, admittedly, with the new popularity of positivism, which is inclined to assign a, or even *the*, certainty coefficient to immediate sense-perception; though even positivism has felt obliged to retain the old gods of certainty in the new guise of tautologies. When we take the discussion one stage further and recognise that Christian theology is inextricably allied to its historical foundation, then we are faced with the position that faith is bound to be a second-class form of knowledge, doomed to uncertainty about its subject, left with sneaking doubts in an area where above all one wishes for certainty, namely, concerning one's ultimate salvation. In this context, it is easy to sympathise with a theology which seeks to place a person's relation to his salvation beyond a peradventure, to give him some sort of assurance that there *is* a way in which he may reach his goal. That way is the leap, the leap of sheer decision. What has to be pointed out, however, is that the leap, the decision, will remain utterly non-significant without some contextual historical knowledge, without some information about who Jesus Christ was, how he lived, what was the purpose of his death, what was the nature of his resurrection. Even a leap cannot take place in a vacuum, nor can a decision be made except within a framework of reference.

But, secondly, a theological circumstance might be said to have led to the suspicion of historical knowledge in relation to faith. There is, I should say, a too great readiness, an almost indecent haste, to be done with the detail of historical knowledge. There is not enough of a rearguard action calculated to save the historical foundations of the faith from the demolition of the sceptics. It is almost all too easy, and where things are as easy as that a theological reason is not difficult to find. Nor are we disappointed. There is behind this acceptance of the sceptical epistemology of history a fear that if historical knowledge were to turn out to be genuine knowledge, then faith would rest on something less than Christ himself. It would mean that a man might come to faith, not by means of a decision, but by a process of historical thinking. There is an ultimate difference between historical knowledge and faith; to move from the one to the other is to change categories. Once this separation has been made, once historical knowledge and faith are presented in the rigid terms of contradictories, no one who stands in that tradition will ever succeed in bringing them together again. Here lies the greatest single bedevilling feature of the whole controversy over kerygma and myth, a controversy which will go on endlessly unless we go behind it to the issue which Kierkegaard refused to face – how historical knowledge and faith are related to one another, for related they most certainly are.

Thirdly, it may be of interest to notice how widely this Kierkegaardian premise is accepted by thinkers who differ vastly in other ways. As long ago as 1929 Paul Tillich wrote these words:

> The Christological question is the question of Christ as the center of our history. This question, moreover, is entirely independent of the problem of historical enquiry into the facts behind the rise of the Biblical picture of Christ. The exposition of these facts can only lend probabilities – and with respect to the historical Jesus, a very faint probability. No religious certainty, no religious belief can be supported by such researches. (*An Interpretation of History*, ET, Scribner, New York, 1936, pp. 264–5. The original article appeared in *Religiöse Verwirklichung*, Furche-Verlag, Berlin, 1929)

I find Tillich here curiously ambivalent. Standing in the main stream of Kierkegaardian scepticism, he seems nevertheless determined to relate Christ to history, hoping to be saved from the uncertainties of history by means of the alchemy of faith. Tillich brings his analysis well within the range of logic and epistemology with his actual use of the term 'probability', which is a clear acknowledgement of the second-class character of historical knowledge, and of the necessity to remedy this deficiency by the introduction of some other source of knowledge.

There is, too, a passage in Barth, made famous by its quotation by D. M. Baillie (*God was in Christ*, Faber & Faber, London, 1948, p. 17) and by Alan Richardson (*History, Sacred and Profane*, SCM Press, London, 1964, p. 134; which see also on pp. 125ff for our present theme):

> Jesus Christ, in fact, is also the Rabbi of Nazareth, historically so difficult to get information about, and when it is obtained, one who is so apt to impress us as a little commonplace alongside more than one other founder of a religion and even alongside many later representatives of His own religion. (From Karl Barth, *The Doctrine of the Word of God*, ET, 1936, p. 188. Translation slightly amended by D. M. Baillie, *loc. cit.*)

In this quotation, the scepticism concerning the historical figure takes an interestingly different form, namely, that of denigration of the person, or rather personality, of Jesus Christ; and it is worth asking whether this sort of judgement is not in fact equivalent to a rejection, albeit unconscious, of the scepticism of Kierkegaard. Brunner however provides the pure milk of the agnostic word when he writes (*The Mediator*, ET, Lutterworth Press, London, 1934, pp. 156 and 168):

> Dependence on history as a science leads to a state of hopeless uncertainty.

Pure echoes of Kierkegaard come through in the next words.

> Therefore when a person refuses to build his relation to the eternal on anything so unsafe as historical science, he is acting rightly; for such a building is indeed a glaring example of building one's house upon sand.

We may round off this short review of the element of historical scepticism in modern christology with a further quotation from Bultmann:

> the acknowledgment of Jesus as the one in whom God's word decisively encounters man . . . is a pure act of faith independent of the answer to the historical question whether or not Jesus considered himself the Messiah. Only the historian can answer this question – as far as it can be answered at all – and faith, being personal decision, cannot be dependent upon a historian's labor. (*Theology of the New Testament*, I, p. 26)

Here the divorce between faith and history which has been endemic in this tradition from Kierkegaard onwards makes itself quite explicit without apology. This divorce has many wider implications for christology, which we might consider were we examining the historical model and its place in christology. For the moment we are interested chiefly in the implications for the psychological model.

CONSEQUENCES OF HISTORICAL SCEPTICISM

Historical scepticism then has had observable consequences in the form of two denials, first, of the possibility of constructing a biography of Jesus; and secondly that later generations (that is, after the ascension of Jesus) could have any contact with or knowledge of the personality of Jesus. The first denial – namely of the possibility of a biography of Jesus – is obviously perfectly correct, if it means that we are unable to give, to use the words of Käsemann (*Essays on New Testament Themes*, ET, SCM Press, London, 1964, p. 45), 'the fabric of a history in which cause and effect could be determined in detail'. The denial is correct, but one wonders whether the same kind of denial might not be made of any piece of biography, namely, that it is impossible to specify with any finality the ultimate springs of motivation that prescribe action. The danger is that we should become so bewitched by this denial that we fail to see that of itself it does not prohibit our making *some* valid historical judgements about the life of Jesus. In reaction against the defeatism and scepticism to which his above-quoted remark seemed to be leading him, Käsemann does admit very soon that 'there are still pieces of the Synoptic tradition which the historian has to acknowledge as authentic if he wishes to remain an historian at all'. Perhaps we ought to point the further moral, which Käsemann ignores, namely, that the authentic pieces of the Synoptic tradition ought to be accepted by the Christian theologian, if he is to remain Christian.

The second denial – that of contact with the *personality* of Christ – is one which to my mind is too readily dismissed as an irrefutable consequence of the previous denial. Once again it is valuable to notice what is being denied and what remains after the denial. What is being denied is that we know how Jesus developed psychologically from childhood to manhood; how he arrived at his messianic consciousness so-called; how indeed mind and will operated in his two-nature person. These are all significant and permissible denials. What is not necessarily implied by these denials is that we are ignorant therefore of what might be called 'the mind of Christ', of how he thought about the Father, about his own death, about men and women. It is not 'uncontrolled imagination' (Käsemann's phrase) that speaks of these subjects. Without some fill-in of that kind in our conception of Christ, without some understanding of what he thought or of his motivation, it is difficult indeed to say whom we are speaking about when we speak of Jesus Christ. He becomes simply an X recurring in a series of propositions about the kerygma; an X, moreover, concerning whose internal nature we are forbidden to speak even on the basis of the series of propositions. In short, my reply to such a view would be that if we are unable to speak of the *personality* of Jesus, we are *ex vi terminorum* forbidden to speak about Jesus.

This much is clear: if the psychological model is to be discarded, then modern christology is on the verge of reintroducing its own brand of docetism. The Word was made flesh, but made flesh in a manner which escapes all the ordinary psychological observations that one would make about a human personality. The early docetists wished to save the unchanging Logos the embarrassment of change and suffering, while their latter-day followers would save him the embarrassment of psychological qualities and characteristics; he is human but in no way known by us, which is to say in no way at all. The great tragedy is that at the very moment when psychological science has enabled us to understand more fully than ever before what is involved psychologically in being human, our scepticism should be preventing us both from understanding what form Christ's humanity took on the psychological side and consequently from knowing how much light the incarnation might throw upon the understanding of the human psyche.

THE CASE FOR THE PSYCHOLOGICAL MODEL

D. M. BAILLIE

But it would be quite wrong to give the impression that the case for the psychological model was one which had been lightly abandoned. In fact, circumstances both within christology and without have combined to secure for it a place or at least a live option on the christological scene. Let us look at them in that order, beginning with D. M. Baillie (*God was in Christ*, pp. 12ff). He puts his finger upon one of the most important circumstances within christology of significance for the retention of the psychological model: he drew attention to the more permanent contributions of 'liberal Protestantism' to the understanding of the person of Jesus Christ. These lay in the area of its definition of the humanity of Christ and they turn out on examination to lie in the psychological field. He mentions the human limits of the knowledge of Jesus Christ, the facts that Jesus grew in knowledge as he grew in stature, and that he is not to be considered to be absolutely omniscient from the moment of his appearance upon earth in the stable at Bethlehem. Sergius Bulgakov is reported (op. cit., p. 13) as having taken up this very emphasis in a Russian Orthodox interpretation of the person of Jesus Christ, holding that though Jesus himself claimed to be Son of God, 'even this apprehension of His own Personality remained subject to the conditions of human growth'. This emphasis represents a break with those elements in patristic and medieval thought which feared to compromise the omniscience of the divine nature of Christ by allowing any ignorance in his human nature. Baillie detects the humanising tendency also in the preparedness of liberal theology to connect the miracles with Christ's humanity. Whereas traditionally they have been regarded as manifestations of the divine nature of Christ, liberal theology wishes to see them also as works of human faith. What he did, others could do: they too could 'move mountains'.

A further human circumstance to which Baillie draws attention is the character of our Lord's moral and religious life. His mission was fulfilled in terms of the human drama of faith fighting against tremendous odds and being victorious; his temptations had the quality of a genuine struggle against an evil power which threatened to overwhelm him; and the agony of Gethsemane and Calvary bore all the marks of human suffering, loneliness and rejection. Jesus too had a personal trust in God, he looked to the Father for strength and comfort; he, too, prayed, and looked for an answer to his prayer. So genuinely, then, was the humanity of Christ presented by the school of liberal theology that there was no going back upon this insight. Perhaps this assertion might now have to be defended in face of the dehistoricising tendencies of modern theological scepticism which we have just been examining. It could be defended, I believe, by reference to the way in which these same theological sceptics approach the New Testament literature: they do accept the human character of the Jesus of the records and ascribe to the primitive Church the deifying tendencies apparent in the Gospels. It is the latter which are particularly open to scepticism. The former are conceded as not in fact consolidating the claims of the theological picture of Jesus Christ.

GÜNTHER BORNKAMM

D. M. Baillie was writing from the standpoint of the theologian. It is to me of greatest interest that Günther Bornkamm, with whose rejection of biographical and psychological description we began this discussion, should nevertheless embark, in the course of the book from which the quotations were taken (*Jesus of Nazareth*), upon a study which draws heavily upon what can only be called psychological material. He speaks of Jesus' sovereignty in dealing with situations in accordance with the sorts of people he encounters in them (op. cit., p. 58). He has clear tactics for dealing with different people – drawing them out of themselves, meeting their objections, testing their sincerity and so on. His dealings with people as well as his public utterances bear the distinctive character of authority. He becomes genuinely involved in situations, angry at the power of disease, gently and tenderly blessing little children. And so the entire description unfolds itself, as Bornkamm rehearses the way in which Jesus understands and presents the theories of the kingdom of God, the will of God and the claims of discipleship; the narratives of his death; the messianic question and so on. This whole approach to the subject of Jesus of Nazareth, coming as it does on this side of the extensive scepticism which we have been examining, and seeming almost, to begin with, to be paying lip-service to it, would be quite impossible without some reinstatement of the psychological model, without some recognition that it is permissible to discern what Jesus was intending, what his attitudes were in certain situations, how he understood his life and death and resurrection. Even if we feel that at times inverted commas ought to be inserted before and after the name of Jesus, this suspicion in no way alters the character of the exercise which Bornkamm is executing.

But before we hasten to say that Bornkamm is a rather odd exception, we ought to read again what Bultmann has to say on 'Jesus' idea of God' (*Theology of the New Testament*, I, pp. 22ff), where he speaks quite freely of Jesus being certain that he is acquainted with the unswerving will of God; that he knows the world's futility and corruption in God's eyes; that he shares the Old Testament view of God; and in even more sophisticated terms, that he released the relation between God and man from its previous ties to history, and desecularised man by placing him on the brink of eternity. Admittedly Bultmann, as distinct from Bornkamm, proceeds thereafter to the delineation of the primitive eschatological community's view of the message of Jesus, of God's judgement, the sacraments, the Holy Spirit, and so on. However, even when Bultmann comes to speak of St John's Gospel and its dominant ideas, he cannot escape speaking as if of Jesus, and not simply of St John's teaching about Jesus. Once again the psychological implications of the whole discussion come into evidence. The mind of Jesus or of 'Jesus' is still the subject of the exposition.

The conclusion seems therefore to be establishing itself that while there is widespread almost total rejection of the possibility of any psychological study of Jesus – a rejection shared equally by Barth and Bornkamm, Bultmann and Käsemann, to mention but a few – there is an equally inevitable tendency on the part of all of them to discuss attitudes, motives, ideas, reactions, and even feelings of Jesus. That rejection and this tendency are in the end of the day contradictory; and it can only have lasted because either the nature of the psychological model was misunderstood, that is, was taken to imply a total understanding of the psyche of

Jesus, a rather preposterous notion anyway; or because more of these theologians were much less radical in their scepticism than their explicit statements would lead us to believe.

EXPOSITORY PREACHING AND THE PSYCHOLOGICAL MODEL

Another circumstance within the theological field which has aided the revival of the psychological model has been the popularity of expository preaching. If one were to try to track down in human terms the secret of the power of the preaching of Professor James S. Stewart, he might at first mention the carefully chosen descriptive language, the constant practice of interpreting Scripture by Scripture. But the secret, I feel, lies in the way in which Professor Stewart so represents the biblical situations, so reconstructs the motives, attitudes, reactions of our Lord to those whom he confronts, that we ourselves are drawn into these self-same situations, ourselves confronted, challenged, judged, forgiven. Without some kind of psychological penetration into the mind of Christ, without some kind of exposure of his will, his purpose, his heart to the ears and minds of the congregation, not only would true preaching be nullified, but the way of our knowing Christ would be cut off.

At different times, and in different parts of the world, I have been required to give advice to divinity students obliged to preach before their training had been completed. In these situations I have said two things. First, that they take great care not to impose or inflict their newly learned theology upon the message of Scripture which they were endeavouring to preach, that is, not to suspend theological essays on textual nails. Secondly, they should choose as the basis of their sermons situations from the New Testament or the Old which lend themselves to descriptive exposition and to interpretative development; that is, they should allow the message to grow out of the situation and out of its constituent parts. The purpose of such exposition is, stage by stage, on the human side to lead the congregation to the point of involvement and response to the present Christ. But that kind of preaching is destroyed by any scepticism we may have about the psychological model or the possibility of speaking validly about how Christ thought or about what he intended. The ever-continuing attraction of H. E. Fosdick's devotional literature, particularly *The Three Meanings*, may be traced to this source: it takes as its overruling aim the introduction of the reader to the person and personality of Jesus Christ. Some of that literature inevitably bears the stamp of the theology of sixty years ago, though not nearly so much as the neo-orthodox critics of Fosdick like to think. But the aim no one dare gainsay, without indicating some better aim for devotional literature, and I know of none.

THE CONTEMPORARY INTEREST IN PSYCHOLOGY: ITS RELEVANCE TO CHRISTOLOGY

But if christology is going to react in any way to the culture within which it expresses itself, then it has to take account of certain circumstances in the contemporary scene which compel us towards a certain sensitivity to psychological questions. Anyone who has attempted to expound the two-nature theory to a group of senior Bible-class members will know that one of the very first questions raised in discussion afterwards is that of how a two-nature person operates psychologically. Leonard Hodgson stated one aspect of the problem when he wrote:

> To-day it is the knowledge of the Incarnate Christ which is in the forefront of the (christological) discussion. . . . We ask now how we are to think of one person with two consciousnesses, with divine omniscience and human limitation of knowledge. (*And Was Made Man*, Longmans Green, London, 1928, p. 10)

In other words, does the fact that Jesus had two natures imply that there were two streams of consciousness in his personality, two series of judgements, attitudes, reactions, each appropriate to the nature concerned? These questions arise even in the interpretation of biblical passages, for example, those dealing with Jesus' temptations, with his agony in Gethsemane, with his cry of dereliction from the cross. When Jesus prayed (Mk 14.36), 'Abba, father, all things are possible unto thee: take away this cup from me: nevertheless not what I will, but what thou wilt', would it be correct to say that the human will was here aligning itself with the will of the Father, and/or with the will of the divine nature? A not uncommon reply to this kind of questioning is that it bespeaks an irreverently inquisitive mind, an indecently prying curiosity, which should be replaced by an adoring worship of the fact of the two-nature person. The fallacy of this reply is that it fails to appreciate how completely our generation has come to think in psychological terms, particularly, and I may add appropriately, when it is thinking about *persons*. In what other terms can one, dare one think? This, it seems to me, is the point of bankruptcy for those christological theories which make such great play of rejecting the clues given in the New Testament to any understanding of the psychology of Jesus.

Christological doctrine is not alone in suffering from the contemporary organised suppression of psychology in the dogmatic reference. The doctrine of the Holy Spirit has been perhaps even more impoverished. Many accounts of the Holy Spirit and his work stop short of the point where the issues for our day really occur – the point of his involvement in the decisions, the wills, the emotions, the cognitions, attitudes, character, reactions of ordinary men and women. We wrap up the whole situation in a parcel labelled 'paradox' and have nasty names like 'synergist' to fix on people who try to unwrap the parcel. This defect in our exposition of the work of the Holy Spirit has led to an almost complete lack of moral psychology in Protestant ethics. The relation of the human will to the Holy Spirit has been so enveloped in mystery that it has been left to extra-ecclesiastical groups like Alcoholics Anonymous to create a structure of moral recovery which has its ultimate foundations in the resources of the Christian faith. For this same reason, this silence concerning the relation of the Holy

Spirit to the psyche of the human being, we have failed to provide our people with adequate doctrinal instruction because we do not possess the adequate psychological scaffolding with which to erect a devotional structure.

THE DOCTRINE OF THE SELF

A further circumstance, external to technical christology but extremely pertinent to it, which makes contempt for the psychological model somewhat old-fashioned, is the quickened interest in philosophical circles in the *self*, the recognition of its status and importance. This interest and recognition have taken many forms. Perhaps the I–Thou philosophy of Martin Buber was the initiation of a process which spread into the whole of Western Christian theology from the 1930s, though there were more strictly philosophical intimations of this kind of interest before Buber. It was left to Buber to give it a language – I and Thou, as Austin Farrer once pointed out, are somehow different from you and me – and to indicate the lines which a personalist metaphysic could well follow.

A score of theologians took up the theme of the uniqueness and integrity of the self: Karl Heim in *God Transcendent*, Daniel Lamont in *Christ and the World of Thought*, Reinhold Niebuhr in *The Nature and Destiny of Man* and, perhaps most significantly for our purpose, John Macmurray in *The Self as Agent*, to mention but a few; and it was embodied in the whole existentialist movement. The self is not a loosely connected series of phenomenal occurrences; it is not a complex of mental states and processes in balanced co-ordination; it is a centre, a standpoint, an agent to make decisions and to fulfil itself in action rather than in knowing, a subject in its own right to be treated and dealt with in a manner appropriate to itself. Because of the ultimate destiny under which Jesus lived, preached and died; because of the profound character of the decisions which he had to make; because of the manner in which he related himself to the totality of existence, to God, to human guilt, to death; his selfhood has come to have a peculiar fascination for a generation which in its thinking about the human situation operates naturally and freely with dramatic psychological models of the self. It would be absurd to ask a generation which thought in such terms suddenly to discard the central idiom of its thought in its understanding of Jesus Christ. It is just this absurdity that is proposed by those who insist that the psychological model be rejected, and that we speak no longer in terms of the personality, that is, the self, of Jesus. In that rejection, it should be noted, we abandon also the insight which knowledge of him can throw upon human selfhood.

These, then, are some of the circumstances which make a wholesale abandonment of the psychological model a hazardous adventure. They have also induced certain christological writers to offer forms of the psychological model as a basis for christ-ology. To these we shall now turn.

KENOTICISM RELATED TO THE PSYCHOLOGICAL MODEL

The psychological model played a great part in one particular christology which exerted a dominant influence in Britain for some fifty years of the present century, namely the kenoticist christology. This influence operated in Britain through the writings of P. T. Forsyth and H. R. Mackintosh. However critical we may be of kenoticism, and it has become fashionable nowadays to reject this theory, it is important to realise what the problem was which kenoticism was trying to solve. It was an attempt to meet two demands: the first, the orthodox christo-logical affirmation of the two natures of Jesus Christ, and the other the necessity to acknowledge the full humanity of Jesus Christ in the terms established by liberal theology. The latter demand was not an unduly difficult one to meet. The human nature of Christ was presented very much as humanistic or liberal interpretations had pictured it: the apologetic value of kenoticism lay in its adopting as much of that sort of interpretation as possible. Kenoticists varied, however, when they came to define how exactly the divine nature was to be constituted. The spectrum of variation has ranged from the assertion that the divine nature is represented by the divine *hypostatis*, through such as that the Logos 'reduced himself to the Jesus of a human soul' (Gess) or that he surrendered 'the glory and the prerogatives of deity' (H. R. Mackintosh) to the quite positive statement of Thomasius of Erlangen that while the Son of God laid aside his omnipotence, omnipresence and omniscience, he nevertheless retained in the incarnate life his love, holiness and justice. But the claim held in common by all the exponents of kenoticism is that it is the Logos, however fully or indifferently characterised, who is the subject of the human life, activities and experiences.

For a number of years now kenoticism has been criticised severely – by William Temple and earlier by Dorner, and in more recent times by D. M. Baillie and W. N. Pittenger – on what have now become traditional grounds. First, kenoticism introduces what can only be regarded as a rather improbable transaction within the Godhead prior to the incarnation, according to which Jesus arranges to come to earth with some only of his divine attributes. Secondly, if this demission of power, this depotentiation, is genuine then other quite fundamental problems arise over how and by whom the cosmic functions previously fulfilled by the Logos are now being executed. Thirdly, there is genuine doubt over the ontological continuity between the Logos and Jesus. So great is this doubt that the question must be asked whether kenoticism does not effectively violate the Chalcedonian thesis of the perfect Godhead of Jesus Christ. The divine nature is so reduced as to be no longer identifiable as such in its completeness. Fourthly, since the kenosis is associated with the incarnation, and since with his glorification at the ascension the Logos resumes his full stature of deity in a *plerosis*, it is no longer possible to affirm that in glory the Logos retains his human nature.

All that has been noted in the now traditional criticism of kenoticism can be made without much modification to the views of H. R. Mackintosh stated in his *The Person of Jesus Christ*. His compromising of the divine nature of Jesus Christ is clearly illustrated by such sentences as the following:

> (Jesus') life on earth was unequivocally human. Jesus was a man, a self-consciousness; of limited power, which could be, and was, thwarted by persistent unbelief; of limited knowledge . . . ; of a moral nature, susceptible of growth and exposed to lifelong temptation, of a piety and personal religion characterized at each point by dependence upon God. In short, He moved always within the lines of an experience humanly normal in constitution, even if abnormal in its sinless quality. (op. cit., pp. 469f)

So much is standard issue for kenoticism. The remarkable part of Mackintosh's theory – a part which has thrown more light upon more christological theory than the whole of his kenoticism – appears when he rounds off his kenoticism with a statement about revelation, namely, 'The Eternal has revealed himself notably in a human being who lived at the beginning of the Christian era' (op. cit., p. 471). He had anticipated this view four pages earlier when he spoke of 'the fact of Christ' becoming 'for us a transparent medium through which the saving grace of God is shining'. Mackintosh's christological progression has therefore been somewhat as follows. He began with an allegiance to the Chalcedonian type of two-nature theory, which he modified in two directions, first, by reducing very considerably the content of the divine nature, and secondly by affirming the totally unequivocal character of the human nature (ignorant, weak, etc.). So impressed is he now by the humanity of the human nature of Jesus that he seems to be aware that it would be compromised if it existed in one person with the divine nature. This problem he solves by saying that the human nature *reveals* the divine nature which does not therefore exist *in* Jesus Christ in the same way as does the human. There is, I feel, a certain prophetic quality in this part of Mackintosh's thought in so far as it anticipates both the role that the concept of revelation is going to play in christological theory in the fifty years following his writing and the difficulties created by the introduction of the model of revelation into the christological scene. That is the subject of our next discussion.

MODERN ENHYPOSTATIC THEORY MODIFIED IN TERMS OF THE PSYCHOLOGICAL MODEL

In the meantime, I should like to examine another form of the psychological model, namely, that attempted by H. M. Relton in *A Study in Christology* (SPCK, London, 1927). Relton adopted as the basis of his christology the enhypostatic theory in the form propounded by Leontius of Byzantium, the theory that while there are two natures in Jesus Christ, only one, the divine nature, has a *hypostasis*. The human nature is not allowed to be *anhypostatos*, but is enhypostasised in the divine *hyypostasis*. When this theory is looked at from a psychological point of view, then the question inevitably arises of whether in Jesus there are therefore two streams of consciousness. Relton attacks this problem quite boldly, almost foolhardily, by saying at once that there is in Jesus Christ one single consciousness and not a double self. The consciousness is that of the God–man. Before he was incarnate, the divine Logos was already possessed of whatsoever he required to be able to lead a truly human life. In other words his deity was not a disqualification for his being human, something of which he had to be shorn to enable him to live a genuinely human existence. For a further amplification of his position he chooses a view once stated by Apollinaris, that there is in God a human element. In other words, 'human' and divine' are not two contradictory terms: they are complementary, 'the less being included in the greater'. Divinity is perfect manhood. The God–man may be said therefore to live a truly human life because he was always the Son of God and always had within his divine nature the perfection of humanity. Indeed, manhood is at its highest and best when united with God. There is no difficulty for Relton in affirming that the Logos is the *hypostasis* of the human nature of Christ, as of the divine, and that his consciousness is unitary, and develops according to the laws of growth governing finite human consciousness.

It is important to notice at the start of any discussion of Relton's view what exactly he has done. He has translated the term 'nature' by the term 'consciousness', and he is even prepared to say (op. cit., p. 226) that the unity of Christ is to be located in the unity of his self-consciousness. He rather blunts the edge of the equation, however, by going on to say that the self-consciousness of the God–man is the subject of the two natures. Quite apart from the question of whether it is permissible to equate 'nature' and 'consciousness' – a confusion of categories which we shall later examine – it makes a nonsense of the whole exercise if we subsequently try to combine them in the same sentence, using them as if they still had different meanings.

Secondly, Relton is certainly making a sound point when he says, by implication, that traditionally in christology too much has been made of the contradiction between human nature and divine nature, and that more should be done to explore the appropriateness of human nature to the purposes which God is seeking to achieve in the incarnation. At the same time, however, the statement that there is an element of the human in God is much too vague to be of any great help. For we require to know what features of humanity are in God, say, will, intelligence, or what? Without some indication of that sort, the statement is simply the converse of saying that man is made in the image of God – the converse, or more naively, a logical implication, for if man is made in the image of God, by definition there is in God an element of the human.

Further, thirdly, no good purpose is served by saying that divinity is perfect humanity. For quite apart from the fact that this view begs the question of whether there is more to divinity than the perfection of humanity, it leads to unsatisfactory conclusions in three ways. By his emphasis upon the identity of human nature and divine nature, Relton removes all necessity for the incarnation. God, on these terms, already has human nature: he does not require to 'assume' anything. On the other hand, if Relton really does mean that there is a difference between ordinary human consciousness and divine consciousness, then he is guilty of heterodoxy in either of two ways. Either, he may be saying that whereas ordinary men have ordinary consciousness, in Jesus Christ this form of it is replaced by the divine form, i.e. perfection. This view is effectively Apollinarian.

Or he may simply be saying that the human nature is absorbed in the divine consciousness, and we have then one nature, one consciousness – which is Eutycheanism. In a word, the composition which Relton prepares consists of too many constituent parts; it follows too closely the directions to the bride to get 'something old, something new, something borrowed . . .', to achieve any really stable conclusions.

E. L. MASCALL AND THE PSYCHOLOGICAL MODEL

A further example of the way in which the psychological model might be made to work comes from the writing of E. L. Mascall (*Christ, the Christian and the Church*, Longmans Green, London, 1946, pp. 53ff) even although he is himself rather hesitant about discussing the psychological implications of the enhypostatic two-nature theory which he accepts. Starting from the now famous remark of Leonard Hodgson's that the question of the knowledge of the incarnate Lord is the major christological issue of recent times, and admitting, rather reluctantly one feels, that 'the question of Christ's human consciousness having been raised we cannot avoid discussing it' (op. cit., p. 54), Dr Mascall propounds his own theory of the nature of the knowledge which Christ had. It has wrongly been assumed in the past that there are only two alternatives on this subject. The one is that of Chalcedonian and patristic christology, according to which the knowledge of Christ is co-extensive with the knowledge of the Logos, and the babe in the manger is thought to be contemplating the procession of the Holy Ghost, the theorems of thermodynamics, the novels of Jane Austen and the date of the battle of Hastings. The other is the kenoticist reaction to that sort of christology, and its view is that Jesus Christ, being truly human, shares in human ignorance, which as we have already seen H. R. Mackintosh believed. Jesus Christ in his earthly life acquired knowledge in the same way as does every human being, by sensation and perception, by trial and error, by being taught and by learning.

There is a third possibility, namely, that there should be two kinds of knowledge in the human mind of Jesus: first, that which he has acquired in a purely human way as we have just described it and, secondly, that which has been infused into it from the omniscient divine mind. There is the necessary human limit to the extent of this infused knowledge so that the possibility never arises of the two bodies of knowledge becoming identical with one another. The other circumstance which is relevant to the communication of knowledge from the divine mind to the human is the precise requirements of the situation in which Jesus is placed. In other words, we are asked by Dr Mascall to conceive of a 'stratification' of knowledge in Jesus' human mind, and we are offered, comparing natural things with supernatural, an example. A 'perfect' lecturer, knowing thoroughly both his subject and the capacities of his class, will impart to them at each stage of the course just as much knowledge as they can competently absorb. Even where he is himself aware of short cuts he will take a long way round, because he knows that the class will be able to follow the latter. The illustration is defective, of course, in that the lecturer's own knowledge has in its turn been acquired, whereas the divine nature of Jesus Christ possesses full knowledge from all eternity.

Dr Mascall was extremely reluctant in the first instance to submit this psychological model, and it is therefore perhaps more than a little unfair to press him concerning it. Yet it seems to me that there are two difficulties which his exposition must eventually encounter. On the one hand, if it is assumed that the divine person is the subject of the knowledge of both the divine mind and the human mind, it is difficult to avoid the conclusion that he both knows and does not know the same fact at the same time. There is no escape from this difficulty by saying that this knowing and not knowing a certain fact is a common feature of normal psychology. For example, a certain piece of information which I once knew may not be in the process of actually being recalled by me at a given moment, and I may in one sense be truthfully said not to know it at that moment. As soon as it is recalled for me by someone else, I may again quite truthfully say that, of course, I knew it. I both did not know and did know this piece of information. That example cannot be validly extended to the knowledge of Jesus Christ. For if the divine person knows some fact through the omniscience of the divine nature, this fact does not require to be recalled for him by someone else in order that he should know it; and the ignorance of the human nature is the ignorance of never having known, and not the ignorance of the mind which once knew and is not in process of actively recalling a given fact. Therefore, if the divine person is taken as the subject of the two natures, he is both omniscient and ignorant at the same time.

On the other hand, I do feel that the example of the 'perfect' lecturer mentioned by Dr Mascall points to a rather different construction, namely, that the two natures are really rather like two persons, one communicating information to the other as need requires and as capacity allows. This construction avoids the difficulty of the previous interpretation of Mascall's view, and it does entail a genuine ignorance on the part of the human nature, and genuine knowledge on the part of the divine nature, there being no *tertium quid* omniscient and ignorant at the same time. But the price at which this rationalisation of Dr Mascall's view has been achieved is one which is higher than he would be prepared to pay – the price of heresy, in fact, the Nestorian heresy; for the two natures have been converted into two persons. But the illustration, based as it is on two persons, a lecturer and his class, does at least point in the Nestorian direction.

CONCLUSIONS CONCERNING THE PSYCHOLOGICAL MODEL

I should like to summarise now some of the conclusions which are beginning to emerge from this investigation of the psychological model. The first, and perhaps the most obvious by now, is that when the psychological model is made the basis of christological expansion it apparently invariably ends in some form of heresy – heresy judged, that is, by the Chalcedonian

Definition. In the older conservative theology the heresy was that of docetism: no genuine reality or growth was allowed to the human nature of Jesus Christ. In the enhypostatic modifications of the Chalcedonian christology, an Apollinarianism which was always suspected of being present in the purely dogmatic presentation clearly comes into view. In Relton, in spite of his enhypostatic sympathies, it is Eutycheanism which characterises his christology. Mascall, whose dogmatic sensitivity must be well-nigh impeccable, employs illustrations which make sense only in Nestorian terms. In short, there is scarcely a single classical christological heresy which has not been reproduced in the modern period in the effort to produce a working psychological model for christology.

Secondly, so comprehensive is the evidence that it is difficult to avoid the view that the fault does not lie simply in the inability of the searchers to find the successful orthodox psychological model. There would almost appear to be something inherently logically impossible in the whole enterprise. Perhaps we ought to qualify that conclusion by adding – so long as we accept the Chalcedonian two-nature model as the norm for the expansion of the psychological. There's the rub. Some years ago now Dr Mascall made illuminating comments on this very conclusion, though it is a pity that he did not pursue its proper implications. He said,

> Christological doctrine is not primarily psychological but ontological. No amount of discussion of our Lord's psychology can have any *direct* bearing on the Catholic creeds and the Chalcedonian definition. (*Christ, the Christian and the Church*, p. 54)

While these comments, as I say, are illuminating for our present discussion, they are not altogether accurate. Dr Mascall seems to have forgotten the extent to which psychological considerations were very much part of the decades of christological controversy which finally yielded the Chalcedonian Definition. The Arians – whatever we say about them – like most heretics (and indeed, if the Scriptures be accepted literally, also the Devil himself) all knew their Scriptures very well; and they argued from a lively knowledge of what Jesus said and did, of how he felt and suffered and from many psychological considerations. It is quite wrong to present the Chalcedonian Definition as if it were the outcome of a series of meetings of the middle-eastern section of the Aristotelian Society. Nor is it easy to persuade any thinkers bred in schools of pragmatism to admit Mascall's implied distinction between logic and psychology. Nevertheless, with these reservations I am convinced that his judgement is a sound one – though I think that it ought to be stated the other way round, to meet my first objection, thus: the Chalcedonian Definition can have no *direct* bearing upon the discussion of our Lord's psychology. If that judgement is accepted, then we have put to an end the necessity to judge and dismiss every psychological model because it has failed the Chalcedonian test. The movement from the two-nature model to the psychological model, the application of the norm of the one to the other, is a category error.

Thirdly, if we pursue the implications of that position, then we shall give up trying to translate the ontological categories of the two-nature model into psychological terms, and saying that a = b and c = d and so on. There is no such dictionary. Even words like nature or person which might occur in both contexts are not equivalents. It was at such a point that the expansion of the psychological model by writers such as Relton and even Mascall failed: they felt obliged to remain within distance of the two-nature model and to be plotting their position by reference to it. The future of the psychological model, therefore, lies not in its validation by a Chalcedonian test but in the explanation and expansion of all its own possibilities. To quote Professor G. S. Hendry (*The Gospel of the Incarnation*, SCM Press, London, 1959, p. 91), who was examining this very subject though for a rather different purpose:

> If Christ is a true and complete man, it must be possible to raise the question of his person in terms of psychology and ethics . . . for it is of the essence of manhood that it is susceptible to ethical and psychological interpretation.

That process of ethical and psychological interpretation remains as necessary a part of christological thought as do the ontological and existentialist analyses which have so long dominated the scene.

Finally, we have already noticed (see above, p. 135) that H. R. Mackintosh moved from a kenotic form of the psychological model to what we shall later be calling the revelation model. Before we leave the psychological model we may note how appropriate that transition is. The psychological model understandably dealt more with the human nature than the divine. Professor Hendry's point was that it is of the essence of *manhood* to be susceptible to psychological interpretation. If the implied restriction is imposed and the divine nature seems automatically to elude the psychological model, some mechanism becomes immediately necessary to relate the human nature to the divine. It enables us to probe the human nature to its deepest limits, while exempting the divine nature from that sort of analysis. There are, of course, other functions which the revelation model performs, and other norms for its employment; and to these we shall turn. In the meantime, I should like to enter a plea for the extension of the psychological model, in some respects at least, to the divine nature, for how else can we properly speak about 'the mind of Christ' or indeed 'the will of God'?

6

THE REVELATION MODEL

Here, until 1964 we would have been approaching the totally, universally accepted mid-twentieth-century christological model. Barth might disagree with Brunner on the extent and nature of the effect of the fall of man upon the image of God in man, or about the range of revelation. Barth and Bultmann might disagree about how history and myth are related to one another in the Gospel; Pittenger might criticise the christology of the kenoticists; but to a man they would rally to a single standard when the question was raised of whether the term 'revelation' is the right one to apply to Jesus Christ. Revelation is what Christianity is about. Revelation is the totality of the faith. To deny revelation is to be not a heretic, but a blasphemer. Suddenly, publicly, in 1964 in the midst of this universal, ecumenical chorus, there was heard a strident, discordant note – though perhaps the word 'note' is not appropriately applied to such a lengthy, detailed and sustained analysis of the case for revelation. I refer to F. Gerald Downing's *Has Christianity a Revelation?* (SCM Press, London, 1964). The publication of that book makes it unnecessary for me to say some of the things that I meant to say. It will affect some of the things I shall have to say, because I shall be obliged to orient myself by its position. But since Mr Downing's purpose was rather different from mine in this present exercise, I expect to say things to which he has not given his attention.

A matter which we have not so far examined is that of how the human mind arrives at the models with which it operates in extending its christological structures. By this time it must be clear that they are not given by the Holy Spirit to the mind of man: they bear too many marks of human ratiocination for us to accept such a naive suggestion. Downing does certainly show that those who think to absolutise the revelation model by claiming that it is part of the scriptural witness to Christ are guilty either of false exegesis or of theological incompetence to understand what is involved in the revelation model. But it would be wrong to think that we have dismissed the revelation model by showing that it is not given in Scripture in so many words. (Downing himself does not think so because, in addition to demonstrating the inadequacy of the biblical texts thought to validate revelation, he contributes a very thorough analysis of theological uses of the term.) Since, however, so many of our contemporaries regard this model as absolutely normative for all christology and theology we may perhaps best begin by outlining the structure of this model.

THE STRUCTURE OF THE REVELATION MODEL

THE OLD TESTAMENT

I should like to take as my starting-point an analysis of the revelation model which I worked out a number of years ago (see *The Reformed Theological Review*, 1956, 1957). At that time I began by reviewing the biblical texts which included words that might be translated by the English word 'reveal', but my doubts about the validity of that procedure which I stated then have now been more than confirmed. The basic revelation model takes the form *A reveals B to C* but this form requires to be qualified as we apply it separately to the Old Testament and to the New Testament.

When we try to make this model operate by giving Old Testament values to the symbols, at first it appears that A and C are the variables and B is the constant. In order to derive a real revelation situation from the model, we give to A the value 'the drying up of the Red Sea' or 'the burning of the bush that was not consumed' or 'the firmament'; to B the value 'God', and to C the value 'Moses' or 'David'. The revelation situation then reads, 'The drying up of the Red Sea reveals God to Moses'; 'The burning of the bush that was not consumed reveals God to Moses'; 'The firmament reveals God to David the psalmist'. The revelation model is thus seen to entail a triadic relation, a three-term relation, the three relata being revealer, the revealed and the recipient of the revelation. If any one of the three is missing there is no revelation.

On examination, the initial simplicity of our model will be found to have deceived us in respect of each of its constituent terms. The triadic character of the model remains as its fundamental structure, but the terms require to be carefully qualified. Let us look at each in turn.

Modification of A

A is that circumstance, thing, event in the world which reveals God to the believer. But in fact, if it is to appear in the model at all it has, in being A, to be more than A. Take the simple case of the drying up of the Red Sea. We may describe this event (as many in 1940 similarly described the weather conditions surrounding the rescue of allied troops on the Dunkirk beaches) in terms of possible, though perhaps unusual, climatic conditions obtaining at that time in the sea between the great land masses of Africa and Arabia; conditions precisely created by immediately previous and long-term causes to which it could be related in terms of barometric pressures, air temperatures, wind velocities, and tides. But so long as the Red Sea event is related only to previous events in the space-time continuum, it can have no place in the revelation model. It has to point beyond itself, to have, as it were, a perpendicular as well as a horizontal reference, in order to appear within the model. The burning bush might be described as a trick of the sunlight, as some kind of optical illusion, or as a form of mirage, which could be precisely accounted for in terms of the laws of light and optics. But when the burning bush appears in the revelation model *A reveals B to C* it rejects the natural or naturalistic description as total, and it claims a character which may even conflict radically with that description.

Without the possibility of its pointing beyond itself, A could not appear as a member in the revelation model; at best it might demonstrate the validity of the laws of light or optics. The stars in their courses, in the same way, might be described naturalistically by reference to the laws of astrophysics; but when the firmament is said to declare the handiwork of God we have gone beyond that description of the stars, not eliminating it altogether, but incorporating it in a fuller interpretation which regards the stars as symbolic of an order operative in the ethical as well as in the natural sphere. In order to represent this fact in the revelation model, I propose to qualify A by x and to say that *A(x) reveals B to C*, A(x) meaning that A in addition to its natural description bears a supernatural interpretation which permits it to appear in the revelation model.

A very similar point has been variously made by two theologians widely separated in time and outlook, St Thomas Aquinas and H. H. Farmer. St Thomas wrote (*Summa Theologica*, I.2.ii; *Summa Contra Gentiles*, I.12):

> God is only known through his effects (*per suos effectus*) or through the things he has made (*per ea quae facta sunt*).

The natural order was not for St Thomas exhaustively describable in terms of natural laws; it had the further character of 'being an effect', of pointing beyond itself to a reality upon which it was dependent for its being and characteristics. In other words for St Thomas the x in A(x) means that A has the further non-natural quality of 'being an effect of'. Here we see rather readily why there should be so much disagreement between the theist and the non-theist over the validity of the classical proofs of divine existence. The non-theist regards the term appearing in the premise upon whose character the argument turns as being solely A; and he denies that it has the qualities which the theist uses in the construction of the arguments. The theist, on the other hand, begins not from A but from A(x) and he has no great difficulty in showing that if A is an effect, then it must have a cause. This form of the argument is therefore not unjustly criticised for being simply the unwrapping of a definition, the explication of a tautology. On such a reading, of course, the proofs of divine existence are assumed to be derivative in the first instance from revelation situations, an assumption which is not entirely unwarranted as one discovers if he tries to state whence the notion of the world as an effect could have been derived.

In a quite different setting H. H. Farmer speaks of the world as 'God's symbol' (*The World and God*, Nisbet, London, 1939, pp. 68ff) and explains his view in terms similar to those we have used:

> The triadic relationship of God, man and the world, involving that both man and his world should have significance for God, and a relative independence over against God as well as over against one another, involving also that man would know God through the world yet not be separated from God by the world, is doubtless very mystifying for the reflective mind, especially when the religious man goes on to affirm that none the less all things live and move and have their being in God.

In fact if I might modify what Farmer says, the world is an incomplete symbol, in the sense that it is a symbol for a relationship whose nature is indicated but whose two, or three, terms are not stated. It is the incomplete character of the world as symbol which gives St Thomas' arguments such plausibility as they have and prevents them from being at least obvious tautologies. It is this incompleteness which is called the *contingentia mundi* and forms the basis of all metaphysical theories which deny that the world is self-explanatory.

Modification of B

By this time, we have become suspicious of the simplicity of the original model, *A reveals B to C*; and we cannot but pursue our suspicions. What is it that A(x) reveals to C? Since it is still the revelation in the Old Testament that we are discussing, we cannot say that it is God's essence that A(x) reveals. We are obliged to say that it is some purpose of God's, some aspect of his being or nature, some attitude of his to the behaviour of his people, some statement of God's, some reaction to events in the world, and so on. Thus, it might be God's anger with Sodom and Gomorrah, his resolute purpose to free Israel from the hand of the Egyptians, his will for the way in which men and women should live in society and how they should honour him as their creator and saviour, or his continuing willingness to forgive them their sins. So once again we modify the model, to say that *A(x) reveals B(y) to C*. B(y) then appears as the completion of the incomplete symbol A(x). If the world is symbol, God is that of which, or he of whom, it is symbolic. If the Red Sea in its odd behaviour is symbolic, we know now that it points beyond itself to the reality of God's intention to save his people Israel.

Modification of C

The modification of the third term in our revelation model is one which has proved to be of tremendous importance in the history of theology. The modification arises for the following reason. While C is the end-term in the process covered by the revelation model, he is not a passive recipient. Indeed, he may be active in two ways. On the one hand, he may strenuously resist the whole endeavour of God to reveal himself to him, and the process may be in danger of frustration and defeat at this very point, because of man's sin. On the other hand, while he may bring all the power and insight, of which he is capable, to the revelation situation, the appropriation of it is something well beyond his capacities. So the doctrine of the Holy Spirit, or of the indwelling grace of God, has begun to appear in the Old Testament, though it is given its fullest and clearest expression in the New Testament. We qualify the C in our model with the terms Holy Spirit to give C(Holy Spirit). I make this modification without any commitment on how the believer and the Holy Spirit are related to one another in this process, beyond the rejection of Pelagianism. We have then for the Old Testament what I shall call model one: *A(x) reveals B(y) to C(Holy Spirit)*.

THE NEW TESTAMENT

We may make our first attempt to form a revelation model for the revelation of God in Jesus Christ recorded in the New Testament, by adopting and adapting that which we evolved for the Old Testament in the following way. *A(x) reveals B(A) to C(Holy Spirit)*. A(x) has the kind of connotation which it had before. A is the ordinary human life of the man Jesus, as it would appear to the people of his day regardless of whether they believed in him or not, his life as it would be written down by a modern scientific historian. The x draws attention to the fact that this life points beyond itself to a reality which is not inspectible by empirical reason, but is known only to faith. Once again A(x) is an incomplete symbol; so far the nonmaterial reality to which A points and of whose significance it is the bearer, has not been specified.

It will be observed that we have altered the second relatum in the model from B(y) to B(A), and the purpose of the alteration is twofold. On the one hand, we want to do justice to the claim made by theologians who use this model that in Jesus God reveals not just one of his attributes, or some aspect of his nature or even his whole purpose for mankind, but his very self; and so the B is retained in the model and the y because it denoted only an attitude, reaction, purpose or attribute of God, is eliminated. At the same time, on the other hand, it is obvious that in Jesus the naked glory of God's majesty is not beheld, and that we have to do, in the first instance, with the Word *made flesh*, God in Christ Jesus, God as a man among men. For this circumstance, I would use the symbol B(A), God in Jesus Christ. At this stage I am making no suggestions about how the B and the A are related to one another. Perhaps some form of kenoticism may readily appear to enable us to say that B(A) represents the divine nature, as it is accommodated to the limitations and privations of human existence. But there is no obligation on us to say how B and A are related beyond insisting that they are compresent.

The final term in the model C(Holy Spirit) remains it would seem unchanged, though two comments might be made. First, the Holy Spirit now directs the believer specifically to Jesus Christ in revealing God, so that his work is limited and defined by the finished work of Christ. Secondly, it is not possible completely to tidy up terminology, for the actual work of consummating the revelation is at one point in the New Testament assigned not to the Holy Spirit but to the Father. At Mt 16.17, after Peter has confessed Christ to be the Son of the living God, Jesus says that it is not flesh and blood that has revealed this fact to him, but 'my Father which is in heaven'. So then we have as model two, *A(x) reveals B(A) to C(Holy Spirit)*.

We have not quite done full justice to all that is said about the revelation of God in Jesus Christ, and particularly to the fact that God as he is known in Jesus Christ, our B(A), is substantially or even consubstantially the same as God is from eternity to eternity. This fact, it will be recalled, was the basis for Barth's rejection of the *consilium arcanum* of Calvinism, the decree according to which God predestines apart from Christ, that certain people, the reprobate, from the mass of sinners, will be damned to hell, while others, the elect, are saved in Jesus Christ. It was unthinkable that God should hold back some aspect of his nature, some secret purpose, when he was making his mind and purpose known to all mankind in Jesus Christ. In having to do with God as he is in Christ, we have to do with God as he is in and for himself. It seems necessary, therefore, to add model three to the other two, and to say: *B(A) reveals B(E) to C(Holy Ghost)*. To give values to the terms in the model: The God–man, Jesus Christ, reveals God as he essentially is to the believer inspired by the Holy Spirit. Model three also entails that the believer who wishes to know more about God as he is in himself will be obliged to return constantly to the God–man, Jesus Christ. In this sense, the revelation in Jesus Christ is exclusive. Model three is too the point of departure for the search which has constituted traditional christology as we know it, the search for a formula to describe the relation of the B in B(A) to the B in B(E); a search, also, which has led to the explication of the doctrine of the Trinity when the relation of the Holy Spirit to the other two terms in the model has been raised.

BIBLICAL TEXTS ABOUT REVELATION

It is necessary before leaving this discussion of the revelation models to say something of their relation to the biblical texts which are normally offered in support of a doctrine, or a concept, of revelation. It has to be admitted at once that the triadic character of model one is not borne out by the majority of Old Testament texts. A wide range of Hebrew words has been called in as evidence, notably, *galah*, reveal; *ra'ah*, see; *'amar*, say; *saphar*, tell; *yada'*, know; and their several Hebrew modifications; but Downing's list (*Has Christianity a Revelation?*, pp. 21ff) of the ways the term 'reveal' is used in talk about God – of theophanies, of 'open' activities of God, of God's communication of secret information about the future, or of God's opening of men's eyes to see a vision – accords more with a dyadic view of revelation than with a triadic. There are two texts – in Ps 97.6, 'The heavens declare his righteousness, and all the people have seen his glory', and in Ps 19.1, 'The heavens declare the glory of God and the firmament shows his handiwork' (to the psalmist) – which with slight additions could be cast in the triadic mould, as indeed we did with one of them above. But I am rather inclined to think that Downing's exegesis is more accurate when he says (op. cit., p. 24) that these are texts not about revelation at all, but about praise – the praise offered to God by the heavens and the whole firmament. 'Praise is for the sake of praise and not for edification.' Nor is the case much better when we come to the New Testament. The most common reference of the term *apokalyptein* is consistently eschatological; while the only text (Lk 10.22 = Mt 11.27) which bears the clearly triadic character of our analysis is either open to such a variety of possible interpretations, or so much a *hapax legomenon*, as not to be a sufficiently reliable basis for a total theory of revelation, or for anything approaching our models two and three. It has always seemed to me to be a strange anomaly that the concept of revelation which has become such a popular term in modern theology should have so little biblical basis for its employment. The anomaly is all the more serious when it is remembered that strong claims are made by revelation theologies to be also biblically based. I have no desire to labour those points now. But I would like to anticipate any premature dismissal of the revelation model on the score of its being non-biblical. It is a necessary part of theological construction that it employs in the deployment of its material many concepts which are not biblical. The Chalcedonian Definition would have won no recognition whatsoever had it been required to pass the test of strict biblical literal documentation. The justification for any model will lie in the success it has in yielding insight into the basic christological material. Downing argues (op. cit.) at con-siderable length that the revelation model fails that test as well, but before agreeing with his sombre judgement I should like, with the help of the above analysis of the revelation model, to explore some of the variations in its use even by theologians who are in close sympathy with one another.

FORMS OF THE REVELATION MODEL

A. A. M. FAIRWEATHER

The first example I take is to be found in A. A. M. Fairweather's *The Word as Truth* (Lutterworth Press, London, 1939, p. 7). This book is a comparative study of the epistemology of St Thomas Aquinas and Karl Barth. I am not concerned with the general themes of the book so much as with three statements made on p. 7, because they provide an interesting contrast with the more modern position, and show how very dissimilar statements can be made with the use of the revelation model. Sentence one: 'God cannot reveal himself by his pure presence.' Sentence two:

'Revelation cannot therefore direct our understanding to God himself and quite alone.' Sentence three: 'God manifests himself only in and through what is not himself, as God in continuity with some reality which we can perceive.' The noteworthy points in this position are as follows. We have to begin with, in sentence one, a denial of the dyadic character of the revelation situation. Revelation is not a theophany, the naked appearance of God before us, and in sentence three we have the recognition of the triadic character of the model: God, the reality through which God reveals himself, and ourselves as the recipients of revelation. This is stated in a rather interesting way, however, by saying that it is through what is *not* himself that God reveals himself. This view is a close reflection of St Thomas' theory that God is known through his effects, through what he has made. Revelation, any revelation, therefore entails some kind of diminution of God's stature, some form of *kenosis*, some assumption that God achieves what appears a priori to be quite impossible, that he should be known in and through what is less than he is. In fact we have now a possible alternative form of the revelation model – *Non-B reveals B to C*.

Next the quotations from Fairweather draw our attention to a fact which we have so far ignored, namely, that the revelation model has perhaps a still more complex internal structure than we have been prepared to admit. A paradigm revelation sentence would be: God reveals himself through history (or nature or Jesus Christ) to believers; or in model form: *B reveals B through A to C*. This form would, I agree, be theoretically the more correct but in the Old Testament passages we mentioned, 'The heavens declare the glory of God' (to the psalmist), and in the common account of the New Testament situation, 'Jesus Christ is the revelation of (i.e. reveals) God to the disciples', there lies justification for taking the direct non-reflexive form of the model.

Further, by saying that God manifests himself as God 'in continuity with some reality which we can see', Fairweather draws attention to the difficulty of describing the relation between God and the reality through which he is revealed. It is obviously not an analytic relation, so that by examining this reality we could discover God within it. Revelation does not imply pantheism, or even panentheism. Nor is it a relationship in which God so transforms that with which he is in continuity in revelation that it is deified. Human nature is not changed into divine when the Word is made flesh. Nevertheless whatever God has touched in revelation carries for evermore that stamp. This is the truth in sacramentalism.

I wonder, finally, however, whether Fairweather wishes to accept all the implications of his second statement, namely, that 'Revelation cannot therefore direct our understanding to God himself and quite alone.' He may simply be reiterating the point that in revelation it is not God out of all relation to reality that we know. But it is perhaps important to draw attention to the fact that in spite of the presence of the reality which is not God, we nevertheless do know God in himself. It is not simply a case of knowing God + p, God + q and God + r, but that despite this conjunction the identity of God is established and his purpose and will for us identified. God is in a sense, therefore, isolated; our understanding is ultimately directed to himself and to him alone. I should add that Fairweather does later go on to mention the immediacy of knowledge of God which takes place 'in, with and under' the various media of revelation. But the quotation examined draws attention to a possible false extension of this kind of theory.

EMIL BRUNNER: THE MEDIATOR

The variation in the use of the revelation model to which I previously referred could not perhaps be more dramatically illustrated than by contrasting Fairweather's sentence, 'God manifests himself in and through what is not himself' with the opening sentence of the English translation of Emil Brunner's *The Mediator* (Lutterworth Press, London, 1934, p. 21): 'Through God alone can God be known.' I find this statement exceedingly ambiguous. It might mean at least three things.

First, it may be an emphatic way of affirming that in our knowledge of God, it is God who takes the initiative. It is only because God has decided to be known, only because he has chosen to emerge from the depth of his hiddenness that men know who he is and what his purpose is for them. I think that this interpretation gives us the clue to the wide prevalence of the notion of revelation in modern theology. It is an attempt to do justice to the way in which God breaks into our lives. We find him because he has first found us. Religion, in other words, is revelation and not discovery. Brunner makes the big break with those who share many of his other views, when he adds that, 'this is a principle common to all religion'. It is no longer possible to argue that the distinctive thing about Christianity is that it has revelation. What distinguishes it is the content of its revelation. It is not difficult to see how Brunner reaches his conclusions about natural theology from this premise. In all religion, in all revelation, God is taking the initiative with men.

Secondly, Brunner could be making another point, and perhaps is, namely, that sin has so laid hold of man that he is unable of himself to see God, in nature, in history or in Jesus Christ. God has to break this power which blinds man; he has to open man's eyes and only then does revelation take place. On this reading, Brunner is drawing attention to the presence of the Holy Spirit on the side of C, the believer, in our revelation models in all forms. God in his Spirit crosses over to our side to ensure that the purposes of his self-revelation will not finally be frustrated.

Let us look at a third possibility, for it is this that Brunner, I think, really intends, namely, that in the revelation situation, since God is God, he cannot reveal himself through anything less than himself. He must reveal himself through himself. But let us now see what this view entails when applied to our revelation models. Model one, *A(x) reveals B(y) to C(Holy Spirit)*, is directly controverted by Brunner's statement; for on this model God is not the medium through which revelation takes place: God is the subject of revelation. Here Fairweather is correct: God is known through what is other than God. Model two is the application, with slight modification, of model one to the revelation in Jesus Christ. *A(x) reveals B(A) to C(Holy Spirit).* Once again, if Brunner's account is correct, God is made the medium rather than the subject of revelation. It is only when we come to model three that we do see a possible interpretation of Brunner's sentence which is acceptable. Model three was: *B(A) reveals B(E) to C(Holy Spirit).* God as he is in Jesus Christ reveals God as he is in himself to the faithful believer through the inspiration of the Holy Spirit. In this case God could be said to be both the medium and the subject of revelation, though we have to remind ourselves that model three presupposed model two for its right understanding and development. What is certainly clear is that we cannot give a simple yes or no to Brunner's formula, nor does it make any real sense if we take it by itself.

KARL BARTH ON THE SUBJECT OF REVELATION

It is impossible in any treatment of the revelation model either to omit reference to Karl Barth or yet to do anything approaching justice to all that he says. Out of the many matters that might be mentioned I wish to select only three. The first is a statement almost identical with that quotation from Brunner which we have just been examining, but Barth makes it in a much more sophisticated way. In *The Doctrine of the Word of God* (ET, 1936, p. 340) he sets down the revelation situation in three sentences: Sentence one: 'God reveals Himself.' Sentence two: 'God reveals Himself through Himself.' Sentence three: 'God reveals *Himself*.' He is making three emphases in this order. In the act of revelation, it is God who takes the initiative, and the whole event has its roots in divine grace. He executes the revelation not through any medium less than himself, but through his *alter ego*. Finally, as a result of this process, he genuinely reveals himself to man, and not just a part of himself or some aspect of his being. In this Barth effectively reduces revelation to our model three: *B(A) reveals B(E) to C(Holy Ghost).* This concentration upon the revelation of God through God, of B(E) through B(A), has led to that neglect of the second model, which bases the revelation event upon a historical person, Jesus of Nazareth, which we already observed to be a residual element of Kierkegaardian scepticism in Barth (op. cit., pp. 351, 353).

Barth later makes an interesting comment upon the content of the revelation whose divine source and character is thus so firmly guaranteed. He says that the revelation attested by Scripture is that 'God reveals Himself as the Lord', and that this is an analytical judgement. Leaving till our next paragraph the use that Barth makes of this unusual summary of the content of biblical revelation, we may relate his account of it as an analytical judgement to our revelation models. Barth has his own account to give of what he means by an analytical judgement. Normally an analytical judgement is taken to be one in which analysis of the subject reveals the predicate to be contained by definition within it. Barth gives a slightly more difficult account of the matter. The revelation judgement is analytical 'because the distinction between form and content cannot be applied' to it. What I think he means is that whereas in other circumstances an alteration of form would entail an alteration of content or the possibility of alteration of content, in the case of revelation, the fact that God exists in the form of a man does not entail any change in his nature from what he had been from all eternity. The content remains identical in the two situations; otherwise we would be obliged to deny the occurrence of revelation. The point is a good one to make, but whether it is altogether safe to make it in this way is another matter. The impression Barth may just create is that by examination of B(A), God as he is present in Jesus Christ, one automatically recognises that B(A) is equivalent to B(E). If we know what the term 'triangle' means, we know by analysis of this concept that a three-sided rectilinear figure has three angles. But in our model three the transition from B(A) to B(E) – from the recognition that God is present in Jesus Christ (as he is present in John the Baptist) to the assertions that the fullness of God dwells bodily in Christ and the God thus present is co-essential with the Eternal God – is itself the subject of revelation and not the result of analysis.

We turn now to a second matter Barth raises in relation to revelation. One of the main uses, of course, made by Karl Barth in *The Doctrine of the Word of God* of the revelation model is that by summarising the content of biblical revelation in the 'analytical judgement' mentioned above, he provides a basis for the doctrine of the Trinity, what he calls 'the root of the doctrine'. The interpretation he gives of how the doctrine of the Trinity is related to Scripture, through a whole series of media – the concept of revelation ('We come to the doctrine of the Trinity by no other way than by an analysis of the concept of revelation', op. cit., p. 358), the summary proposition about revelation, and even the constituent terms in revelation, Revealer, Revelation, Revealedness – is one of the most elaborate exercises in modern hermeneutics that I have ever encountered. But Barth is saying in effect that there is a threefoldness in the revelation situation, the triadic structure which we embodied in our revelation models, which qualifies it to provide a basis for the doctrine of the Trinity. Against the suggestion that we could arrive at the threefoldness of God simply by juggling with the logical structure of the notion of revelation, he replies very firmly that this sort of doctrinal extension of the revelation can only be carried out with the Christian model of revelation and with no other. What Barth does not indicate clearly enough is the quite unhistorical character of the exposition he gives of the root of the doctrine. Revelation considerations in no way affected the course of the great trinitarian controversies in the third and fourth centuries; and even now they would carry conviction only to those who were prepared to accept Barth's rather esoteric approach to the subject. What Barth does make clear is the fact that the doctrine of the Trinity is not in the Bible, that it involves 'availing itself of other concepts than those contained in the (biblical) text before it' (op. cit., p. 354). Once this character of the doctrine is recognised, then there is never any question of 'reading it off' from a biblical script. It is a very complex process of interpreting, checking, analysing and expounding that finally yields us the doctrine; and it is exceedingly difficult, at some stage in that process, not to yield to the argument from tradition.

Thirdly, in *The Doctrine of the Word of God* Barth has, we have just seen, operated a fairly conventional model of revelation. The source of the revelation is the Revealer. The medium through which he is revealed is the Revelation. The result for the person apprehending the whole event is the Revealedness of the Revealer. All rather wordy, but basically simple. B reveals A to produce revealedness for C. On this model, the medium of Revelation is the whole event of Jesus Christ, the incarnation in its composite totality. There appears, however, somewhat later in Barth's writing, a model with a rather different internal structure. The modification is, I believe, of major importance for the understanding of how the revelation model is tending to be used today by Barth's followers. The explicit quotations giving this revised model are not extensive. What I would claim is that if we do use this revised model we make much more sense of Barth's more recent writings than we do by adhering to the early model. Within the framework of very strong assertions that no dualistic thinking must be allowed to divide the human from the divine, Barth says quite clearly (*Church Dogmatics*, ET, IV/2, 1958, p. 115. Cf. II/1, pp. 16f) that 'the divine essence (nature) expresses and reveals itself wholly in the sphere of the human nature'. Also, 'the saving act of God takes place in the man Jesus of Nazareth. The power and authority of God are revealed by him and to him, in his words and in his actions' (op. cit., p. 99). These quotations are definitely not against the run of play. Three times on earlier pages (namely, pp. 96ff) Barth has spoken about the human essence of Jesus Christ being the *organ* of the nature or work of the Son as the Mediator, a judgement curiously reminiscent of the famous sentence attributed to Nestorius, 'Mary bore a man who was the organ of Godhead.'

What are we to make of this revision of the revelation model? Barth does seem to be saying quite definitely that the revelation which takes place in Jesus Christ takes place through the human nature. We seem to have reverted to Fairweather's position: God is revealed through what is not God. The charge of Nestorianism cannot quite be made to stick. It would if Barth were saying that in Jesus Christ there are two complete persons present in exactly the same way at the same time. He is saying something rather different, and much more subtle, namely, that the human nature is there in the ordinary empirical and inspectible way, but that the divine nature is 'there' only as it reveals itself through the human nature. It is 'there', we might say, revelationally, or if words meant what they said, apocalyptically. On this reading the relation between the two natures is to be understood not in terms of compresence or logical *enhypostasia*, or yet of *communicatio idiomatum*, but in terms of this quite peculiar and unique relation of revelation. If we were to accept such a view, we might then be able on the one hand, to go to the extreme with the kenoticists – and in fact Barth begins to approach that extreme in the volume referred to (IV/2, e.g. pp. 484ff); and yet, on the other hand, to affirm to the full the deity of the divine nature with its complete attributes all revelationally present in Jesus Christ. We have now effectively reached the position detected in H. R. Mackintosh (see above, p. 135). To revert to our models: Barth on this reading has telescoped models two and three to give *A(x) reveals B(E) to C(Holy Spirit)*. It is the relation of revelation which constitutes the situation, binds it in a unity and justifies Barth's insistence that there is no dualistic thinking here. My own feeling is that if the revelation model is to be made to work in our time it has to take this form, and not the form which Brunner and the earlier Barth had favoured.

HIDDENNESS AND REVELATION: GÜNTHER DEHN

This presentation of the revelation model facilitates the inclusion in our talk about the revelation of God of some very mystifying statements about the hiddenness of God in his revelation. If God can be known through God alone, then there can be no room for hiddenness. The medium must be as clear as the *revelation*. It is when we introduce what is not God and affirm that God is known through what is not God that we lay the foundation for a whole range of statements about God's concealment, statements which have a long history in Lutheran theology, and which are part of Barth's standard talk about revelation. A typical example is to be found in Günther Dehn (*Man and Revelation*, Hodder & Stoughton, London, 1936, pp. 65f):

> God is concealed even in his revelation . . . even among Christians there is a continual desire to get into contact with God directly in his revelation. . . . But God resists this desire by remaining always, even in his revelation, the hidden God . . . God becomes man . . . God's activity is interwoven with the events of human history (and in it) is not directly distinguishable from the history of mankind.

Indeed so effective is this process, that God does indeed conceal himself at the very point of revelation. I agree that some of this kind of talk comes very close to being nonsense, and that it forms a very easy point of departure for all who want to take the leap. But if there is any sense in it, it lies here, in its indication, perhaps a little sensationally, that God reveals himself through what is not God, a man who is carpenter, whom we have known since childhood and talked to, who is maybe a little bit odd, but such a fine fellow that we look upon him as one of ourselves. If revelation had been written all over this man, if he had come with the unmistakable mark of the divine upon him, if there had been no concealment, then he would have been accepted at least by those who were supremely responsible for his death. The Pharisees, however we dislike them now, however we pillory them, were not God-haters. Nor had they given up looking for the Messiah. If they had been given a sign, one tiny sign, they would have accepted. But no. He was concealed. There Dehn is correct. There too is the case for saying that the revelation comes through what is not God, the other-than-God which so often effectively conceals it.

DIFFICULTIES FOR THE REVELATION MODEL

I should like next to examine the role which the revelation model may fulfil in modern christology and the status which is to be

accorded to it, together with some of the problems which it
creates and of which its more ardent supporters are curiously
imperceptive. Let us look to begin with at some of the quite
basic difficulties which Gerald Downing raises (*Has Christianity
a Revelation?*). I shall set aside the fundamental problem of
biblical foundations for the term – not because it is unimportant,
for it seems to me to point to a quite radical revision of the
way in which many so-called biblical theologians interpret their
task – and instead concentrate on some of the more strictly
systematic issues. For example, there is a whole series of
difficulties which Downing encounters in the many accepted
phrases about revelation. The term 'revelation' is associated
with unveiling, with making clear something that is already
hidden. But when we apply this term to Jesus the result is not
exactly what we want – for all that might be meant is that God
appears as Jesus; or to adopt the language of D. D. Evans, we
'look on' Jesus as God. But this usage does not do justice to
what happens in me and to me when Jesus reveals God to me.
The notion of finality when applied to revelation creates
trouble, for revelation is essentially an open-ended process. It is
something that happens and must go on happening so long
as men and women find God revealed to them in Jesus Christ.
The here-and-now character of revelation prevents us from
calling it once-for-all, except in some paltry sense such as that
Jesus Christ was seen only at a certain period in human history
and then 'once-for-all' time. Downing makes a brief reference
(op. cit., pp. 224f) to a sentence about revelation which Barth
has introduced into modern theology, namely, that 'revelation
is self-authenticating'. Though he does not treat the view
with the fullness it deserves, he does put his finger upon the
basic problem which it must face, that of explaining the differences between allegedly 'self-authenticating' experiences of the
self-same God. As he had just said, 'consistent solipsism is
impregnable', nor, may we add, does the assertion of the
objectivity of a self-authenticating experience logically imply the
objectivity of the entire character of the subject claiming self-
authentication.

WHAT IS REVEALED?

At the end of the day, perhaps Downing might be said to be rejecting the concept of revelation simply because it is not borne out by the evidence.

> God's love may well be too profound for us ever to understand. But it is not traditional teaching to suggest that it is self-contradictory. If any 'mystery' is 'revealed' to present-day Christians with their kaleidoscopic beliefs, it is a mystery of diversity, and that by definition is not 'God'. The traditional image of the 'mystery of God' is an ocean too deep to plumb; but the total course of Christian theology makes it look like a maze so complex that everyone gets lost in his own way. If there is a 'revealed mystery', it is this that is 'revealed' . . . The theologian is using a word that normally describes 'making clear' to mean 'leave unclear'. (op. cit., p. 229)

There is a certain tang to this sort of criticism, and it may even seem to have an iconoclastic quality. But it is difficult to resist the conclusion that it is largely justified by the sharp conflict that exists upon so many fronts in contemporary theology, and by the bitterness of so many of these conflicts, with its denial of the love that lies at the heart of the Christian faith. Downing sums up his scepticism concerning revelation as the clue to Christianity by the quite outspoken questioning of the whole idea that God intended 'to reveal himself' in Jesus Christ. He may do so – our Christian hope is that he will – in the end-time; and what he has done in Jesus Christ will prepare us to know as we are known – then. But 'a "revelation" of what cannot now be seen is not a "revelation"' (op. cit., p. 238). The great contribution of Downing's book, despite critics, is that it points us in the direction where we shall find more effective models to describe Jesus Christ, and models that are also much more biblical. These are the models of redemption and salvation. These models, as we shall see later, cannot adequately be sustained by the revelation model.

PERFORMATIVES PARASITIC

Before leaving the summary of some of Downing's position, I may perhaps mention two points that merit further consideration. The first is that there are certain circumstances which make the extension of the 'performative' analysis of language to religious language not entirely valid, for this reason: If we take a typical performative statement – such as the Queen might make, 'I hereby appoint you High Commissioner to India' – we can see that this statement is not a description of anything but the actual execution of an appointment. What must, however, be noted is that it occurs within a context which may have to be described if someone says that he does not know who the Queen is, or why she should be making an appointment to an office carried out six thousand miles away, or what a High Commissioner is. In other words, a performative statement is parasitic. For this reason we can never resolve religious statements altogether into 'performatives'. By their very nature as 'performatives' they entail for their understanding what we might call 'host' statements, some at least of which must be descriptive. The linguistic analysis of religious statements cannot finally, therefore, replace the ontological enquiry concerning the descriptive account of the contextual framework of the performatives.

The second consideration that ought to be kept in mind in trying to make an assessment of Downing's rather searching analysis is that while it is true that the word 'revelation' strictly relates to the process of making known what was previously unknown, or unveiling what was previously hidden, in most recent theology it has come to be used synonymously even with the very term which Downing proposes as an alternative to revelation talk – salvation, or with reconciliation and redemption. In one sense this fact lends still greater weight to Downing's criticism; for if it does not make much sense to say that the revelation remains hidden it makes perhaps even less sense to say that some men are redeemed and are not aware of it or that they are partially redeemed. It is significant that in Barth, as the *Church Dogmatics* theme unfolds itself, it is the fact of reconciliation in Christ which increasingly comes to take the strain of the argument, while the idea of revelation to some extent recedes. It is not without interest and relevance to Downing's analysis that the term 'revelation' has at many hands come virtually to lose all connotative sense and to operate solely as a denotative term. The result is one of the clumsiest redundancies or at best periphrases of modern christology, the phrase 'the revelation of God in Jesus Christ', which is used so frequently and unthinkingly that it means no more than the name 'Jesus Christ'. I am not forgetting that the name 'Jesus Christ' was for primitive Christians, perhaps chiefly for Jewish Christians, itself a connotative phrase; but in the gentile world as in the modern world it became almost solely denotative. When it has reached that stage it is no longer a christological model.

REVELATION AND REDEMPTION: WHICH IS MORE ULTIMATE?

We have observed how Downing wishes to substitute the soteriological for the revelation model, and how Barth shifts the emphasis from revelation to reconciliation. Both of these moves are, I am convinced, due primarily to the fact that the revelation model fails to sustain an adequate analysis of the death of Jesus Christ. Let us take a basic soteriological proposition: 'The death of Christ reveals the love of God to sinners.' This proposition may be integrated in the context of either of two quite different theories about the significance of the death of Christ.

On the one hand, we may say that the attitude of God to sinners has been solely and consistently one of love towards them. God had tried many methods under the old covenant to help them to understand this attitude of his to them. All had failed, so in the end he sent his own son to live among men and to die self-sacrificially, as a supreme illustration of God's love. Through Christ's death, no change was effected in God's relation to man: no obstacle between God and man was removed. In a sense nothing happened objectively. A very compelling illustration was offered.

On the other hand, a fairly definite attempt may be made to take up where the previous theory left off, to agree that indeed the death of Christ supremely reveals the love of God but it does so for a very definite reason. Between the sinner and God there stands the mass of human guilt which is an offence to God. Whereas God loves the sinner, this mass of guilt must be removed before that love can express itself in God's acceptance of man. God in Jesus Christ accepts the responsibility for this guilt and Christ bears in his body the pain and suffering for this guilt. In Christ, man the sinner, his sins forgiven, is acceptable to God. It is through these happenings, these objective events, that the love of God is illustrated or revealed.

It seems to me intolerable that such a range of soteriological variation should be comprehended within one phrase. It has certainly enabled those who have been unwilling to reject openly so-called 'objective' theories of atonement to employ language which was sufficiently ambiguous to conceal their allegiance. In a word then, the revelation model fails to extend into a sufficiently unambiguous soteriological structure to justify its exclusive use in christology.

REVELATION MODEL AS A FORMAL STRUCTURE

Again, it is not always appreciated that the revelation model is a strictly formal structure. It states that a certain formal relationship holds between B and A for C, but in itself it does not supply us with the content of B or A. For example, it has been argued that if it is true that Jesus Christ reveals God, then the deity of Christ is *ipso facto* demonstrated. But such a demonstration is not by itself valid. It requires to be supported by some concealed premise such as that of Brunner's which we have already examined at length, namely, through God alone can God be known. But without some such premise, and as has been said before it is not an easily supportable premise itself, no conclusions can be drawn from the revelation model by itself as to the content of B or A. Someone who wishes to argue that God may reveal himself through sunsets, or good music, or inspiring poetry, or some of the repetitive processes of nature, cannot be ruled out of court by any appeal to the revelation model *simpliciter*.

In fact, I would go farther and say that the controversy over natural and revealed theology is not a controversy over the revelation model at all, but over the values which the controversialists have endeavoured to import into the model. If you like, it is a quarrel about definitions. One side has said that revelation takes place only in Jesus Christ, or logically: no instances of revelation are other than instances of revelation in Jesus Christ; and the other side has said that revelation takes place in nature, in human moral effort, in human history, and so on. In terms of revelation, one side is as entitled to its definition as the other, for the revelation model *per se* may be given either set of values. One side can only gain the edge on the other, or at least seem to do so, when it substitutes for the revelation model one of its soteriological alternatives, and appealing to Scripture, 'There is none other name under heaven . . . whereby we must be saved' (Acts 4.12), argues that even if there is revelation outside of Christ, it is 'sound and fury, signifying nothing'. This is not the place for any further elaboration of this moth-eaten controversy, but I do sometimes wonder whether it ought not to be settled by a simple appeal to fact. If there are indeed some people who can honestly say that God reveals himself to them apart from Jesus Christ, and if we are to presume that they know what revelation means (say, from their awareness of revelation in Jesus Christ), then I wonder whether it is valuable or indeed proper to prosecute the controversy against them.

REVELATION MODEL AS A SECOND-ORDER STRUCTURE

Another way of stating the case that I am now making is to say that the revelation model is a second-order model which derives its meaning from other first-order models. A comparable case could be made for saying that the assertion of the deity or the divinity of Christ is a second-order statement about him. The first-order statement occurs in the form of the primitive Church's declaration that in Jesus Christ God has fulfilled all his promises to Israel. So effectively does the range of fulfilment surpass human capacity that it seems to have reached a degree of accomplishment that only God himself could achieve. The affirmation that 'Jesus is God' is then made. In some senses, the revelation model may quite justifiably be taken even as a third-order model, because it depends for its assertion, and for its content, both upon the first-order statements which the Bible makes concerning Jesus, and also upon a whole group of theological statements which have found their way into creeds and confessions and stand in very close proximity to the biblical statements.

If this argument is correct then we have to say that Jesus Christ is the revelation of God because he is God incarnate; and we cannot say that the affirmation of the deity of Christ rests upon the prior declaration that he is the unique revelation of God. Revelation is not a theological conjuror's hat out of which we may draw the rabbits of the several doctrines of the Christian faith. The model of revelation is in fact dependent upon these models for its content and indeed for its form. For that reason, it becomes almost impossible to sustain Barth's positions, on which previously we kept an open mind, that we come to the doctrine of the Trinity by no other way than by the concept of revelation, or that the root of the doctrine is to be found in the revelation structure. In the hierarchy of doctrines the doctrine of the Trinity stands too high to be a derivative from a third-order doctrine such as that of revelation.

REVELATION MODEL AND THE PSYCHOLOGICAL MODEL

As a result of the previous aspects of the revelation model upon which we have been commenting – that it is formal and that it is a second- or even a third-order model – it tends to combine with other models (in addition as we noted above to giving way to them). This procedure is not always without its complications. Some of these we have noticed in connection with the two-nature model, and the psychological model. When the revelation model is combined with the two-nature model, one or other of two consequences follows.

Either, we have the rather curious circumstance that the divine nature is part of the situation which is the medium of revelation or, in some extremer forms of this view (Brunner and Barth, at times), that the divine nature is alone the medium of revelation and the human nature becomes an optional extra. I am not sure that we are not quite close to impermissible nonsense when we try to say that the divine nature can be both the medium and the subject of revelation (that is, without the additional apparatus of forms two and three of the revelation model). For *ex hypothesi* the medium of revelation is known directly, and if the medium and the subject of revelation are identical and thus known directly, there is no occasion for revelation.

Or, and this is, we said before, the only real alternative: the human nature *per se* is the medium of revelation (Barth on rare occasions) and it mediates the divine nature to us. This combination of the two-nature model with the revelation model would entail an almost entire rewriting of christological theory, and a very radical recasting of the two-model theory. Very little of the Aristotelianism which has been engrossed in modern enhypostatic theory would remain, as indeed would little of enhypostatic theory.

The combination of the revelation model with the psychological model would lead to a christological theory not unlike that which we have just mentioned. The chief difference would be that the human nature would be construed in more strictly psychological terms than would be available for Barth with his rather radical Kierkegaardian historical scepticism. This combination enables its expositors to give a more thoroughgoingly human account of Jesus' earthly life, the critics might say even an ebionite view, and relieves them of the recurring problem of explaining how a divine mind can be at the same time omniscient and ignorant, the same person omnipotent and weak. The essential and obvious humanity of many of Jesus' actions in the New Testament has induced biblical theologians with a systematic bent to employ the revelation model to enable them to connect biblical accounts of these actions with standardised systematic theological interpretations of them. Here lies part-explanation of a practice to which Downing refers (op. cit., p. 20 n. 1), namely, the wide use of this model by biblical theologians despite the absence in the Bible of any general occurrence of the term to describe God's actions or purposes – in the New Testament the revelation model provides a bridge between the biblical narratives and the systematic christological picture of Christ. But it is a procedure which is not entirely unexpected because of the formal character of the revelation model: by its nature it derives content from beyond itself.

APOLOGETIC AND KERYGMATIC VALUE OF THE REVELATION MODEL

To turn now to a quite different matter: the revelation model has often been thought to have great apologetic and kerygmatic value. The kerygmatic value, it is said, lies in the fact that in proclaiming God and his mercy and goodness, we are not under obligation to lay out the pathways which men and women must take to find God. He has already come to them. He has 'revealed' himself. He has appeared. The apologetic value of such a concept, it is said, is that it relieves us of all obligation to prove that God exists, or that he has done this or that, or that a certain interpretation is the only valid one to impose upon a given set of phenomena. This assessment of the value of the revelation model savours perhaps more of the safe seclusion of the pulpit than the rough-and-tumble of the common room, and one wonders how much longer it can continue to bewitch the insensitive and imperceptive.

Let us examine the situation more closely. The kerygmatic statement – that God has appeared among us – carries a prima facie persuasiveness only because the revelation thus asserted is taken to be dyadic, two-term, a direct face-to-face confrontation. But in fact this is not so. The situation kerygmatically described as God having revealed himself is that of a man called Jesus acting in this way and that and saying this and that. Immediately the stage is set for a very long argument about whether that claim to revelation is a fair interpretation of these words and actions. That argument does not concern me at present. But the fact that it can begin shows that the revelation situation is not dyadic but triadic (as we have all along contended) and that before the revelation model can be employed there must be at least some idea, some general notion, accepted to which revelation is referred. Within the context of the Old and New Testaments this condition is fulfilled. The Jew can speak significantly of the God who was known to Abraham and Isaac *revealing* himself to the people of Israel in their sufferings in Babylon. The God who subsequently reveals himself is already identified by the people of Israel and acknowledged by them. In the New Testament Peter, had he been so moved, might have spoken of the God who had promised salvation to Israel revealing his salvation to men finally in Jesus Christ; and the proclamation of revelation would again be significant because God was known to his hearers.

But where there is no prior knowledge or acknowledgement of God, revelation propositions have no weight. If I say to an unbeliever 'God is revealed in Jesus Christ', this proposition means no more or no less than the term 'God' means. If God has no existence, the proposition cannot assist his revelation. Propositions asserting the revelation of God presuppose some prior knowledge of God if they are to have any significance. The assertion of God's being and God's revelation cannot significantly be made in one proposition. When we pursue this course, we begin to develop a sympathy which Protestant theology has not had for many decades now, for the proofs for divine existence. For among the many other things they may be trying to do, there is this: they are endeavouring to establish a value for the term 'God' which might make a revelation proposition not just meaningful but actually possible. In short then, the revelation model has no real place in an apologetic situation where we are conversing with total unbelievers. It has a place in a kerygmatic utterance only where it is made in the context of some degree of accepted belief in God.

PART III

PROCESS CHRISTOLOGY

7

DAVID R. GRIFFIN

The christological models so far considered have been controlled in their expression by the norms imposed by the Chalcedonian Creed and its derivatives, as well as by the metaphysics which in turn conditioned them. We turn now to a selection of christological views which claim a rather different metaphysical inspiration and medium of expression and control, namely, the process philosophy associated with the names of Alfred North Whitehead and Charles Hartshorne. The examples of such process christology will come from the writing of David R. Griffin, John B. Cobb, Jr and Norman Pittenger. Certain differences in method, however, between this process christology and the Chalcedon-related types may be considered in advance. For example, first, it will have been noticed that the corpus of Aristotelian metaphysics drawn on by the Chalcedonian christologists, both orthodox and heretical, was fairly well defined, and the logical principles in accordance with which it was operated were almost universally accepted. The writings of the process philosophers, by contrast, have never quite achieved the quasi-canonical status given to Aristotle's, nor has there been a logical system to be employed in the extension of the process philosophy into areas not anticipated by its founders. Consequently, secondly, the process christologists draw on different aspects of process philosophy, interpret it differently, and their dependence on their sources is to be seen more in terms of influence than of literal transposition. The rather selective method which they have adopted in using process material differs considerably from the adherence of the classic Chalcedonian christologists to a common metaphysic and its accordant logical method. Thirdly, there are in the process christologists greater differences from one another than is the case in more classical christology, differences which amount to independence of one another. Comparisons among them then become difficult, particularly as there is no process canon by which to judge them, and even at this early stage we may wonder whether, in its absence, we have to fall back on the Chalcedonian norms, and whether it is a category mistake to do so.

DAVID R. GRIFFIN

We begin with Griffin who, in his *A Process Christology* (Westminster, Philadelphia, 1973), founded his treatment of the subject firmly on a process basis and, building meticulously on this foundation, has given us a classical example of its type. We shall concentrate upon chapter 8, 'God's supreme act of self-expression', where he sets out the substance of his presentation.

PROCESS FOUNDATIONS AND THE HUMAN ANALOGY

Griffin (op. cit., pp. 206ff) opens his case with the claim that Whitehead's philosophy meets three criteria which Langdon Gilkey once required of any ontology adequate to the needs of contemporary theology, and therefore of christology. These criteria are: first, that the analogical categories used to describe divine deeds and self-revelations should be 'intelligible and credible', and that, since human action is the sole action that we know, the analogy with God's action has to be found in that sphere. Secondly, such an ontology will have to make provision for speech about 'special' acts of God, of which, if we may anticipate in order to give the drift of the argument, the event of the incarnation is the 'supreme' act. Thirdly, the ontology contemplated will have to secure that these ends are achieved without entailing some miraculous suspension of the normal processes of 'natural causation'. The ontology of events implicit in Whitehead's philosophy, with its views that 'actual entities are events (actual occasions)' (Griffin, p. 207), will prove to be the means of meeting these criteria, and the demonstration of this achievement provides the structure of the form of process christology which Griffin favours.

Taking up the theme of the human analogy as the most intelligible way of understanding God, Griffin develops for us the content of the human side of the analogy. Given that a moment of human experience is an instance of an actual entity, and the human mind consists of a series of such occasions, a 'living person' is the technical process name for the human mind (op. cit., p. 208). The mind exists within an organism which is both body and mind, and it is called a 'corpuscular society' in view of its many – a billion is mentioned – components; and also a 'monarchical society' in view of the dominance within it of the mind. The mind, by the route of the brain, is the recipient of innumerable impulses and stimuli which have come in the first place to the body; on receipt of these influences, the mind 'constitutes itself' in return with its decisions sending impulses back along the same track via the brain-cells to all parts of the body. There are two aspects to this mind–body relationship which are of importance to the development of the analogy. On the one hand, the mind in its domination is sympathetic and kindly towards the other members of the society, especially in imparting to them their 'initial aims'. On the other hand, it is itself sensitive, as it were from within, to what happens to these members according to their feelings.

Having earlier spoken of the human mind as a series of events or occasions of experience, Griffin extends his account to say that it is 'a certain abstract essence' which converts this series into a unity, continuing from occasion to occasion (p. 211). Comprised within this 'essence' are, principally, purpose and character. Purpose is the underlying drive of the personality which motivates all that the person does. Character is the subjective quality of the person, seen particularly in the person's attitude, openness and responses to others. Such responsiveness to others in turn contributes to the acts of 'self-constitution' of the person. Purpose and character are interdependent and together reflect the person's personality.

Griffin now extends the basis of the analogy by examining the mind–body relationship more closely, to distinguish 'acts of the person', the primary from the secondary. The former are the acts of 'self-constitution' which, as we have just seen, take place when the mind receives stimuli from the brain or its past and responds to them in decisions to be executed by different parts of the body. These latter actions when executed are the secondary acts of the person. The primary actions of the person are invariably identical in structure, in that the mind always influences the body, which is also responsive to efficient causes from its past, by offering it aims. The parts of the body respond to these influences as 'partly self-creating subjects'. Since the primary activities of the mind are structurally the same, it is in the secondary activities, or external acts as Griffin sometimes calls them, that the 'special acts' of the person are to be found. Such acts have three distinguishing characteristics (op. cit., p. 212). First, they must be such as to reflect the person's essential character and purpose, as defined above, and not simply run-of-the-mill undistinguished and insignificant actions which anyone could be performing at any time. Secondly, the action must spring from a genuine intention of the agent, so that it authentically 'expresses' his purpose and character. Thirdly, to be regarded as 'special acts' these activities must reach a very high degree of actual achievement of the aims entertained by the agent.

APPLICATION OF THE HUMAN ANALOGY

Griffin now applies the human analogy thus described to our thought about, and description of, God. God, a living person, in the process terminology which Griffin uses, is a strand of occasions of experience which, as we saw in the human person, is nevertheless a unity through the persistence of that abstract essence which defines his person. In almost totally traditional theological fashion, this abstract essence is said to include the

divine attributes of omniscience, omnipotence and everlasting-
ness, as well as his personal attributes of purpose and character.
The distinction made earlier between acts in a primary and a
secondary sense is applied fairly literally to the actions of God.
God's primary actions are in his case also self-constituting as he
responds to stimuli from the world, and his responding decisions
become the initial aims which, when objectified 'by the actual
entities', form the world as it comes to be (p. 214). But acts of
God in this primary sense are all structurally the same, so that
there takes place no violation of the normal causal relationships
in the world – which, it will be recalled, was the third
requirement of an ontology adequate for christology, which
Griffin had extracted from Langdon Gilkey (see above, p. 178).
Moreover, the identity of purpose and character in God's primary
acts appears in the nature of these acts, as he seeks by his love for
them to induce them to fulfil the highest possibilities he has
communicated to them indirectly through entities in the world.

So, if we are to discover the nature of the 'special acts' of God,
which by definition will be different from his universal activities,
we have to examine the secondary sense in which God's acts may
be considered. Once more Griffin applies the human analogy –
this time, of the three characteristics of human external special
acts. Since all events in the world issue from acts of God in which
he provides an initial aim for them, it is necessary to identify
what constitutes a 'special act' of God. The first requirement is
that it should express God's essential being, character and
purpose, and to be effectively credible, God's vision of reality
should be expressed through the words and deeds of a human
being (p. 215). The second requirement is based on the premise
that God provides initial aims for finite actual entities which fall
within the range of the possible in their circumstances, and so
acknowledges that there will be differences in content of God's
aims for these entities. Some will approximate more closely than
others to his essential being, and so to being 'special acts'. Thirdly,
God offers to each entity an initial aim composed of ranked
possibilities, lower and higher, among which the person can
choose. If such choices, freely made, reflect God's nature to 'an

unsurpassable degree', then we have not only a 'special act' but a 'supreme act' of God.

THE PERSON OF CHRIST

Having set up his criteria for the identification of a supreme act of God, Griffin applies himself, following the order set, to the determination of whether Jesus meets the criteria, First, he contends that in his life and message Jesus proclaimed love as the essential being of God and its priority over his justice, his readiness to forgive, and his joy that men and women were already participating in the Kingdom of God now come among them. Secondly, Jesus' message did not spring *de novo* out of history, but had its roots in the past and in the religion of Israel, with its teaching about creation, God's purposes for all his creatures, and his will for them. Against that background God had pronounced his aims for Jesus, which were of a supremely high nature and approximated to the point of identity with God's own 'subjective eternal aim for the world' (op. cit., p. 218), so that God's particular aims for Jesus were inclusive of God's aims for the whole created order. These aims were so completely fulfilled by Jesus in his whole life and message that he expressed comprehensively the very being and nature of God, as love towards all his creation. Thirdly, emphasis has to be laid on the fact that in this process Jesus of his own volition, and not through any coercion, elected to obey God and to make known, at the price of sacrifice, God's purpose and will for the whole of the world and God's creatures.

At this point Griffin furthers his account of the person of Jesus by employing the revelation model which we have considered above. It is because Jesus has been recognised to have fulfilled the supreme aims of God for his whole creation and to stand in this quite unique relation to God, that men and women have been able to speak of him as the decisive and supreme revelation of God. But not only have they in fact found him to be so; for them it is also fitting that Jesus should be so regarded, because of the content of the aims which are God's general aims for creation, which God has given him and which he has fulfilled as his particular aims. The distinction may then be drawn between the objective side of the situation, which is God's self-expression in the life, words and mission of Jesus, in the past; and the subjective side, which in a single unrepeated assertion he says is 'a soteriological statement' (op. cit., p. 220), the revelation in the present to men and women who have now appropriated the significance of what happened there and then. The distinction is, in effect, one which is familiar to us from Barth, between the objective possibility of revelation (the incarnation) and the subjective possibility of revelation (our apprehension of, and obedient response to, the incarnation).

Having dealt with the view that Jesus reveals the nature of God and his Kingdom, Griffin turns to consideration of the way in which Jesus' life and deeds are revelatory of God's agency in the world and in relation to the world. The relation between God and the world is, he holds, a two-way relation. On the one hand, contrary to the implications of the doctrine that God is impassible, he cites as the accepted position of his book that God does respond with love and sympathy to the joys and sorrows of his creatures. The life, mission and deeds of Jesus are central to the revelation of this aspect and character of God's activity in the world. This contention is, I believe, marred by a rather outdated account of 'orthodox theology', which in many of its modern expressions has a great deal to say about God's being afflicted in all the afflictions of his creatures, and is much less dependent on the Aristotelian idea of the 'unmoved mover of the spheres' than either Whitehead or Griffin appears to realise. On the other hand, thinking of the relation of God to the world, Griffin holds that this relation is characterised by persuasiveness and lack of coercion and control. Nowhere is this fact more clearly revealed than in the crucifixion of Jesus, where God desists from that very interference with human action which would have expressed his uninhibited omnipotence. Even the taunts of bystanders as Jesus hung on the cross could not move him to invoke the power of God for his deliverance. Once again, Griffin's case would stand without the doubtful evidence from one narrow type of theology which now has few followers. In short, then, the case for the claim that Jesus was and is both the supreme expression and decisive revelation of God's essential being and of his activity in, and in relation to, the world rests upon the content of the aims which God has given him, which reflect directly 'God's eternal subjective aim', and upon his obedience to these aims.

THE SPECIAL PRESENCE OF GOD IN JESUS

Griffin rounds off his construction with the examination of a question which has to be faced by all christologies, namely, in what way does the presence of God in Jesus differ so greatly from his presence in other men that it may be regarded as special? His reply follows closely but not uncritically the christological views of John Cobb. Adopting a definition of the self as 'that relatively continuous center within human experience around which experience attempts more or less to organise itself', Cobb refines it to the point where it is equated with an 'I' which supersedes and controls both the emotional and the rational elements in the human psyche. With this notion of the 'I' in mind, he distinguishes between the Hebrew prophets, on the one hand, in whose psyche there is a struggle between, say, the call to declare God's word and their own reluctant inclinations, and Jesus, on the other hand, in whom there was no opposition between his prehension – to use the process term – of God's aim and the other prehensions which formed the content of his experience. This prehension of God was in effect the centre of his psyche and the determinant of the part played by the different elements of his experience. Here lay the source of his authority, both as God's supreme activity of self-expression and as the supreme revelation of God. He re-affirms a point made earlier, that while the aims which God has given to Jesus and which have been fulfilled by him are particular to him and unique, nevertheless they comprised God's aim for the ultimate good for the whole creation. He rounds this passage off by using a notion of which Cobb makes so much in *Christ in a Pluralistic Age*

(Westminster, Philadelphia, 1975), that Jesus, by fulfilling these aims so completely and thereby the purpose of the whole creation, was the supreme expression of the Logos, himself the true character and purpose of that creation.

COMMENTS AND CRITIQUE

A CATEGORY LEAP

In the christology which Griffin offers, we are being asked to make what might be called a category leap. For in the study so far, we have been examining christologies which in one way or another remain within touching distance of the ontology which had its roots in Aristotelian metaphysics. Their key concepts have been drawn from that source, and though there has been considerable variety of interpretation, as we have passed from one language to another we have not failed to observe the control which the parent ontology has exerted even over these interpretations. But ever more pressingly, the question is raised whether Aristotelian ontology is still acceptable as the source from which normative concepts for a present-day christology are to be drawn. Langdon Gilkey, as noted by Griffin, made a special plea for a credible ontology, implying thereby that the Aristotelian option was no longer an option. So, too, did the Roman Catholic representatives on the Anglican–Roman Catholic International Commission, when the *Final Report* in 1981 seemed to be acknowledging (p. 21) the difficulty of adhering to Aristotelian language to describe the presence of Christ in the Eucharist. But such uneasiness with Aristotelian ontology seems to have taken a long time to reach theology, for dissensions were being voiced as early as Locke, Berkeley and Hume. It is therefore to Griffin's credit that he has bitten the bullet and conscientiously endeavoured to construct a christology which eschews Aristotle and uses process philosophy, which is certainly one of the most consistently presented and logically argued of the modern possibilities. Griffin's use of the process concepts appears early in his presentation as he develops from them the content of the human analogy, so central for his case; and his extension of it into his *analogatum* of the person of Christ is consistently worked through.

But even in his category leap, Griffin does not abandon the components of traditional theology and christology. For example, he refers (op. cit., pp. 213f) to God's 'abstract defining essence', which includes both the classical unique attributes of omniscience, omnipotence and omnipresence, and his 'personal attributes' which comprise God's unchanging and eternal character and purpose. So it has to be remembered that Griffin makes this explicit commitment to classical theology. For as the chapter unfolds along the lines of the process notion of the di-polarity of God, he introduces such ideas as that God constitutes himself each moment, *pace* his unchangingness, receiving and responding to the experiences of the creatures in the world. Here, too, there is a bond with traditional theology; for these responses in which God gives to the entities in the world their aims for their own true good are themselves the expression of his love.

The dilemma confronting anyone attempting to plot out a novel christology, as Griffin does, is to decide how much of the old christology and its supporting theology you must take along with you to ensure that what you are offering can be seen to be genuinely 'Christian'; and, on the other hand, how extensively you are going to introduce your new ontology and its components. We have just observed how he has retained elements of the traditional doctrine of God. In the strictly christological field, he lays down certain markers. For example, he states very clearly (op. cit., p. 180) both his problem and his ambition, when he says that the problem for a christology based on Whitehead is not how God could be present in Jesus, but how God could be present in Jesus in a special way, so that Jesus would be the unique revelation of God's nature. It is doubtful if we have had a better definition of the christological task in the history of the subject from Athanasius to Moltmann. He severely castigates Schubert Ogden (op. cit., p. 220) for saying that there is no ground for holding 'that God has acted in Christ in any way different from the way in which he primordially acts in every other event'. Another concern of traditional christology which he adopts is the description of the way in which the human element and the divine are thought to be related to each other. This is always a subject of controversy, yet if he ignored it, such neglect would earn him the charge of inadequacy. There is yet another classical issue which Griffin handles very expertly, when he observes that it is not sufficient to say of Jesus that he is God's supreme act of self-expression. What has also to be demonstrated is that Jesus is the decisive revelation of God. His point is that without recognition by at least some men and women that Jesus stood in a quite unique and special relation to God, that self-expression which God effected in Jesus would not be self-revelation. The same case is made by him when he describes God's self-expression in Jesus as the objective side of the situation, and the knowledge of God and reality which is revealed to men and women in knowing Christ as the subjective side of the situation. Finally, Griffin, in what I suspect is an attempt to bring in the notion of 'incarnation' which otherwise is absent from the construction, refers to his presentation as a discussion of the presence of God in Jesus (op. cit., p. 228), which he develops along lines suggested by John Cobb, as we have seen. So it has become clear that in his christology Griffin, while employing several process concepts, has charted his course by reference to major points which appear in most traditional christologies. Our next step is to assess his success in reaching his destination of saying in process terminology what has been said about Jesus in traditional christology.

ASSESSMENT

PARALLELS WITH DAVID HUME

Difficulty arises at the outset when Griffin describes to us the nature of God. He uses the human analogy, which equates the mind or psyche constituted by a series of occasions of experience with the person, this series coming to form a unity through the carry-over of an 'abstract essence' from one occasion to another. But this essence is far from 'abstract', for it includes specific characteristic human qualities, as well as the person's character and purpose, as defined above (see above pp. 179f). God, regarded in terms analogous to these used to define the human person, is said also to be a living person, 'a sequence of occasions of experience' (op. cit., p. 213), with a defining essence which in his case is composed of the classical attributes of omniscience, omnipotence and omnipresence, as well as certain personal attributes. It is the notion of 'essence' or 'abstract essence' which gives me pause. For it has always seemed to me that the great contribution of process philosophy to Western thought lay in the fact that it filled the vacuum created by the deflation of that substantialist metaphysics which had dominated fairly consistently from the time of Aristotle onwards, as has been noted, to the time of Locke, Berkeley and Hume. In fact, what Hume wrote on the subject of substance and qualities has an uncanny relevance to our present discussion, when he wrote (*A Treatise of Human Nature*, Oxford University Press, London, impression of 1928, p. 221) of substance as 'an unknown substance' 'feigned by the imagination', and also (op. cit., p. 222) as 'that unintelligible chimera', in which is thought to cohere the different qualities of the object. Hume extends the argument to the human mind and person, arguing in the same way (op. cit., p. 259) that the personal identity which we ascribe to the mind of man 'is only a fictitious one', and proceeds from 'the operation of the imagination' upon the train of perceptions which enter the mind. When we remember that Griffin had said that 'a "person" is not a single entity but a strand of occasions' (op. cit., p. 211), we have to ask, in the context of Hume, what can be the status of the notion of 'abstract essence' said to provide continuity of personality. It looks all too like Hume's 'chimera', a fiction of the imagination, and, besides, it seems to rely too much on the substantialism which process philosophy was breaking away from. In fact, I have never read any attempt to relate process philosophy to Humean empiricism, as encountered in the *Treatise*, yet, as indicated above, the parallels are close. Hume, however, never abandons his opposition to substantialism, employing other methods rather than resort to a form of it (Griffin's 'essence') to account for the impression of identity or continuity in things or persons. The matter, however, does not end there, for this problem in the *analogans* inevitably protracts itself, as we have seen, into the *analogatum*, the nature of God. We are left wondering how the defining essence of divine traditional and personal attributes, which has an unchanging character, with all the characteristics of Aristotelian substance, is related to the process in which God reconstitutes himself in receiving the experiences of his creatures and in his responses to them. I have the fear that Griffin requires something like that concept of substance to give identity, integrity, self-consistency and continuity to a series of occasions of experience which would otherwise cease to be, after experienced – a problem as old as that with which his critics charged Heracleitus when he formulated his philosophy of flux. Perhaps such a way out of his problem is simpler than the method which Hume evolved with his introduction of the notions of 'belief' and 'imagination', which, in effect, also retained a form of the doctrine of substance.

THE DEITY OF JESUS CHRIST

One of the most important yardsticks for the assessment of a christology is the manner in which the writer describes the deity of Jesus Christ. While he never uses the term, Griffin clearly has the idea in mind as he seeks to determine the difference between the relation of God to Jesus and his relation to the creatures of the world. On p. 206 (op. cit.) he writes, that 'speaking intelligibly of God's special action or presence in Jesus has been one of the most difficult conceptual problems for Christian theologians in modern times'; while at pp. 218ff he severely criticises Schubert Ogden for holding that God has acted in

Christ in no way differently from his primordial action in every other event. Griffin himself seeks to meet the issue by employing the resources of Whitehead's philosophy, as we observed (see above pp. 178ff). The christological question that we now raise is: are Griffin's concepts of God's supreme act of self-expression in Jesus and of Jesus as the decisive revelation of God, together with the argumentation that he deploys to support these concepts, co-terminous with the traditional understanding of the deity of Christ? The sum of his case is as follows: Jesus has received from God aims which are quite special and unique to himself. These aims include a specific view of reality and particularly of the Reign of God, from the future breaking into the present, the supremely desirable good and ultimate joy, which it is his mission to proclaim and to persuade men and women to accept. These aims are identical with God's subjective aims for the world and all men and women. In such terms is Jesus described as God's supreme act of self-expression. On the other hand, men and women have recognised that the aims given by God to Jesus, while special to him, were nevertheless God's own aims and universal in purpose and character, embracing the whole of creation. So comprehensively did Jesus fulfil these that men and women judged him to stand in such a special relation to God that he was appropriately regarded as God's self-revelation of his nature and agency.

As to the question whether Griffin has in such terms secured the deity of Christ: agreed, he never claims that he has established or demonstrated the deity of Christ, or that it was his intention to do so. All he is arguing for is a credible christology based on process philosophy. Yet the issue of deity cannot be balked if the christology is to take its place alongside the others we have been examining. My fear is that the case for deity cannot be proved. What has been said of Jesus is that he receives from God the very special and unique aims which are at the same time God's subjective aims for the entirety of the created order. Now in his analysis of the Divine Being, Griffin spoke of the abstract and defining essence of God, which includes his traditional formal attributes as well as his personal attributes, what could be called

God's essential nature. But whereas christology, as usually understood, has always wrestled with, even when it has not always
satisfactorily dealt with, the question of how and how far Jesus
shares that nature, Griffin does not raise the matter at all. Once
(on p. 214), he uses the term *homoousion*, which describes the
relation of the Son to the Father in the Nicene Creed, but the
subject to which it refers in the sentence – 'it'– is of uncertain
identity, beyond the fact that it clearly is not Jesus who is
intended. It would appear, then, that Griffin advances his
christology by considering the relation of Jesus not to God's
nature, but to God's *acts*.

What slightly puzzles me is that Griffin does not take his
argument on from there and demonstrate that so special are the
aims God has given to Jesus, so comprehensively has he fulfilled
them, that in his whole being Jesus is to be identified in nature
with the Father. An argument such as that would be wholly in
line with patristic method; for in relation both to Christ and to
the Holy Spirit they argued that the acts done by Christ and the
Spirit were such as could be done only by one who was divine in
very being. They were far beyond the capacity of creatures. Again,
though Griffin never resorts to statutory trinitarian language,
what he is in fact describing are the *opera ad extra Filii*. What I
am suggesting is that it would have been a short step to say that
the quality of Jesus' fulfilment of the special aims given to him
by God was such as could only have been achieved by one who
was of the very nature of God, related to God in terms of the
opera ad intra.

Two addenda might be made by way of linking this last
comment on Griffin's christological method to his claim concerning Jesus that there was something special in his relationship
to God. First, he argues very forcefully (op. cit., pp. 221ff) that
when the fact that Jesus was God's supreme act of self-expression
was apprehended by actual men and women, then it would be
appropriate to say that Jesus was the decisive revelation of God.
Recalling a theme which was prominent in the discussion of the
revelation model (see above, pp. 156–8) namely that 'Through
God alone can God be known', and applying it to Griffin's

revelation statement, we may fairly conclude that Griffin is making the highest claims for Jesus' relationship to God. But it also means that his process christology ultimately depends on the revelation model for its validity and validation.

In a rather strange twist to the end of his presentation, Griffin employs another notion, namely, 'the presence of God' to lend strength to his case for his account of Jesus. But to do so he expounds, albeit not entirely uncritically, an account of the matter given by John Cobb, Jr. What comes out of his commentary on Cobb is that for Griffin not only did the special presence of God in Jesus constitute his selfhood, with all the rest of his life and mission centring upon it, but his consciousness of God's presence gave him an authority possessed by no other human being. I have referred to this piece of argumentation as a 'strange twist' in the presentation partly because the notion of the presence of God is one for which we have not been prepared in the previous discussion, partly because we are left wondering whether it is an alternative way of describing the fact that God has given Jesus special aims and these aims are also God's subjective aims, or whether it is a concept additional to the previous descriptions of Jesus which brings this process christology into line with traditional accounts. Whatever the reason for introducing the concept of the presence of God, my judgement is that when we say with St Paul, 'God was in Christ', or with the Nicene Creed, 'I believe in one Lord Jesus Christ . . . Very God of Very God . . . Being of one substance with the Father', we are saying more than that Jesus received and amply fulfilled the special aims given to him by God. Now, such a difference in content of statement might not have mattered if Griffin had all along held to a full process position, that is, without the somewhat controversial idea of God's abstract and defining essence. But given such a notion within this chapter, it was always open to Griffin, had he wished, to describe the presence of God in Jesus not simply in terms of aims and actions, but also in terms of the presence in Jesus of the very nature and being of God. But at that point a halt has to be made, because we seem to be lashing Griffin too firmly to a metaphysic from which his metaphysics, if consistently followed, would release him.

THE WORK OF CHRIST

It has been argued from time to time in the earlier chapters that the ultimate criterion by which any christology is to be judged is the nature of the soteriology which it implies or allows. I fear that by such a standard the process type of christology advocated by Griffin fares rather badly. The subject of soteriology occurs at two points. The first is on p. 217 (op. cit.), where, after saying that one of the elements in the newness of the message of Jesus was the priority of God's love over his justice, Griffin affirms that this love is expressed in the radical offer of forgiveness, the acceptance of which is the way of entry into God's Kingdom. As the account stands, the theology behind the forgiveness, while it connects that forgiveness with God's love, would seem to be no more than that of *'Dieu pardonnera; c'est son métier'*. The second reference to soteriology occurs (op. cit., p. 220) when Griffin describes the statement, 'Jesus is God's decisive revelation' as 'soteriological'. His meaning is that Jesus, being God's decisive revelation, is the source of the 'cognitive approach' of men and women 'to reality'. So authentic is this apprehension that it validates the claim made on behalf of Jesus to be in a special and unique relation to God, both as his supreme self-expression and as his decisive revelation. So much of the language of both these references is coded, so circular is the argumentation, that any criticism is in danger of being based upon misapprehension. One or two things are clear. For example, assigning prior importance to the concept of revelation in what is said to be a soteriological statement, leaves the content of the revelation undefined. In our previous criticism of the revelation model (see above, pp. 166–8) we argued that – and it is particularly true of soteriology based on the revelation model – this model is parasitic upon other soteriological models; for example, if we say that the death of Christ reveals the love of God, we have to resort to one or other of the soteriological models to describe in what way the love of God is the key to the understanding of the death of Jesus. This criticism is applicable to Griffin's account in so far as he has connected the love of God with forgiveness. Further, it is not made clear by Griffin in what way Jesus, through his comprehensive obedience to the aims set him by God, contributes to what was called the cognitive approach to reality, which was in some way salvific. The problem is that we are not told what the special aims are that God has given Jesus, which he obeys so comprehensively. On the one hand, the aims may simply be that through the proclamation by Jesus of the whole message concerning God, his love and his forgiveness, men and women may come to knowledge which will effect their salvation, a word we may justifiably use in the light of Griffin's mention of soteriology. On the other hand, the special aims given by God to Jesus may include such action by Jesus as is described in the New Testament. The trouble with this interpretation is that, whereas Griffin refers extensively to the acts of God, he does not balance these references with similar accounts of the actions of Jesus, such as appear in a traditional soteriology which describes the 'work' of Christ. Also, that process is wrongly understood if the human faith involved in it is interpreted solely in terms of cognition of a so-called approach to reality (presumably, of God's love and forgiveness). Once again the problem may be one which arises from the use of the notion of cognition along with the concept of revelation, which tends to have an intellectual overtone. Barth cancelled such a suggestion by equating revelation with redemption, but that is scarcely an option for Griffin who, on the whole, eschews the language of traditional dogmatics. The question remains whether it is possible to discuss an essentially dogmatic theme, namely, christology, without recourse to traditional dogmatics or dogmatic terminology, a subject to which we may have to return after examining other process christologists.

8

JOHN B. COBB, JR

John Cobb, Jr had established himself as the authoritative theological exponent of process thought, with works on natural theology, the doctrine of God and the evangelical and homiletic relevance of process philosophy, and his contribution to the problem of the essential nature of Christianity, before he offered his now classic presentation of what might be called a process christology, *Christ in a Pluralistic Age* (Westminster, Philadelphia, 1975). That book, once again, is not an ivory tower, sterilised account of his subject; it recognises certain cultural changes in Western and Third World thought which are highly significant for christology. It will form the main source for this exposition. However, in a subsequent symposium (reported in *Encountering Jesus: Debate on Christology*, ed. Stephen Davis, Westminster/ John Knox, Philadelphia, 1986), partly under the pressure of these same cultural circumstances and partly in response to critical discussion of his revised christology by Davis, John Hick, Rebecca Pentz and others, Cobb modifies his form of process christology to a point where the question must be asked whether he still remains faithful to his original insights. But his restatements in that symposium and his responses to critiques from the others supplement his original presentation and provide material for our own assessment of his christological theory.

From an early point in *Christ in a Pluralistic Age*, Cobb expresses a deep sense of the decline of the image of Christ in contemporary society and the corresponding loss of the redemptive power of that image from all but those living within the closed circle of the Church. Despite this gloomy assessment, the book leaves the reader with a sense of optimism. This sense arises from the thesis, extended throughout the book and expressed in a whole range of contexts, that the image of Christ has nonetheless not disappeared from what he calls 'our basic vision' (op. cit., p. 19), but is to be identified 'within the concrete reality of our history and our time' (ibid.). The christology which he has promised in the title of the book may fairly be described as a specific form of the process model, namely, the 'creative transformation model' which, when applied to the images of Christ, Logos and Jesus, provides us with a christology with a distinctive and, at the same time, very interesting shape. Cobb is himself rather reluctant to allow the name 'christology' to be attached to his theory, preferring to regard his work as a series of studies of different items of christology. Whether we accept his modesty or not, it is clear that he has, like Griffin, made a brave attempt to sketch out a christology which aims to substitute the process metaphysic of Whitehead and Hartshorne for the traditional metaphysic of Aristotelianism.

CREATIVE TRANSFORMATION

This model, 'creative transformation', which will prove to be central to the author's whole interpretation both of the person and the work of Christ, would appear immediately to have strong overtones of classical christology. Yet Cobb does not offer it as a transcript of the terms of classical christology. He prefers to source it in a quite different location, namely, two works by André Malraux – *The Voices of Silence* (tr. Stuart Gilbert, Doubleday, New York, 1953) and *The Metamorphosis of the Gods* (tr. Stuart Gilbert, Doubleday, New York 1960). In these works, according to Cobb, Malraux does two things. First, he traces briefly the history of Christ in Western art, illustrating how the image of Christ has changed, from Byzantine times, when Christ was presented as the omnipotent and omniscient ruler of the universe, through post-Augustine interpretations of Christ as very much in the image of the Father, with a growing humanisation of Christ through thought of the immanence of God, culminating in the fifteenth century 'when Christ had become Jesus, and Jesus had become a man among men' (op. cit., p. 35), appearing in an ordinary human environment. This humanisation of the Christ-figure had already appeared preliminarily in the fourteenth century, in the individuation of human beings, with secular persons sometimes replacing religious statues in public buildings. A new phenomenon appeared with the emergence of the self-awareness of the artist in the sixteenth and seventeenth centuries, accompanied by the realisation of the autonomy of art itself. However, even then art still retained its Christian character, though with emphasis upon the impoverished, the tortured, the compassionate and the crucified experiences in human existence which Christ had shared; and it was not until after El Greco and Rembrandt that the Christ-image was marginalised in Western visual artistic production.

The second theme which Cobb derives from Malraux's sketch of the history of art is perhaps more speculative and interpretative and less historically factual. It is that, as the visual figure of Christ disappeared from Western art, the same Christ who had been (as we would say) the empowering genius of that whole artistic process continued to operate but as an interiorised, subliminal driving force. 'That means that Christ is found in the present, in the real, contemporary, everyday world' (ibid., p. 38). As a consequence, individual artists were imbued with a 'distinctive spirituality', and through union with what in a previous age had been articulately acknowledged as Christ, they were empowered with an awareness of new creative ability, capable of 'transforming the world'. It must firmly be denied, however, that there is any discontinuity from one to the other of the art-forms in which the Christ-figure is portrayed, whether as Byzantine pantocrator, or cast in the image of the Father in the Romanesque presentation, or as humanised in the humiliation of crucifixion. Nor is there any discontinuity from classical, Byzantine or Renaissance art to those expressions which in modern art emanate from the driving principle already mentioned. In the latter expressions, humanity itself is seen as 'christified', and the artists involved are 'bearers of a sacred meaning and responsibility' (ibid.). So this change from artistic creations in which the Christ-figure and his role are overtly recognised, to what might be called the second, the modern, stage in which he is marginalised and even evicted but remains, as it were anonymously, the creative driving force, involves no invasion or envelopment of the artistic field by forces from without. Even the autonomy and the absoluteness inspired by the Christ-figure of the earlier stage remained, to be assumed by art itself; and the creative, transformative, redemptive, unifying and ordering process associated with that transcendent figure passed into the lives and activities of artists themselves.

But at this point Malraux enters a caveat, to ensure that before we prematurely identify Christ with this creative transformative process in modern art, we make several points clear. The first is that this creative principle will be in evidence in human activities other than art – in science, philosophy and the Christian Church, and its presence there must be acknowledged. Malraux fears that not to do so will amount to 'dividing Christ'. The second point is to recall the autonomy inherited by modern art from its Christ-inspired predecessors and to qualify the absolutism which it induced; by humanising its forms, art will now see itself not as the expression of a Western culture but as comprising the whole sphere of human artistic expression, such as those of the Sumerians, the pre-Columbans and the Buddhists. The other way to describe this process is to say that it draws out the universal character of the transforming power, observed initially in Malraux's account of classical art. Thirdly, these two previous positions imply not only that Western art, even Christian art from which this analysis sprang, is now relativised; but also that the pluralism which it affirms is now to be internalised within the formula.

APPLICATION AND EXTENSION OF THE ANALOGY TO CHRISTOLOGY

Cobb adopts Malraux's position as stated and carries it forward analogically into christology. Traditionally Christian faith has been correlated with a Christ who is transcendentally of one nature with a God who is absolute and totally superior. This absolutism has been eroded over the past two centuries by several influences. The chief of these was the development of the discipline of 'history of religions'. Attitudes to these religions changed gradually from the exclusivism which rejected them as enemies of the true faith, through a grudging admission that they formed a propaideutic to Christian faith, to a sympathy towards them and an empathy which regarded them as appropriate to cultures very different from that in which Christianity had been born and developed. In a paradoxical way, Karl Barth, who was in this century responsible for the re-affirmation of the exclusivist position, nevertheless unintentionally helped the history of religion stances to flourish. In a sense he turned theology in upon itself with his early adoption of Anselm's methodological principle, *credo ut intelligam*, and his account of theology as *fides quaerens intellectum*. But at the same time he offered a cast-iron distinction between 'theology', focused on Christ, and 'religions' worshipping other gods and maybe none; the former premised the condition of faith, and the latter sought objectivity. One qualification to this statement would require us to recognise that the practitioners, as distinct from the analysts and observers, of these other faiths would claim that in order to understand their religions a requirement not dissimilar to faith also has to be made. The other theology of the twentieth century which Cobb uses to establish his introductory case is that of the liberation movements. Christ is the power from which emanates – indeed, Christ is – the 'creative transformation of consciousness, understanding and imagination', which achieves freedom from traditional structures of society, politics, economics and sexuality for new forms of existence. Of this theme we shall hear more.

PLURALISATION, RELATIVISM, INDIFFERENTISM AND INTERNALISATION

Cobb, then, considers three consequences of this preliminary analysis which are highly relevant to his argument, some of which might even appear prima facie to invalidate his case. He nevertheless uses them to conjure virtue from their vices, because of their contemporary popularity in religious studies. The first is the affirmation of pluralism. The spread of the study of religion has involved some kind of empathetic relation, short of actual belief, to the religions concerned, and consequently a desacralisation of the subject of worship. Since this methodology has to be applied to all religions, Christians are faced with the problem of their relation to Christ as he appears in the Christian tradition. The difficulty is compounded by the second implication of Cobb's account, namely, that the pluralism just mentioned would normally entail relativism. If all religions are subject to the same process of desacralisation and objective analysis, then one tradition is as good as another, each being appropriate to the culture in which it is cradled and the best option for those concerned with it. As we shall see, Cobb not only counters the evil of indifferentism implicit in this relativism, but also positively embraces the pluralism which had become an embarrassment to Christians more accustomed to the claims of exclusivism. In order to do so, he employs an argument which is not altogether immediately apprehensible, though it seems to involve two elements. The first is that Christians may be persuaded towards pluralism when they are empathetic, and consequently openly receptive, to all religious traditions, presumably because of their validity for their practitioners. The second element in the argument, which is the reason for the first, is that such Christians have come to understand that Christ, as the previously expounded 'process of creative transformation' (*Christ in a Pluralistic Age*, p. 60), is active in all these traditions, albeit as 'the anonymous Christ', to use Rahner's term. This process is operative within Christian theology and creatively transforms its relationship to its own past, its doctrine and its established morality. In that process, the classical exclusivism is transformed and the way opened up for the adoption of pluralism. At this point in the argument, indifferentism is rejected, because the pluralism Cobb contemplates involves a positive appreciation of the value of other traditions, and for Christians that entails the very special relation to Christ, as freshly understood, which is faith. The third consequence of Cobb's initial constructive steps in his christology is the result of what he has said in the other two. 'Christ as creative transformation is the principle of pluralism' (op. cit., p. 60), so that Christian faith now 'internalises' within itself both pluralism, as it has been exegeted and with all its implications, and the relativism which has been shown to be a conceptual partner to that pluralism. Hence the title of Cobb's book, *Christ in a Pluralistic Age.*

LOGOS, CHRIST, AND CREATIVE TRANSFORMATION

After his rather innovative and modernistic approach to christology – for as we heard, he is not advancing a complete systematic christology – Cobb is nevertheless moved to plot his position on what might be called a traditional chart, by giving us his interpretation of the central subjects in any christology.

His view of Logos, for example, stands close to that expressed in the Prologue to St John's Gospel. The Logos, as an 'eternal aspect' of Deity, is the transcendent ground of all meaning, the principle of coherence and order, the origin of all purpose in the universe, and the source of all potentiality and possibility, and of their relevance. These phrases, which have a classical patristic resonance, can readily be given a process gloss as Cobb establishes connections with Whitehead, who would identify the Logos as God in his Primordial Nature; and for St John's 'he it was by whom all things were made', Cobb would read, 'the Logos, as the initial phase of the subjective aim of all things, is their fundamental impulse towards actualisation' (op. cit., p. 76).

According to the Christian tradition, this transcendent Logos exists in an incarnate form, bearing the name of Christ, to whom it would be no error to attribute the transcendent attributes of Deity. The occurrence of the transcendent in the immanent form Cobb construes as a special case of 'causal efficacy in general' (op. cit., p. 72). But such causal efficacy cannot be properly understood in substantialist terms, which preclude the embodiment of one entity in another, for they cannot occupy the same space at the same time. The causal efficacy concerned is to be understood in terms of relations between successive human experiences, where the dynamic present is in creative synthesis with many vital elements from the past. This synthesis gathers up many previous experiences of the person, some provided through the brain or other parts of the body, others deriving from the experience of other persons. So if we think of the synthesis thus created as the later experience, we can regard it as reactualising and completing what has gone before, the past from which it came. It might be said to 'incarnate' all that it composes, while the latter 'constitutes' it. Thus does Cobb interpret the incarnational process, Christ being the incarnation of the Logos in the realm of living things, particularly human beings, and carrying into these realms and making effective within them the creative transformation which is of the very being of the Logos. So the Logos remains the transcendent principle of order and the source of all possibility; Christ is the immanence and incarnation of the Logos; and through Christ the creative transformation which is the mark of the Logos irradiates all 'authentic speaking, . . . sensitivity of feeling and free imagination' (op. cit., p. 77), and so directs all whose faith, trust and hope are in Christ to identification with the divine process.

Certain characteristics of the Logos emerge from naming the incarnate Logos 'Christ'. For example, that process of creative transformation which the Logos as incarnate promises and actualises, and which can on occasion elicit hostile reaction, in fact effects release from bondage to the past and opens up a new future. In that future, because the Logos incarnate is Christ, we are assured that the cosmic Logos is love. It is love which calls us to love others, to have such empathy with them that our self-constitution embraces their past. The actuality of God's love for us creates the possibility and, to a degree, the actuality of our love for God. Cobb acknowledges that for Christians the content of the concept of 'love' derives from Jesus, and thereby indicates how heavily dependent his christological approach is upon traditional Christian christology – a point to which we shall return.

IS JESUS, CHRIST?

The very considerable presence of the Christian corpus of belief in Cobb's christology appears again in his description of the relation of 'the Nazarene carpenter' to the Logos. The question he is now posing is: does the power of creative transformation, already established and accepted as the distinctive character of the Logos and the Logos incarnate, Christ, reside in Jesus? To support his claim that it does, he quotes in evidence two sets of circumstances. The first is the creative transformation, quite radical in some cases, effected by the works and words of Jesus upon concepts and ideas which were already present in Judaism – the understanding of the nature of God as Father, as compassion and love, as bountiful and indiscriminate provider, as one whose forgivingness extended to the agony of a cross. But such creative transformation would not in itself be enough to establish Jesus as Christ. The more required – and this is Cobb's second body of evidence – is that Jesus should have the power to bring about such creative transformation in men and women who, in our day and age, hear his message and learn of his deeds and are thereby creatively transformed. Without that evidence, Jesus would be but one of thousands in the past who have shaped the course of history. It is the evidence which Kierkegaard would have produced for his affirmation of the power of Jesus to make us 'contemporary disciples' of his, no matter in which century we lived. It is the authority which the words and works of Jesus exert over the lives, decisions, motivation, feelings and perceptions of ordinary men and women, radically and creatively transforming them, that validates the confession, 'Thou art the Christ' (as in the words of Simon Peter's confession at Mt 16.16).

But Cobb goes further in order to clarify the nature of the creative transformation which Jesus efficaciously accomplishes in those affected by his words and works. It is not enough that their self-justification is challenged by the assurance that God authoritatively forgives them and creates the opportunity to begin anew. Even in face of the traditional teaching about our justification in Christ, the offer seems to remain incredible and the statement of the belief lacks power. In an echo of the famous words of Paul Tillich, 'we seem to be unable or unwilling to accept God's acceptance as decisive for our own self-understanding' (op. cit., p. 113). Such accepting of God's acceptance only comes when Christians are so closely related to Christ that they are said to be 'in Christ', receiving through him the grace and power which transform them into new creatures proving the will of God, receiving the forgiveness which eliminates all self-justification and self-condemnation and effects a full redemption, living a life in the joy, the peace and the hope which radiate from God. Having up to this point drawn on traditional accounts of the central Pauline notions of 'in Christ' and of 'I in Christ, and Christ in me', Cobb now turns to existentialist/process concepts to give an alternative reading, on the ground that the old substantialist metaphysic is no longer credible. In line with his previous strictures on substantialism as a medium to describe the relation of the Logos to Christ (above, p. 202), he argues that the self, the 'I', cannot be construed as 'a self-identical substantial entity' (op. cit., p. 130), which can be related only externally to other substances and cannot include these relations within itself. On the contrary, the 'I', the self, is to be regarded as the ultimate subject of thinking, feeling and willing, and of overt activity. As such, it is the central point of reference for the conscious life of the self, integrating and selecting for prominence the various states and relevant past experiences. Sometimes that process may take the form of conforming not just to the past of the 'I' but also, as in Paul's case, to some centre originally from outside itself, namely, 'the salvation occurrence of Jesus Christ' (op. cit., p. 125), who might be said to invade the self. Accordingly, the 'I' comes to be constituted in what Cobb calls a process of 'coconstitution' – in the case of Paul, by Christ as the dominant partner, which is a reasonable transcript of Paul's 'I, yet not I, but the grace of God' (1 Cor 15.10), but also by the personal past experience of the self.

JESUS: THE HUMAN SELF AND THE INCARNATE LOGOS

Cobb has now a prepared platform from which to approach one of the major problems in classical christology, even though he does not state matters in these terms. From the observation that the human 'I' or self may be coconstituted by past or present mental or physical experiences or anticipation of others in the future, as well as by the presence within the 'I' of Christ, he adds that sometimes tension may arise between these two co-constituting elements. But another structure of existence is conceivable – one in which the presence of Christ 'chimes in' with the self's appropriation of its past experiences and their ordering, and there is a complete compatibility and continuity between the personal past and the lure to self-fulfilment which is due to the creative presence of the Logos. Did such a situation exist, we would be face to face with the incarnation of the Logos in its complete sense (op. cit., p. 140). In such a structure of existence, which Cobb would identify with 'the incarnation of the Logos', there would be no question of the presence of the Logos destroying the identity and the continuity of the human self. On the contrary, the human 'I', whose past contains experiences of 'pleasure and pain, hope and fear, longing and compassion', as well as anticipations of a novel future, now has at the centre of its existence the Logos who presents and fulfils the call to novel self-realisation by the 'I'. In other words, the Logos stands at the centre of the 'I' as the principle appropriating, ordering and integrating both the elements from past experience and the creative novelty which the Logos projects for the future.

So far Cobb has been describing a structure of existence which is, as far as his argument has proceeded, no more than a theoretical or logical possibility. But the drift of the argument is transparent, for he immediately affirms that what he has described is the person Jesus Christ. His whole life and message were determined by the immanent Logos, and so he was at one with God's will for him and with God's purposes not just for himself but for the whole world. His actions and activity were God's, and he was unique. This fact lends fresh weight to two sets of circumstances which Cobb has previously examined. The first was to validate the use which Jesus (according to the Scriptures) made of his power of creative transformation, particularly of some of the dominant themes of Judaic thought – in brief, the revelation of God claimed for him by his disciples. Whereas each of us is bound by particular, limited and egocentric perspectives on the human situation, which distort our judgements of others and our self-assessment, Jesus, by contrast, holds a different perspective, of impartiality and disinterest; his 'I' is wholly ordered from the Logos as centre. The second point to which Cobb returns is whether the authority and efficacy which Jesus demonstrated in his own time and upon his disciples and contemporaries extends to our day and generation; this raises the question whether light can be thrown upon that matter by the recent analysis of the nature of the 'I' of Jesus. Using the metaphor of 'a field of force', Cobb starts from the conviction which as Christians we all hold, that when we stand within the field of force surrounding Jesus, we experience a right relation to God. While we may frequently be aware of tensions within the self, at other times such tensions are harmonised with each other into novel and exciting forms. These latter occasions result from the special presence of the Logos incarnate with and within us. The experience of such coalescence of personal purpose and the will of Jesus may well be a union of suffering and joy, with the cross as its supreme expression. Such experience is renewed and maintained by 'repeated acts of remembrance' (op. cit., p. 143).

Those who are drawn within it find the salve which these acts create, for the self-justification and guilt it implies.

TOWARDS A PROCESS CHRISTOLOGY

By now a sufficient contribution has been made to what might be called 'an alternative christology with process elements' to enable us to set it alongside certain articles in the classical creeds. For example, because of the process rejection of substantialism which we have already encountered, it is not possible to affirm that Jesus Christ is *homoousios*, of one substance, with the Father. Yet Cobb maintains that the truth expressed at Nicaea and Chalcedon is faithfully conserved in the statement that God himself is fully present in Jesus in so far as in him is the Logos incarnate who constitutes his selfhood. Indeed, Cobb might well have quoted Col 2.9, 'In [Jesus Christ] the whole fullness of the Godhead dwelt in bodily form.' As regards the element in the Chalcedonian christology, that Jesus was co-essential with us in humanity, once again anti-substantialism has to make way for views which we have already met. In the structure of human existence, the self may be constituted by experiences, principles and interests, past and present, with egotistical tendencies at odds with God and his purposes; or the self may equally at times be coconstituted by the Logos, who sets up a new centre within the self and coalesces with past experiences and anticipations of novelty and self-fulfilment in the future. In the former case there arises conflict between the self and the Logos, and that way lies the origin of sin and rebellion against God. There is but one in whom that tension does not exist and has never existed. For the Logos is all-determinant of the human 'I' in Jesus, in all its dispositions, purposes, feelings and allegiances. So Jesus shares our humanity, in the form of 'the structure of our existence'. But when he does so, there is no question about sinless or sinful humanity, so much discussed in recent years. For in that human existence the Logos and the past of that existence coalesce, and there is no occasion for that conflict between the self and the purposes of the Logos, with the lure of the future which they present, which is the source of anxiety, guilt and sin.

Cobb presents the Chalcedonian theme of the human and the divine in Christ in another way by beginning from a position implicit in what he has just said. There exists in all humanity a measure of the presence of the Logos, affirming the future potentiality of that person, a potentiality which in ordinary persons is never fully actualised. Only in the case of Jesus does the Logos achieve maximum presence within, and so optimum determination of, the human existence; or as Cobb alternatively states it, only in the case of Jesus does the human existence constitute itself in accordance with the lure of the Logos (op. cit., p. 171). The two forms of the description are important, for the former acknowledges the initiative of God in the event of the incarnation, while the latter does justice to the freedom of Jesus to choose to constitute, or rather to coconstitute, his selfhood with the Logos. So he does, then, move beyond the strictly Chalcedonian position (with its view of the humanity of Christ as *anhypostatos* or impersonal, as interpreted, for example, by H. R. Mackintosh in *The Doctrine of the Person of Christ*, T. & T. Clark, Edinburgh, 1912, pp. 385–90) to one which accords better with the *enhypostasia* of Leontius of Byzantium or Leontius of Jerusalem, when he explicitly says, 'the coalescence of the Logos and humanity in the one person who is Jesus, far from diminishing or depersonalising Jesus' humanity or transmuting it into something else, enriches and completes his humanity' (op. cit., pp. 171f). The assumption behind Cobb's reasoning here is that humanity is at its perfection when it is totally aligned and identified with the will of God as expressed in the lure of the Logos, and that coalescence is actualised.

COBB REFLECTS

Before we embark upon an assessment of the very interesting form of christology which Cobb has to offer, we have to allow him the privilege of second thoughts (*Encountering Jesus: Debate on Christology*). What he offers is not change for change's sake, but he seeks, rather, to meet what he regards as a standing obligation on theology, namely, to rework continuously the inherited tradition of Scripture and doctrine by synthesising it with concepts, ideas and attitudes which are current in contemporary society and culture. In the event, he considers two such convictions, liberation theology and feminism, which have gained increasing influence in Western theology over the past 25 years.

LIBERATION THEOLOGY

Recalling the dominant concept in his previous approach to christology, namely, creative transformation, Cobb begins by asking whether it can be creatively transformed by the wisdom of liberation christology, which is strongly in evidence in Latin American, Afro-American, Asian, African and Korean theology. To achieve a positive answer, he follows a circuitous track. Beginning from the Gospel witness to the unambiguous and unconditional support of the poor by Jesus, Cobb claims that his concept of creative transformation can be combined with, and itself transformed by, the notion of liberation, the transformation resulting in a heightened conscientisation towards the universal needs of the poor and the oppressed and a new sensitive awareness of them. But such conscientisation is immediately seen to have two defects: first, it presents a very middle-class, elitist cultural face; and secondly, it suggests that the poor themselves lack this awareness and fail to be Christian until they too are 'conscientised'. He then sets out to meet these difficulties and does so in two stages. First, he affirms the core theme of liberation theology, that Jesus identified with the poor who know the reality of their condition from within it. For us, the lesson is that in listening to the poor we are listening to Jesus. Though Christ is present in the poor, those who see him there still have to work with urgency for the relief of their misery and suffering. Secondly, such conscientisation dare not expend itself solely in practicalities, however obligatory these may feel. It has to evolve its own logic, its own 'rhetoric' as Cobb calls it, of a rigorous kind that will construct effective socio-economics to control, alleviate and eventually eliminate the conditions that produce poverty and injustice.

But in what has become a very convoluted argument, Cobb now (op. cit., p. 152) returns to his question, whether the concept of creative transformation has to be modified to incorporate the insights of Christ's self-identification with the poor. He claims, though it is a claim that is eventually scarcely upheld, that the concept of creative transformation can accommodate the truth about Christ's identity with the poor if we concentrate on the idea of Christ as the truth. This truth appears in John's, 'I am the way, the truth and the life', the truth, which we saw when considering the Logos, 'which is the way all things cohere in God' (ibid.). So Christ is the way the Logos exists in the world; and now, conversely, the way the world, inclusive of its suffering, is in God.

In a further stage of his argument, and in order to answer his question about creative transformation and accommodate the emphasis upon 'truth' which he has just introduced, Cobb now embarks on a rewriting of the section of the doctrine of the Trinity which deals with the *opera Trinitatis ad extra*, the works of the Trinity in relation to the created order, as distinct from the *opera ad intra*, the internal operations of the *personae* in relation to one another. Cobb says that these individual *opera ad extra* were assigned to one or other of the *personae* on grounds of appropriateness; but later all three *personae* were regarded as being active in all *opera ad extra*, with the exception of the Second Person. In the latter case, it came to be said that it was the Logos, the Word, who was incarnate in Jesus. The change in what had become an accepted usage, which Cobb now wishes to make, is to say that it is the whole Godhead in Trinity who is incarnate in Jesus, and that the name 'Christ' denotes the relations of God, without limitation, to the whole of the rest of the universe. The one who is incarnate suffers with those who suffer as well as rejoicing with those who rejoice, and is named Christ. He, too, is the one in whom all things consist; he is present in all things, and he is the truth. This Christ is the truth, not simply as knowledge of things but rather as understanding of their comprehensive fulfilment in God. Finally, because this notion of truth is the inspirer, the sustainer and ultimate goal of creative transformation, it would seem that the former is being given precedence over the latter in Cobb's christology.

THE CHALLENGE OF FEMINISM FOR CHRISTOLOGY

The second movement in contemporary culture which has led Cobb to rethink some elements of his christology is feminism. To several of its contentions he seems to be not altogether unsympathetic. For example, the fact that Jesus is a man may make some women unresponsive to a soteriology which regards him as saviour. Again, he concedes that much of the Scriptures and Christian tradition from the third century onwards carry evidence of a strong patriarchal bias which is unacceptable, though in faithfulness to the teaching of Christ he points out that the Gospels are at many points sympathetic towards women. Going, to a greater extreme, however, Cobb agrees that few will accept the teaching of the Church from any past age as relevant to modern times, but he wonders, nevertheless, whether there is any teaching from the past which might be given a form which would enlist the understanding of future generations. In two particular ways, Cobb seeks to come to terms with the feminist witness. First, coming down to specific matters, he observes that the symbolism of Christ on the cross, and of suffering love itself, carries overtones of the depression of women, who see themselves as the chief subject of such symbolism at the hands of their husbands and sons. As for his adjustment to this view, he proposes, after avoiding the traditional centralising of the cross as the supreme expression of sacrificial love, that there is still a place for sacrifice in personal relationships in the interests of achieving full mutuality. The way of creative transformation, while it implies some sacrifice of the self that is being transformed, leads to the goal of self-realisation as willed by God.

The second adjustment which Cobb makes to his christology in response to feminism is still more substantial. Having just suggested that it was the Triune Godhead who was incarnate in Jesus, he now (op. cit., p. 157) admits that he has not gone far enough to meet the difficulties experienced by feminists, for the three persons in the Godhead present 'exclusively male imagery' (ibid.) – though he might have mentioned that both originals for 'person' in the trinitarian vocabulary, *hypostasis* and *persona*, are in fact feminine. Incidentally, he had mentioned but promptly discarded the suggestion that we might think of the Spirit as being incarnate in Jesus, but there are also problems there, for in addition to his own misgiving that 'Spirit' already had masculine associations, there are grammatical problems in that *ruach* is both feminine and masculine, while *pneuma* is neuter. So he proposes that we name the creative transforming Word or Logos which is incarnate in Jesus, *Wisdom*, which in its Greek form, *sophia*, is sufficiently feminine to satisfy feminist susceptibilities. *Sophia* has the characteristics of both incarnating herself in the world and accepting the world into herself – the characteristics which have already been ascribed to Christ; but she is also present in Jesus as the wisdom of God.

ASSESSMENT

Parts of this assessment have been assisted by the critiques offered by Cobb's fellow symposiasts and recorded in *Encountering Jesus: Debate on Christology*, together with Cobb's final response to them individually; other parts will take account of stances from which Cobb does not withdraw in so far as they are integral to his process commitment.

QUESTIONS OF NAMES AND ROLES

One particular problem with which we are left after reading *Christ in a Pluralistic Age* might be designated as that of nomenclature and equivalences. This is stated quite succinctly by John Hick in his critique of Cobb in *Encountering Jesus: Debate on Christology*, pp. 158ff, where he claims that Cobb offers us three sets of equations, covering his original position and his recent modifications. They are:

(1) Christ = Logos = creative transformation = primordial nature of God
(2) Christ = conscientisation = the poor = the truth = the Trinity
(3) Christ = Wisdom (*Sophia*, fem.).

From this analysis, Hick asks the questions whether the first equation is replaced by a combination of the second and the third; or whether all three are to be taken as one. My own suspicion is that Cobb's use of the terms in his christology is too varied and complex to be compounded into a series of equations, even though Cobb himself writes as if they were in some cases equivalents. So I cannot attempt a quick answer to Hick's dilemma and propose to use his equations as a basis for our own 'critique' of Cobb's presentation. In regard to equation (1), where we have 'Christ = Logos', we have to say that the equality is both affirmed and qualified by Cobb. It is affirmed in so far as, from time to time, he uses the two terms interchangeably, saying, for example, that the Logos indwells Jesus and again that Christ does so. But, to be precise, and Cobb is on occasion precise, Christ is the immanent Logos, his immanence differs from the transcendence of the Logos, but in the difference still remains the Logos. At another time, Cobb differentiates Logos from Christ by saying that the Logos is cosmically immanent in all things and events, whereas Christ is the immanence of the Logos in all living beings, particularly humans – though having made the distinction, he seems at once to eliminate it on the grounds that the human and the inorganic spheres are ultimately continuous in the theory of emergence as Cobb affirms it.

Having accepted, if with hesitation, the equation 'Christ = Logos', we find that the equation is strengthened by a third member in (1), namely, creative transformation, which in the course of Cobb's presentation is clearly equated with both. At an early point in his book, Cobb has identified this, for him, central concept in his christology. It is 'that process in which our imagination and life-orientation can be transformed by lucidity of vision and openness to what we see' (*Christ in a Pluralistic Age*, p. 21). In fairness to our author, he furnishes us with comprehensive illustrations of its significance in the arts and theology, but the centrality allotted to it in a christology does raise questions. For example, while it is undeniable that 'life in Christ' of the kind which is truly Christian is possible only through a process of creative transformation effected in the life of the believer, it has to be admitted that that transforming process is a work of Christ in the life of the believer, and not to be equated with the whole person of Christ. If it is so equated, there must be a reduction in the notion of Christ as person, however that word is understood – in strictly trinitarian terms or modern psychological terms. The equation might be more appropriate to the Logos, who is sometimes spoken of by Cobb as 'the principle of order and cohesion in the universe', but I wonder whether, even in that case, we would not want to regard the Logos as more than a principle and more akin to the being of God. For reasons which we shall examine later, however, we have seen that Cobb in his subsequent revision of his adherence to the concept of creative transformation, which appears in *Encountering Jesus: Debate on Christology*, pp. 141ff, emphasises more the notion of *conscientisation*, that is, an awakening and sharpening of the conscience towards the affliction and distress of the poor. This condition is effected by two considerations. The first is the actual teaching of Jesus concerning the poor, conveyed to us by means of parables, and brought home to believers who find themselves just as really within the field of influence of Jesus today as did the disciples who were with him in Galilee. Strangely, though Cobb has written a chapter on the teaching of Jesus in *Christ in a Pluralistic Age* and the subject is of great importance for this and other parts of Cobb's christology, Hick has not included Jesus or his teaching as a component in any of the three equations we are discussing. The second source of conscientisation, as we noted above, is the message that Jesus 'identified' himself with the poor, as stated so unambiguously by Jesus himself, 'Inasmuch as ye have done it unto one of the least of these my brethren, ye have done it unto me' (Mt 25.40b, cf. v. 45b). Cobb himself then has to face the question of whether a christology based on the concept of creative transformation can comprehend that of conscientisation. His positive answer to his own question is that the concept of creative transformation is itself open to creative transformation, and the move in the direction of conscientisation is one such change; in the rhetoric of his argument a further equation is made of the poor with Christ, which is both a rather rough deduction from the statement about Jesus' identification with the poor and also a suggestion that the '=' is not to be taken too literally, but rather as the articulation conjoining the components of a conceptual system. In this system, the components must not be taken independently of each other, for they are mutually explanatory. For that reason – to answer Hick's questions – equations (1), (2) and (3) are not to be treated separately from one another, nor are they to be conflated, nor is any one to be regarded as superseding either of the others. It might not seem that there is any option left; but on the strength of what Cobb has written, it is more accurate to say that there is movement of thought through the equations at certain points. So having engrossed conscientisation within his system as a qualification of creative transformation, Cobb states the transformation in another way, by saying that it encompasses the *truth* that Christ identifies with the poor (*Encountering Jesus: Debate on Christology*, p. 153) and is the suffering of God with us. In process terms, this truth, this suffering of God with us (and rejoicing with us also), is the consequent nature of God. This truth, derived from Jn 14.6, though it is not immediately seen as equivalent to the original, is said in the end to direct all creative transformation, presumably by encompassing the lure of the consequent nature of God. We have to conclude, I fear, that Hick has not oversimplified Cobb's christology with his series of equations; on the contrary, by nominating them he has helped to bring into the open the confusions and problems of Cobb's theories. One other such problem, to which attention is drawn by its appearance in Hick's equation (2), is the way in which Cobb reframes one now generally accepted part of the doctrine of the *Trinity* (see above pp. 202f). Quite rightly, he affirms that while all persons in the Trinity are involved in each of the *opera ad extra Trinitatis*, only one is appropriated *terminative* with each *opus ad extra*: the Father with creation, the Son with the incarnation and the Spirit with sanctification. While it is said that it is the Son who is incarnate, however, he is confessed as *vere Deus* according to the creeds and we do not need what Cobb considers a change in trinitarian doctrine in order to say 'that the one who is incarnate is the one who suffers in the suffering of the least' (*Encountering Jesus: Debate on Christology*, p. 153). Though Cobb's argument is rather hard to follow here, he seems to be working towards being able to affirm that the world's suffering which is in Christ is also in God. I guess that he is afraid that if it is only Christ who suffers, then, on his understanding of the incarnation, that suffering would not be felt by the whole triune God. So to prevent such a possibility, he argues that it is the whole Godhead who is incarnate in Jesus Christ – which is what the Creeds had said in the first place, and the words of the carol, 'Veiled in flesh the Godhead see'.

Perhaps we may now return to a matter mentioned earlier in passing, namely, that Hick omits *Jesus* from all the equations he attributes to Cobb. This omission is all the more strange, in that the person and teachings of Jesus are important to the development of Cobb's christology. The subject of Jesus now arises as we review names and roles in this christology. First of all, for Cobb the authenticity of the words of Jesus is evidenced both in the immediate effect they had upon his contemporaries, among the disciples and in the nascent Church, and in their influence, which bridges the centuries, upon men and women of our day. This effect and this influence had all the characteristics of creative transformation which Cobb had equated with the Logos. It is a modern form of the proof of the divinity of Jesus Christ, and I have to say that it is a very convincing form of an argument which is as old as christology itself. Secondly, connected with

the previous account of the words of Jesus, there occurs a curious
hysteron–proteron in Cobb's thought. In chapter 4 (op. cit., pp.
85ff), which is the chapter preceding that on 'Jesus' Words and
Christ', Cobb says that 'the Logos is love' (p. 85) and that the
structure of Christian love 'towards the future, towards the past,
towards God' (p. 86) – why not 'towards the present'? – has the
same structure as the creative transformation which Cobb has
just laid down as the key category in his christology, and in
process terms is identical to the structure and working of the
consequent God. Thirdly, the saying of Jesus appearing in Jn
14.6, 'I am the way, the *truth* and the life', serves as the source
for Cobb of the final stage for the process of creative
transformation, which is said to be directed by the truth. Here
we can only say that Cobb has injected into the notion of the
truth both a narrower meaning (Jesus' identification with the
poor) than Jesus intended – though the term has been given
many interpretations in the history of theology – and also a
specialised process meaning, 'the inclusive and ultimate perspective upon all the finite and conflicting perspectives that make up
the world' (op. cit., p. 152). At this point in Cobb's modification
and development of his christology, the reader does wonder
whether in the interests of theory he has adopted a view of 'truth'
which is a long way from Jesus' intention, a consideration
relevant to the assessment of his whole christology.

QUESTIONS OF THEOLOGICAL METHOD

The broadly stated premise from which, in *Christ in a Pluralistic
Age*, Cobb embarks upon his christological presentation or
experiment, as it might be called, is that we live, as he judges,
in a post-Christian age, so that Christianity has become an
anachronism and its main terms are largely meaningless except
to that in-group which is the Church, whose members know the
language. From that alien environment in which Christianity
and Christians now have to live, he extracts two concepts which
have been most influential in the decline of the faith – pluralism

and relativism. Adopting Malraux's view of the place of Christ in the history of art as an analogy for the interpretation of the history of religion and christology, and stipulating the concept of creative transformation as the fundamental hermeneutical principle in such a history, Cobb integrates, as we have seen earlier, both pluralism and relativism within his system. It seems, however, that within a period of little over ten years even that revision of classical christology became outdated, for he now had to adjust his system to incorporate two more fashionable theologies/philosophies, namely, liberation theology and feminism. Once again, he has to modify his system, first by qualifying and downgrading his previously central hermeneutical principle, creative transformation, by giving precedence to what we are told is one form of it – conscientisation, and by subordinating it to the notion of truth; and secondly by introducing the notion of *sophia* as the subject of incarnation in Jesus Christ. While seeming to say that *sophia* is solely the subject of the incarnation – 'Christ names *sophia* as she embodies herself in the world and receives the world into herself' (*Encountering Jesus: Debate on Christology*, p. 158) – he does seem to be saying by p. 172 (op. cit.) that in fact Logos and Pneuma are also each incarnate 'with its own history of use'. Nor dare we forget that he has already proposed that the Triune God, and not the second *persona* in the Trinity, is incarnate in Jesus.

It is difficult to resist the conclusion that Cobb's theological method is singularly unsatisfactory. We have noticed the major adjustments to central concepts that he has decided to make within a decade. We have noted the limited accounts that he gives of the great New Testament notion of 'truth' as used by Jesus, not to mention the variety of views he offers on what is involved in the incarnation. But it is his reaction to feminism and the devices he employs to make christology acceptable to its supporters which reveal the dangers of this sail-trimming theological method. He settles for the notion of *sophia* as the subject of incarnation in Jesus because it is feminine, as against the masculine of Logos, yet its connotation has to come mainly from the Old Testament, and it has finally to be supplemented as a description of the incarnation by the reintroduction of Logos and Pneuma. It is perhaps surprising that these unhappy attempts by Cobb to satisfy feminist sympathisers did not bring a realisation of two important circumstances. The first is that as far as language is concerned gender is different from sex. Admittedly the two do coincide in most languages in obvious cases; but over a vast range of words, subjects which in English are neutral in gender are in other languages either masculine or feminine. Therefore, since feminine language is just as sexist when used of, say, God, it would appear that the only end to the masculine/feminine language controversy is to opt for neutral terminology, because the fourth possibility, common gender, leaves the problem of which single pronouns to use. My prediction of the ultimate resolution of the language controversy is a neutral theism. This conclusion is borne out by my second consideration, namely, that there is never going to be a way in which Jesus, the Saviour of the world, will be designated other than as a man. Cobb himself seems to be aware that many feminists have moved into a post-Christ theological position, conscious that the masculine components of Christianity are so central to the tradition that to excise them would destroy the fabric of the whole. I should have thought that this decision on their part eliminates the need for the kind of drastic alterations which Cobb finally makes in order to accommodate them, remembering always, as he reminds us, that there are un-necessarily partriarchical, almost chauvinist, elements in the Scriptures which have to be amended or omitted. There are, too, feminine elements which have been ignored and now need to be brought out into the open and affirmed – elements to be found in passages in the Old Testament and in the teachings of Jesus.

COBB AND CLASSICAL CHRISTOLOGY

Anyone reading Cobb's account of christology cannot but be aware that he has classical christology in his mind, and that it does receive explicit expression from time to time. For example, at an immediately observable level, we have seen that he employs all the traditional names that we would expect to find in such a study – Logos, Christ and Jesus. He makes very considerable use of the 'teaching of Jesus' for the advancement of his argument on what is traditionally called 'the person of Christ'; while at a crucial turning-point of the latter part of his argument, he enlists some of the more recondite elements of the doctrine of the Trinity (concerning the *opera ad extra Trinitatis*) which, as we have seen, he modifies in order to meet some requirement of his christology. In *Christ in a Pluralistic Age* he writes chapters about 'The Christ of the Creeds' and 'Christ and the Creeds' (pp. 147–73), in which he demonstrates a very knowledgeable acquaintance with the detail of classical christological controversy. There are, however, very important points at which, with considerable ingenuity, Cobb presents to us a christology which has a distinctive process character; and these points stand at the centre of the subject. The first is what might be called the *deity of Christ*, by which Cobb claims that the Logos has an all-determinant influence upon the constituting of the person of Jesus by coalescing totally with his human past, his present motivation and his future aspirations. In the same way the *sinlessness of Jesus* is secured, for whereas in other people there is a tension between the Logos and the human will, motives, desires and decisions which amounts to disobedience towards the will of God; in Jesus there is no such tension because he is aligned to the will and purpose of the Logos and the Kingdom of God. When we come to the subject of the *two natures and the one person* of the Christ of Chalcedon, Cobb affirms the inadequacy of substantialist christology to deal adequately with the subject and turns once again to his process concepts. The human self of Jesus is coconstituted by the Logos, who is the immanence of God in Jesus, and in such a union we have an intellectually credible case of the *enhypostasis* of post-Chalcedonian christology. The perfect incarnation of the Logos, 'the coalescence of the Logos and humanity, in which each becomes hypostatic in the one person who is Jesus, far from diminishing or depersonalising Jesus' humanity or transmuting it into something else, enriches and completes humanity' (op. cit., pp. 171f). There is

here a noteworthy difference from traditional enhypostatic
theories of the person of Christ, which hold that the human *physis*
of Jesus, which is itself anhypostatic, finds its *hypostasis* in the
person of the Logos, hence the term *enhypostasis* to designate the
status of the human *physis*. Both the divine being of the Logos
and the humanity of Jesus are enhypostatised in the person of
Jesus Christ. The possibility of a charge of Nestorianism may be
deflected by noting that Cobb speaks of 'one person who is Jesus',
the human 'I' being comprehensively constituted by the Logos.

It must be recognised that Cobb's system evinces great internal
coherence, and that he is sufficiently sensitive to the areas in
which christological controversy has raged over the centuries
to provide us with a christology which endeavours to remain
within the canons of orthodoxy. He appears to avoid the
heresies of adoptionism, Nestorianism and also, as he would
claim, Eutycheanism, and of denying the divinity of Jesus Christ
and his sinlessness. He shows an allegiance to Scripture and
tradition, to both of which he is loyal in a scholarly way. Why
then are we uneasy about the final product?

The central features of Cobb's christology which give me cause
for concern are his account of the person of Christ, which
depends for its formulation upon his account of the self or the
'I', and his subsequent interpretation of the relation of the
humanity of Jesus to his divinity, represented by the presence in
him of the Logos. He rejects, as we know, any substantialist view
of the person or the self, and states his own position clearly in
two sentences: (i) 'There is no fixed entity or aspect of human
experience that is uniformly designated by "I" '; (ii) ' "I" refers to
the ultimate subject of conscious experience and the ultimate
agent of responsible action' (op. cit., p. 123).

As regards sentence (i), I should like to say that no substantialist would ever wish to say that the self was a '*fixed* entity';
the self is constantly changing in internal constitution, maturing
or deteriorating and so on. Nor would the substantialist say
that the self is 'an aspect of conscious experience' – why only
'conscious'? – for the self is the experiencing entity and could
scarcely be an aspect of itself. So it is difficult to see what exactly

the substantialist is said to be denying in the negative introduction to the positive statement, for all that really remains is
the denial that the self is an 'entity'. But if the denial holds, what
then is the self? For however in the end we define it, it surely has
to be some kind of entity. As regards sentence (ii), we have two
positive statements, that the 'I' denotes 'the ultimate subject of
conscious experience' and 'the ultimate agent of responsible
action'. In the first denotation, the term 'subject' has two meanings: the one is grammatical or logical, indicating that experiences are experiences *of* someone, for they are not self-existent.
Now, if we are to accept Cobb's further term for this subject,
namely, 'centre', then we cannot say, as he tries to do on p. 123
(op. cit.), that it is 'an aspect of experience'. The result is quite
illogical – experiences (of the self) are then said to be experiences
of an aspect of experience, which is also unacceptable. On the
second denotation, the subject referred to *is* an ontological entity,
self-identical and self-existent, who experiences the experiences
intended – which does not mean that, with all their changes, the
'I' may not change. Even then, if there ever comes a time when
the 'I' changes dramatically and, as popular usage has it, 'he/she
is no longer themselves', the self does not disappear. The same
argumentation applies to the other denotation, that the 'I' refers
to 'the ultimate agent of responsible action': actions are persons
acting, who take responsibility for these actions, and are not
simply notional, as distinct from ontological, centres around
which experiences cluster. I have discussed at length (above, pp.
83–113) the question of the place of the notions of nature and
substance in classical christology, and all of that discussion is
totally applicable here. Particularly, I would like to quote the
conclusion reached previously (*The Shape of Christology*, First
Edition, SCM Press, London, 1966, pp. 103f):

> the subject–predicate form, allied so closely as it is to the primary
> substance–secondary substance ontological distinction, while it
> may not stand in a relation of one-one correspondence to the
> latter, is nevertheless one of the ways in which we may legiti-
> mately talk of reality . . . we expect reality to be not unlike how
> we describe it.

In short, the substantialist case seems to me to be still valid; we talk of centres of experience, of subjects and agents, and they have ontological as well as grammatical/logical status.

Indeed, we require such a conclusion if we are going to succeed with our christological use of language. My trouble with the process case is that its exponents never make the correlation between the metaphysical analysis and the language we must use to describe it. We have seen the difficulties which occur at the level of the analysis of the self or the 'I', difficulties very similar to those facing philosophers such as Locke, Berkeley and Hume, who, though writing long before the day of process, nevertheless held anti-substantialist views of the self and thinghood. But the problems met in connection with the human self reappear when we tackle the christological question proper. In addition, two other problems appear, the first being whether the non-sub-stantialist argument is applicable to the Logos; and the second being how the two non-substantialist entities – humanity and divinity – are to be enhypostatically united. Recalling that *anhypostasis*, that is, of the *hypostasis* of the human nature, is the precursor of *enhypostasis* of the human nature in the *hypostasis* of the Logos, we note that the process account of the anhypostasised humanity, namely as a complex of experiences, motives, ideals and attraction by the lure of the Logos, without an ontological centre, almost meets Leontius' demand of *anhypostasis* in the case of humanity, as a condition of *enhypostasis*. I say 'almost' because Leontius would speak of the human nature, which has sub-stantialist connotations, rather than of a complex of experiences, etc. But that sort of reasoning cannot be extended to the analysis of the Logos, for, in uncompromising terms, it is in the *hypostasis* of the Logos that the humanity finds its centre, its subject. That centre cannot be spirited away into a complex of experiences, etc.; otherwise, the coalescence of the Logos and humanity would be just that and would result in a Eutychean christology. So we have reached my second problem as stated above, namely, how the Logos and humanity coalesce in the person of Jesus Christ. Interestingly, Cobb makes an unexpected contribution to the solution of the problem when he says (op. cit., p. 171) that in the coalescence of the Logos and humanity, 'each becomes hypostatic in the one person who is Jesus Christ'. That statement is, for me, resonant of the account which Ephraim of Antioch gives (see above, pp. 101ff) of the way in which the *hypostasis* of the Logos and that of the humanity become a single fused *hypostasis* indicated by the name Jesus Christ. But it is an account which is acceptable only if this single joint *hypostasis* is a genuine centre, with identity and continuity and self-existence, and it is scarcely, if at all, sustainable if the human nature of Jesus and the divine nature of the Logos are regarded as systems of experiences – past, present and future-looking. So the conclusion which seems to be emerging is that the saturation in classical christology and the terminology which it uses make it very difficult for Cobb to break away from the logic and the metaphysics which that christology presupposes and replace it with a process system. This consequence is particularly observable in the account which he gives of the enhypostatic coalescence of the humanity of Jesus Christ and the Logos. It is, I believe, the problem of attempting to graft a process christology on to an Aristotelian trunk.

9

NORMAN PITTENGER

CLEARING THE GROUND

CRITICISM OF ENHYPOSTASIS

More lucidly than in the writing of either of the other two
exponents of process christology whom we have considered,
Pittenger states the logic and the motivation which have
wooed him away from the classical Chalcedonian and post-
Chalcedonian christology upon which he has clearly been reared.
He does so in two books, *The Word Incarnate* (Nisbet, London,
1959) and *Christology Reconsidered* (SCM Press, London, 1970).
The main subject of his dissatisfaction, expressed in both books,
is the doctrine of *enhypostasis* usually associated with the names
of Leontius of Byzantium and Leontius of Jerusalem. It affirms
that in the person of Jesus Christ, while the divine nature (*physis*)
is centred in the person (*hypostasis*) of the Logos, the human
nature (*physis*) which is alleged to have no human person
(*hypostasis*), and therefore to be *anhypostatos* locates its *hypostasis*
in the divine *hypostasis* and so is said to be *enhypostatos*. (The
subject is discussed at length on pp. 94–105 above.) Pittenger's
attack on the doctrine of *enhypostasis*, both in its classical
expression and in the forms of it used by modern writers such as
the Tractarians of the last century and H. M. Relton and E. L.
Mascall of this century, is sharp and direct. He will have none
of Relton's almost ecstatic praise for *enhypostasis*:

> the person of Jesus Christ so conceived [that is, according to the
> doctrine of *enhypostasis*] is the richest and fullest possibility for

man. Man is so 'made for' union with God that centring of his life in God in such a fashion as *enhypostasia* suggests could be the accomplishment of the end or goal of human existence. (Quoted in *The Word Incarnate*, p. 101)

Pittenger responds in kind, rejecting the entire concept in equally strong words, arguing that such descriptions are totally incredible and make presuppositions concerning the nature of God and the relationships which he has with mankind that to most of our contemporaries are utterly absurd.

For example, since the ascription of the *physis anhypostatos* to the humanity of Christ is a presupposition or a consequence (according to your point of departure) of the doctrine of the *enhypostasis*, the human nature of Christ cannot be said to have a true human centre, and this entails a minimising of the humanity of Christ. Pittenger claims for Jesus Christ a body which is a fully and completely human body, together with a human mind and a human soul. Short of that totality, we have no assurance that there may not be some area of our being which has not been exposed to salvation, for according to a saying of Gregory of Nazianzus which is thought to have quelled the Apollinarians, 'What God has not assumed, he has not redeemed' (*Epistle* 101, Migne's *Patrologia Graece* t.37, 181). What I find disturbing about Pittenger's attack on *enhypostasis* is that it ignores a distinction of which he himself is fully aware, namely, between the psychological and the logical or, as he says, ontological role of the terms *hypostasis* and 'person' (*The Word Incarnate*, p. 112). He rubbishes the doctrine – it is 'absurd', 'incredible' – but the charge is applicable only when the doctrine and its constituent terms are regarded as psychological concepts. Pittenger was aware that the patristic writers who used these terms were not using them in a psychological sense. Therefore, if he were really intending to demolish the doctrine, he would have to attack it on its own grounds of logic and ontology. But not to do so was a misjudgement which dates from as far back as Harnack (*History of Dogma*, ET, 1898, vol. IV, pp. 233f, n. 3), and found its way into British christology through H. R. Mackintosh's, *The Person of Jesus Christ* (T. & T. Clark, Edinburgh, 1912, p. 207).

Pittenger focuses his difficulty with christologies which endeavour to give a modern psychological account of the doctrine of *enhypostasis* upon the meaning and use of the term 'person'. For when it is used as the equivalent of *hypostasis*, as has been the case traditionally in English theology both trinitarian and christological, it is overtaken by a change of meaning influenced by psychology, sociology and literary studies. Nowadays, the term means 'the psychological centre of subjective experience. It has a primary reference to the conscious subject of these experiences . . . the organising centre of the totality of experiences; it is the "self"', though even in that sense there is a leaning towards whatever it is that 'establishes self-consciousness and self-direction' (Pittenger, *The Word Incarnate*, p. 112). This account of the 'self' is later going to prove of immense importance in the construction of Pittenger's own christology.

Pittenger, therefore, is very precise and definite about his starting-point in christology: a rejection of the neo-Chalcedonian attempt to amend certain alleged deficiencies in the Chalcedonian formula. More: he rejects the attempts of twentieth-century theologians to prolong the life of Chalcedon by translating its key concepts into modern psychological terms, because in doing so they fail to realise that the Fathers who originally used these concepts were not thinking in psychological terms at all. This modern psychologising method involved a category mistake of the first order. Pittenger himself seems to be abandoning the whole Chalcedonian and neo-Chalcedonian approach to christology, without, as we have already noted, considering the possibility of a logical and ontological assessment of its main circle of ideas, in particular the much-offending doctrine of *enhypostasis*. A point in his defence, though he does not use it, is that perhaps 'the modern mind' cannot read the Chalcedonian Creed other than in psychological terms; Aristotelianism is a foreign language. This fact is particularly evident in the rejection of the substantialist metaphysic which is built into Chalcedonian christology in all its forms: such concepts as substance, essence, being, nature, have an 'inert quality'. Here the way is being prepared for the adoption of a process philosophy to replace substantialism.

BACK TO BASICS

Pittenger seems, then, to have reached the point where there is no way forward, for him or for the modern thinker, in the Chalcedonian christology or any of its sophisticated variations. Confronted as it were by this impasse, and in order to create for himself a new starting-point, Pittenger therefore sets down what he calls 'three essential elements in the christological enterprise' (*Christology Reconsidered*, p. 7), which together express the experience of believing Christians in times past, related as it was to both Scripture and tradition. After expounding these elements, his intention is to conceptualise them into a christology which will make sense to our contemporaries.

The first of these elements is: 'there is a firm conviction that in some fashion we meet God in the event of Jesus Christ' (ibid.). This conviction would be as true of the disciples who experienced the daily companionship of Jesus as it would of those men and women today who encounter in the Gospel of Jesus both the demand and the succour which God offers.

The second element is: 'there is the equally firm conviction that God is thus met in a genuine, historically conditioned, and entirely human being' (ibid.). The claim for the humanity of Jesus Christ has been sustained throughout orthodox christology, with arguments which at times a more advanced psychological understanding of the 'self' would have to regard as less than satisfactory. That criticism would be true even today, on the one hand because there is still in some theological quarters a tendency to lay stress upon the action of God in Jesus Christ, often seeking, out of the most pious reasons, to say that all is of God to the detriment of the understanding of the humanity of Christ. On the other hand, when the human nature of Jesus Christ is acknowledged, more is made of his perfections than of his limitations; rarely, with such notable exceptions as Edward Irving and Karl Barth, is there any willingness to say that it was sinful human nature that the Logos assumed at the incarnation.

The third of Pittenger's foundational christological elements is: 'there is the assurance that God, met in that man, and the man in whom God is met, are in relationship one with the other, in a manner or mode which is . . . the most complete inter-penetration . . . conceived after the analogy of personal union' (ibid.). Here, it appears to me, Pittenger is not only breaking away from the classical expressions of the relationship of the two natures and one person, and to that extent not reflecting the insights of classical christology, but is already adumbrating the position which he himself is going to adopt in his fuller account. It is an example of his particular theological method – to give notice of a position which he is later going to expand and develop into a full theory. He states a preference for speaking of the relationship or union of God and that man, rather than of godhead and humanity. The personal relationship between God and man which he is proposing to use is described in terms of the analogy of love, which is the most gracious and intimate of personal unions. But this relationship has its basis, as we shall shortly see, in the character of God who is himself love – love living, dynamic, indefatigable, unrelenting, tirelessly seeking the response of love from those whom he loves. Conversely, man, who is rational and volitional, is supremely made for love, unsatisfied as long as he does not receive the love he needs. Both of these latter points we shall now explore.

THE ALTERNATIVE METAPHYSIC

Acknowledging the unacceptability in modern times of the substantialist metaphysic on which classical christology had rested for some 1,500 years, and of those particular aspects of it which some twentieth-century theologians have attempted to modernise, Pittenger sets his hand, as already intimated, to offering a replacement in the form of process philosophy, though note has to be taken that the author continues to draw heavily upon Christian content, especially in the area of his doctrine of God. He is convinced that the world-view associated with process philosophy is the most suitable for the presentation of a modern-day christology, which is by his definition the doctrine of the activity of God in the man Jesus (*Christology Reconsidered*, p. 133). So we look first at the significance of the term 'process' against the background of classical substantialism. The cosmos, we are told (ibid., p. 121), is constituted not of substances, essences and natures, but rather of occasions, events, occurrences and happenings – though Whitehead would allow us to include 'actual entities' – and we all live within an ongoing dynamic movement which is creative. These events have both an outer side, of a recognisable generic structure, and an inner side which is more akin to feeling, sentience or experience, and varies in complexity according to its ability to prehend or grasp the process (a concept recently described at length by Charles Birch in *Feelings*, UNSW Press, Sydney, 1995). A further aspect of the process thought so important for Pittenger's christology is the notion of 'emergent evolution'. Previously, evolution had been understood as a process in which the variation and complexi-fication that took place from stage to stage added no novel or hitherto existent elements beyond the original given. But accord-ing to the idea of 'emergent evolution' favoured by such thinkers as William Temple, Jan Smuts, L. S. Thornton and, particularly, Conwy Lloyd-Morgan, and presupposed by Hartshorne in his account of the relationships between God and the world, genuine novelty emerges at each stage. This emergent process receives further interpretation from Lloyd-Morgan, who argues that this emergence is directed by a *nisus* whom he identifies with the Logos, the medium of God's self-expression. It is a position which Pittenger endorses when he later affirms that evolution implies an epigenetic process in relation to an Eternal Reality who is the God of the Christian faith, operative within the whole process through the Logos or Word of God (*The Word Incarnate*, p. 166).

Against the background of that cosmic theory, Pittenger introduces Hartshorne's understanding of the concept of God, said to express 'the basic idea which must govern any conception of God which can claim to be Christian' (ibid., p. 149). Since the conception of God is fundamental to Pittenger's christology in many ways, we must now consider the use which he makes of Hartshorne's highly commended views. Hartshorne rejects the notion of a God who is out of relation to the world – Aristotle's unmoved mover of the spheres, or the end-term in a medieval logomachy; or the notion of a God who is so distanced from the world that any action within it is that of an intrusive alien, spectacular and occasional and having little lasting effect on the movement of the world. As distinct from that misconception, and because the world *is* movement and becoming, development and history, Hartshorne has in mind a God who, though he is being, is not statically so but is constantly and intimately related to the world of 'becoming'. So while Hartshorne does not wish to depart from the notion of being, and even regards God as absolute *qua* self-identical, the 'Supreme Creative Reality, to whom all wisdom, goodness and power belong' (ibid., p. 147), yet God is a relative being, in the sense of being in constant relation with the entirety of the cosmos and all therein. So constant and penetrating is God's presence and operation within the world, not acting from the outside but expressing and realising himself within the world, that Hartshorne describes the world as being 'in' God, as 'the circumambient Reality' outside whom nothing exists; hence the name for this view, 'panen-theism'. So God is operative within every element in creation, proposing potentiality to lure it from its actuality and bringing that potentiality to actuality through love, which is the very essence of his being. God's operation is of varying intensity, from the lowest levels of existence through to the human historical plane, 'informing, moulding, modifying, relating life with life, and event with event . . . for the fulfilment of a purpose which governs the whole enterprise' (ibid., p. 163). This relationship of God to the world and all that is therein is so intimate, however, that God is also affected by it even to the point not only of sympathising with and containing suffering among his creatures, but of actually sharing this suffering, supremely in the cross (ibid.). Since it is of the essence of God's being to love and he is affected in and by the experiences of those whom he loves, and since love is also a relationship of Love and Lover, it is only fulfilled and completed when that love is returned. Then man, through an act of self-commitment in a definite decision to respond to this God of love, begins to achieve that purpose which is God's destiny for him.

PITTENGER'S CHRISTOLOGY

With all the presuppositions and components of his christology to hand, Pittenger now proceeds to put them into place, keeping in mind the three elements which any christological enterprise must conserve, the three criteria which it must meet. The first of these is that justice be done to the conviction that we must meet God in the event that is Jesus Christ. Now, though Pittenger himself gives this principle primacy, I should like tentatively to suggest that we consider it after the other two, asking whether in the event of the presence of God in the man Jesus, as described by him, men and women may and do encounter God.

THE HUMANITY OF JESUS CHRIST

So I propose to move to his second element: that God is met in a genuine, historically conditioned and entirely human being. There are several ways in which Pittenger would claim that he fully expresses this. For example, his oft-repeated rejection of the *anhypostasis/enhypostasis* element in much post-Chalcedonian christology rests on the claim that it gives a false account of the humanity of Christ. Its inadequacy lies in its denial of any human *hypostasis* in the humanity of Christ and its ascription of the divine *hypostasis* of the Logos to the anhypostasised humanity. He argues, it will be recalled, for a genuinely human centre of experience for Jesus Christ. Another way in which Pittenger seeks to do justice to the 'really real' character of the humanity of

Christ is in his portrayal of 'the model which we find most satisfactory for the understanding of Jesus of Nazareth'. He regards as inadequate the Victorian hero, the self-sufficient, self-contained individual, as well as 'the great-souled' if also flawlessly good man of Aristotle's *Nicomachean Ethics* (*Christology Reconsidered*, p. 70). He presents instead one who meets the conditions of true humanity. These categories he itemises and applies to Jesus Christ. The truly human person is to be understood in relation to his past history and the culture from which he springs. Jesus comes to us as a member of a race whose faith had been moulded across a thousand and more years, a fact that is readily observable in his teaching, which draws deep from the corpus of its sacred literature; when he shows his own originality, what he says is only intelligible in the context of that literature and, indeed, is often offered as the interpretation of some aspect of that literature, the unveiling of its profoundest meaning. But supremely, for Jesus, the God of Abraham, Isaac and Jacob is his God and Father, and his whole mission on earth is related to the will of that God for himself and for his people.

Another category of authentic humanity which Pittenger itemises is the recognition of the relationships which he influences and by which he is influenced. It is a principle which has acquired much greater popularity in the four decades since Pittenger penned it, and it takes the form of insistence on the fact that persons are only persons-in-relation. But it carries its own danger of seeming to suggest that it is the relations in which persons stand that determine their personhood and personality. Pittenger comes close to succumbing to this danger when he says that 'every man is constituted to a very considerable degree, by his relationships' which work both ways (ibid., p. 73). Yet surely it is what Jesus Christ is in himself which is the key to understanding the relationships in which he stands and the influence which he has upon them and they have upon him. The important point, however, is that Jesus Christ was immensely influential upon those who were associated with him and also upon those who happened upon him casually – disciples, women friends, publicans and pharisees, members of the occupying forces, a blind man, and so on. Equally, he was dependent upon many, from Mary's care for him in a manger to Simon of Cyrene carrying his cross. He was a genuine member of a society, the pattern of which was as complex as it could possibly have been – politically, economically, religiously, ethically, ethnically and culturally. What Pittenger is implying by this biblical/theological account of the life and mission of Jesus, though he does not press his point, is that the terms 'humanity' or 'human nature', when referred to in christology, have to be spelt out in Gospel history, stories and imagery, and not in the aridities of logical definitions.

A third obligation upon anyone seeking to understand what it is to be human is to take the impact of the person upon subsequent history into serious consideration. Pittenger is not referring simply to memories retained by those who knew such a person. He has in mind the more notional thought that, though we pass this way but once, the world is never going to be quite the same for our doing so. It is a diminishing impact, but less so as we rise in a scale of 'importance', and not at all in the case of Jesus. To him can be traced the origins of the Gospels, through their impact at first or second hand upon the writers and their accounts of the responses made to him by those who met in him, 'as a teacher, a prophet, a spokesman for God', and eventually as the long-expected Messiah (ibid., p. 77). Since his death, 'the process of impact-and-reception' has continued and been given permanent expression in the founding and growth of the community of the Church, the reverberations of which we can still experience.

Pittenger enlarges upon the profile of what it means to be a human person, and how Jesus' humanity conforms to that picture, in a fourth component which sums up the other three, namely, that persons are to be understood only as we focus upon their past history, their present relationships and their impact upon their successors. Their identity or selfhood is both constituted by and understood within this network of relations. Clearly, in terms of such a requirement, Jesus was fully human, gathering up the whole destiny of the past history of his people in his message about the Kingdom, entering fully into the many relationships which contemporary society offered, and living a life, dying a death, being raised by God to live in the hearts of his people and in the worship and activity of the Church till the end of time.

In a fifth feature of what he calls 'the location of the Incarnation', Pittenger (ibid., pp. 67ff) argues that if God is thought to act in a human person, as christology maintains, then God has to be presented as acting within the different circumstances we have been describing. Due regard must be paid to the past history of his people, the complexity of the relationships in which he finds himself, and the influence which he will have upon the history of the Church, the nation, nature and the world. However, since that discussion falls more exactly, within our forthcoming examination of how Pittenger deals with the third desideratum in a contemporary christology (see above, p. 234), which deals with the relationship of God to the humanity of Jesus Christ, we shall not pursue it here.

What is missing from this profile both of humanity in general and of Jesus Christ in particular, is the all-important theme of the 'full Christian theistic meaning of the word . . . man' (ibid., p. 180), namely, that there is in him the potentiality of the image of God and it is God's will for him that this image should be made manifest, though in truth it is often 'dimmed, blurred, and marred, but never destroyed' (ibid., p. 181). So God, or more precisely, the Word of God, the Logos, is the foundation upon which human existence rests. It is not a role which God fulfils passively, for through his Word he energises that response of worship and commitment to his initiative of love and compassion which leads to the partial realisation and manifestation of the image of God. This activity on the part of God through his Word, Pittenger admits, is of varying intensity and predictability, though, he adds, there is also fundamental consistency throughout. So man exists not as a being centred upon himself, not *'incurvatus in se'*, but oriented Godward; in the words of Augustine, *'Tu fecisti nos ad te'*. This theistic anthropology is not only a very necessary complement to what has gone before;

it is also essential to the description of the humanity of Jesus Christ, to which we shall proceed later.

But before moving on to that discussion, let us note three points. First, after rejecting the static and logical definitions of human nature which played so large a part in christological controversies from the fourth century down to the present century, and having declared that process categories would dominate his christology, Pittenger cannot be said to have failed in his promise. The account we have just had of the humanity of Jesus Christ is wholly comprehensive, enveloping the New Testament events, stories and images, relating them carefully to the Old Testament passages and promises, and carrying the process forward to life in the risen Christ and to the community, the Church, which he founded and still enlivens. We have come a long way from the christology which traded in texts from the Scriptures and used building blocks culled from Aristotle's *Categoriae*. Pittenger operates, too, not by resorting to literal biblicism, but by taking full account of the researches of such scholars of his day as Rudolf Bultmann, John Knox, Dennis Nineham, Günther Bornkamm, Ernst Fuchs, Ernst Käsemann and Gerhard Ebeling. Secondly, to select from what has just been said, for it is of great importance in its own right, he has done justice to the historical component in Christian faith and theology. Much is made from time to time of the fact that the Christian faith is based in history and that the events which constitute its core genuinely happened in the course of history, ordinary, mundane history, even though some theologians tried to extricate it and give it more secure status in what they called *Heilsgeschichte*. But Pittenger does not succumb to such enticements. Thirdly, Pittenger does not amplify what he has previously said about the nature of the self and its experiences. Rejecting the substantialist notion of a *hypostasis* in which the human nature (*physis*) inheres, he conceives of the experiences of the human being as having an organising centre, what he has called the 'self' and also the 'person' (*The Word Incarnate*, p. 112). Now, much discussion on the nature of the self has taken place throughout the past century, particularly through the immense

developments in the discipline of psychology and the issues
which have arisen on the borderline between philosophy and
psychology. Without embarking upon any detailed account of
the history of that discussion, we may just note that the position
taken by Pittenger, following some of the process philosophers,
is but one among many. If I am being fair to him, he seems to be
saying, not that the self is a carefully self-regulating system of
experiences, but that it is a kind of Pure Ego around which the
experiences arrange themselves and which, more importantly,
exercises a co-ordinating influence upon them. I hesitate to
identify Pittenger's theory of the self as a 'Pure Ego' theory,
recalling a comment of C. D. Broad that 'it is supposed that a
"Pure Ego" is so disreputable that no decent philosopher would
allow such a thing in his mind if he could possibly help it' (*The
Mind and its Place in Nature*, Kegan Paul, London, 1929, p.
214). Later on (p. 278), Broad points to a confusion which
prevails to this day, among different views of the self, its experiences and the Pure Ego: one, that the self is the Pure Ego without
its states or experiences; two, the self is the whole complex of
Pure Ego and its relations to its states and experiences, as well as
their interrelations with one another; and three, the self is simply
the interlocking network of states and experiences, with no
hypothetical Pure Ego. I would say that Pittenger's position on
the self falls within the first category, largely because he has used
the notion of an ego at the centre organising the experiences of
the person. The self, so construed as the Pure Ego, is the co-
ordinator of its experiences and states at any one given moment,
but it is also the centre of co-ordination, through memory, of
experiences from the past with those of the present, and, through
imagination, of both with the hopes for the future. It is at this
point that my problem arises, for I cannot see how it is that this
centre, this self, this Pure Ego, is not therefore regarded in
ontological terms as a mental entity. It is the subject of its states
and experiences and so has genuinely 'real' existence. It is no
doubt itself subject to process, to growth or decay, education
or propaganda, but it is not itself in the end reducible to a series
of events or a string of occasions. I have considered this matter at

such length because I am convinced that it is central to any assessment of Pittenger's christology, and particularly of his description of the relation of humanity to divinity in Jesus Christ.

THE RELATION OF GOD TO THE HUMANITY OF JESUS CHRIST, OR GOD AND MAN IN JESUS CHRIST

We come now to the third essential element in Pittenger's understanding of the christological enterprise, which is:

> the assurance that God, met in that man [Jesus], and the man in whom God is met, are in relationship with each other . . . [which] must be conceived after the analogy of personal union such as we know in human marriage, or the love of a lover and his beloved. (*Christology Reconsidered*, pp. 7, 12)

This analogy, while perhaps the controlling one in Pittenger's christology, is not the only one, and it will have to be considered along with these others. He uses a number of ways to describe the togetherness of God and man, deity and humanity, in Jesus Christ, and these we shall have to itemise and correlate.

The two movements – from above and from below

Let us begin with a quotation from Pittenger which is so precise and thoughtfully stated that by unpacking its contents we have to hand the main elements of his christology. On p. 188 of *The Word Incarnate* he says:

> The *most complete*, the *fullest*, the *most organic* and *integrated* union of Godhead and manhood which is conceivable is precisely one in which by gracious indwelling of God in man and by manhood's free response in surrender and love, there is established . . . a full, free, gracious unity of the two in Jesus Christ, which is both the farthest reach of God the Word into the life of man and also (by consequence) the richest response of man to God.

Let us now pick up the detail and amplify it from his other central christological views. First of all we are aware that there are in Jesus Christ two movements (rather than two static natures), the one being God's reaching downwards to, and focusing on, the man Jesus (rather than humanity in general), the other, the responding love and surrender of the man Jesus. The emphasis on 'movements' is of course in line with the process approach to these matters and follows what we have hitherto observed in Pittenger's accounts of both God and man. We have already noted that not only is God as Logos present throughout the whole order of creation, providing from within the *nisus* towards the actualisation of the potential of its individual members; he is also thus, especially and graciously and lovingly, with human beings, whose potential he has created and inspired to actualise in varying measures the image of God. But in Jesus Christ alone is the action of God the Word so complete that this image is perfectly actualised, and he is named the Express Image of God, his humanity uniquely and totally open to God. His life is one of all-encompassing conformity to the purposes of God for him, and through him for the whole of creation. So, in phrases which, as Pittenger acknowledges, are reminiscent of Karl Barth (ibid., p. 182), this actualisation, with its double movement, may be said to be 'from above' and 'from below'. On the one hand, God has elected that his will for mankind and the whole of creation will be fulfilled in Jesus of Nazareth, through the Self-Expressive Word who indwells him. But, on the other hand, it must also be said that from the side of manhood there is a responsive and consenting movement of love and commitment to the Word.

In parenthesis, we have to make a final observation on this theme of the two movements which makes the reference to Barth singularly important. When Barth spoke once of the Holy Spirit, he described him as 'God from below meeting God from above'. To round off one of his presentations of the theme of the two movements, Pittenger concludes that the bringing of the manhood of Jesus into conformity with the will of the Logos, and so actualising the Express Image of God in him, is effected by 'the operation of the Holy Spirit' (ibid.). The question of the place given to the Holy Spirit in the incarnation is important generally in christology, and its significance does not go unobserved by Pittenger, who nevertheless occasionally seems to assign to the Logos activities which orthodox theology would regard as appropriate to the Holy Spirit. This confusion of the functions of the Holy Spirit and the Logos seems inescapable. On the one hand, Pittenger is saying that the Holy Spirit is the Divine Person who facilitates the happening of the two movements in such a way that they coincide. The work of the Holy Spirit here would then be regarded as the continuance of his actions in relation to the virginal conception (ibid., p. 183) and the commissioning of the Messiah at his baptism. On the other hand, Pittenger does seem to allow that the Logos performs activities, in order to inspire human responses to the approach of a loving God and human achievement in seeking conformity to his will and purposes – all of which are normally, as we have said, attributable to the Holy Spirit. It was a problem which some years later was to give concern to both Donald and John Baillie when John Hick criticised the christological position adopted by Donald, and supported by John, in his *God was in Christ* (Faber, London, 1948). It is a subject to which we shall have to return, and it is mentioned here in order to look at it in the context of its occurrence.

The unity of divinity and manhood

Pittenger, however, does not tarry long over the notion of two movements without making it clear to us by various statements that he thinks of Jesus Christ as a *unity*. 'The unity of divinity and humanity in [Jesus Christ] is the *coincidence* of the divine and human acts, the act of God and the act of man' (*The Word Incarnate*, p. 181). It is, too, in the context of what we have just heard from Pittenger about the two movements and the two acts that we can appreciate the force of the quotation given in the opening sentence of this section concerning 'the most organic and integrated union of Godhead and manhood' (above, p. 238). But in emphasising this union, Pittenger now goes further in two respects than he has so far. At p. 197 of *The Word Incarnate*, whereas previously he had been speaking of the two movements or acts, that is, of divinity and humanity, he now actually refers to them as natures – 'the true ontological nature of each'. Admittedly he does in honesty acknowledge that he lapses from time to time from his avowed dedication to anti-Chalcedonian language in favour of the process alternative, yet this lapse into speaking of 'nature', also quoted as 'the essential nature proper to both', may be due to his and our inability to abandon Chalcedonian speech altogether; and if the speech, maybe also the metaphysic? One way round the problem is to say that it is characteristic of these two natures of which he is speaking that they are never static (the term unacceptable to Pittenger) but always acting and moving and in process. The Psalmist said it first, 'He slumbers not nor sleeps'. The second way in which at p. 197 Pittenger goes further than he has so far in speaking of the relation of God to man in Jesus Christ, is to state that 'it is a genuine ontological union in the only significant meaning of that phrase'. He applies to the union the German term *Seinsverhaltnis*, 'a relationship of essential being' which, as it occurs in Jesus Christ, is 'living, moral and spiritual'. Once again we have an interesting combination of process and Chalcedonian languages, due largely to the difficulty, if not impossibility, of describing the person of Jesus Christ otherwise than by lapsing from traditional process language.

Having spoken of the union between God and man in Jesus Christ, Pittenger sets out to describe how it is that this union is so close and so stable and in no sense a 'mere association', an accidental happening or two categories of thought to be joined in logical terms. Several times over, he says that humanity in the person of Jesus Christ is so responsive in love to the presence of God in him, so committed to the achieving of the purposes of God, so fully open to the Divine Reality, that it is the perfect instrument, means, organ or *organon* – Pittenger uses one idea or the other on different occasions (e.g., ibid., pp. 92, 130, 181,

188, 277) – for God's Self-Expression or Self-Manifestation in human terms and in the sphere of human existence. At that point we may be tempted to think that Pittenger has taken up an adoptionist position, by suggesting that God the Logos had to wait until in the course of history, a human being appeared who exhibited all the qualities of perfect manhood before initiating the incarnation. But Pittenger is not so naive. He has already made plain (p. 92) that in the eternal providence of God there was conceived by and born of Mary, the Son, the Elect One. From the beginning, his humanity was being 'appropriated and employed' by the Logos for the furthering of the divine will for all creation; while in that operation the humanity was 'appropriating and expressing' the Logos, thus showing his availability for the purposes of the Logos in the world.

I must, however, confess to a certain uneasiness about the fairly prevalent notion in Pittenger's christology of the Logos employing the humanity of Christ as an *organon*, instrument and so on, for the purpose of his Self-Expression. My uneasiness springs from memories of Kant's *Second Critique*, with its severe condemnation of the immorality of treating another person as the means to an end. Such a condemnation would be applicable even when the end was of the very highest order and the means itself dedicated to that end. Pittenger himself seems to have anticipated this very difficulty (pp. 188f) by giving us two related answers. One is that he rejects the suggestion that the humanity of Jesus Christ is an instrument 'in the low sense of being a tool used incidentally for a special purpose', presumably meaning that such a tool would be subsequently discarded, whereas the humanity of Christ would be eternally the instrument which God in his wisdom had prepared beforehand. I still fear that Pittenger has not quite exorcised my misgiving, but he has, with his explanation, emphasised the dualism of the divinity and the humanity of Christ, while still leaving a whiff of the idea of the one using the other. The second answer comes as the eventual completion of the quotation I have just given. He rejects the notion of a 'mere association' between God and man in Jesus Christ, as an adequate description of the intimate and interpenetrating relationship of God and man in him. He goes on to give what he regards as a Chalcedonian account of the matter (p. 188), by saying that in the union of the *organon* and the Word they are integrally one, 'inseparable and indivisible even while they are also unconfused and unchanged in the essential nature which is proper to each'.

Nestorianism?

Mention of Chalcedon raises the spectre of Nestorianism, which Pittenger seems to acknowledge – rather sensitively, by reason of his repeated references to the subject – is a charge that might be brought against his christology. There are two points here, the one historical and the other *ad hominem*. The first is the long-debated question whether Nestorius was himself a Nestorian. While the dualism accredited to 'Nestorianism' was ruled out beforehand and in the event anathematised by two of the famous adverbs of Chalcedon, these strictures, in the judgement of Pittenger, did not in fact touch the authentic Nestorius, who could indeed have accepted the terms of Chalcedon had he had the opportunity. It is a long story and in its detail not relevant to the charge brought against Pittenger. The second point is, as I said, *ad hominem*, namely that his position is, as popularly understood, 'Nestorian'. Pittenger reacts sharply, defending not only those Nestorians who, instead of contemplating a 'mere association' or a 'mechanical conjunction' of the two natures, used the terms εὐδοκία (*eudokia*, delight, satisfaction, good-will, as at Lk 2.14) and συνάφεια (*sunapheia*, union, close connection, and in the human reference, sexual intercourse), but also, often almost in the same breath, defending his own position against the charge, arguing that he is committed to the affirmation of the divinity of Jesus Christ and his totally unimpaired humanity, in a union which he calls 'organic', 'integrated' and 'ontological'. He feels that he fully meets the principle, as opposed to a specific theory, enunciated in Chalcedon, which

Alan Richardson summarises (*Creeds in the Making*, SCM Press, London, 1951, pp. 84f) as follows:

> We are free to suggest any theory about the mode of the Incarnation which commends itself to us, provided we do not lose sight of the fundamental truth that God and man are brought together in the Person of Jesus Christ.

In short, it would appear that it is quite erroneous to attribute Nestorianism to the christology of Pittenger because, in the spirit of Richardson, he claims that 'Our Lord is, for Christian faith, One who is truly divine, truly human, truly a personal unity in which these two are comprised' (ibid., p. 96), and he makes these points frequently and convincingly enough for us to accept what he says; for him, Jesus Christ is one. In such acceptance, however, honesty obliges us to notice that some of the long-standing questions in christology have gone unnoticed, for example, how the person of the human nature is related to that of the divine nature, if Jesus Christ is to be said to have one person – a subject to which we shall return in discussing Macquarrie's christology.

There is one important element absent from this account of Pittenger's defence of the union of the two natures of Jesus Christ as he sees it. It is absent because, strangely, Pittenger himself does not produce it at the crucial stage of his defence. I refer to the notion that the unity of God and man in Jesus Christ is penetrated and sustained by the fact of their love for one another. The constituent parts of that notion are present in all that he has said before. God is present throughout his creation, not least in the loving indwelling through his Logos which energises their *nisus* and provides them with the lure of the potentiality in his purpose for them. This loving indwelling is at its supreme in the presence of the Logos in Jesus Christ. But the humanity reciprocates with a responding love, commitment and devotion, fulfilling that purpose which God in his providence had determined from the beginning of time. At an early stage in *Christology Reconsidered* (p. 12), as we noted, Pittenger claims that the union of godhead and manhood in Jesus Christ is to be understood in terms of the personal analogy of the marriage of the Lover and the Beloved, which reflects his commendation of Nestorius' original use of the word συνάφεια (*sunapheia*), to model the relationship. This analogy goes far to remove any uneasiness left by the notion of the Logos using the manhood of Jesus Christ as the *organon* of his Self-Expression, for it is inconceivable that the Lover and the Beloved would ever have been in the relation of end and means, or employer and instrument. So now we may even make bold to say that the presence of the Logos in Jesus Christ is the Self-Manifestation of humanity, the fulfilment of what God in his love presented as the actualisation in this man of the perfect Divine Image. In the same way we shall say, not that the divinity is revealed through the humanity of Jesus Christ, but rather that the whole, integrated event or occasion of Jesus Christ, the God–man, is the revelation of God.

This understanding of Pittenger's defence of the unity of Jesus Christ against the dualist Nestorian implications of some of the criticisms aimed at him is the key to another way in which he speaks of Jesus Christ, this time returning to process language. He sees a reflection of the unity of Jesus Christ in the description of Jesus Christ as the 'emergence' of God–manhood. This term is intended to affirm the continuity between God's presence through his Logos in creation and in men and women and his presence in Jesus Christ, and also Jesus Christ's continuity with his brothers and sisters in whom that Logos also dwells and whom he inspires. But the term 'emergence' also denotes that the upside of these continuities is a discontinuity: the novelty, the uniqueness of this presence of God with man which is the God–man. Pittenger here is seeking to avoid the implications of a strictly evolutionary theory of Jesus Christ, which would regard him as standing at the end of a process which had begun in the lowest forms of creation, even, as some would say, in the inanimate world, with the Logos energising the upward movement and the creatures responding to the Logos in a process of mutual prehension. On such a theory the reductionist has no difficulty in suggesting that the so-called God–man, Jesus Christ, is no more than a rearrangement of constituents which have been present from the start of creation. On the contrary, Pittenger claims that the God–man is the novelty which, while analogically describable in terms of the previous process of the Logos indwelling creation and creatures responding to his presence, is nevertheless different in respects which distinguish him from all that has gone before. I have to draw attention here to a point to which Pittenger alludes but never, in the two books we are considering, altogether fully explains, which is of major importance to this part of his exposition, namely, the distinction between immanence and incarnation. In a short reference (*The Word Incarnate*, pp. 103f) to a work by S. F. Davenport, *Immanence and Incarnation* (Cambridge University Press, Cambridge 1925), he seems to agree both with the distinction drawn by the author and his use of the term incarnation as the more proper basis for christology than immanence, the latter being the *opus* of the Holy Spirit. But Pittenger takes exception to Davenport on three grounds, the first being the assignment of the Logos only to his presence in Jesus Christ, whereas, as we have observed on a number of occasions, Pittenger finds the Logos operative in, within and throughout creation. The second ground is his rejection of Davenport's reason for affirming the distinction in the first place, namely, because immanence may exist in degrees but incarnation occurs without degrees, is absolute and can occur but once, that is, in Jesus Christ – a subject to which Pittenger returns on several occasions. The third and final objection to Davenport is the latter's acceptance of *enhypostasis*, due, no doubt, to the influence of H. M. Relton's, *Study of Christology* (SPCK, London, 1917), a book which, with its unearthing of Leontius of Byzantium, has more than most others determined the flow of controversy in christology in the twentieth century. Again, it is the affirmation of the impersonal nature of the humanity of Christ which Pittenger cannot tolerate. So passionate is Pittenger's commitment to the unity of Jesus Christ, so varied are the ways in which he argues for it, that we have to conclude that it is quite erroneous to lay at his door any charge of Nestorianism as the term is used by heresy-hunters of any generation. A more extended inquiry would be necessary if we were to reach a conclusion on the question of how far he would go in support of the 'real' Nestorius, for he seems to have sympathies in that direction, but it is questionable whether there is access to sufficiently reliable documented evidence on what Nestorius actually did think to enable us to form an accurate judgement. In any case such a matter is not germane to our present discussion. What remains to be examined, however, is the exact nature of the unity which Pittenger ascribes to Jesus Christ, as well as the degree to which it transcends the dualism which is so central an element in his analysis. The examination of these and similar questions will form the substance of our final assessment of this third type of process christology.

ENCOUNTERING GOD IN JESUS CHRIST

Our exposition of Pittenger's christology has been structured on three propositions which he defines as 'three elements in the christological enterprise'. So far, we have been dealing with the second and third of these 'elements', the one dealing in effect with the genuinely historical humanity of Jesus Christ, and the other with the relations of the divinity and the humanity in Jesus Christ to one another. To complete our presentation we return to the first element, which reads: 'there is a firm conviction that in some fashion we meet God in the event of Jesus Christ'. The illogicality of taking the first last may be atoned for by the considerations that to do justice to it we require to draw on what Pittenger has said in arguing the two other elements, and that it is the most important element of the three, for it asks whether, when the person of Jesus Christ has been interpreted in the style of Pittenger, it is still the case that his christology shows us how men and women encounter the living Christ.

Without arguing for total equivalence of statements, I would suggest that Pittenger, in his first elemental principle, is saying that his christology will have to do justice to what traditional christology has called 'the deity of Christ'. He offers us several ways of conserving this first element. For example, given that God is operative throughout the whole universe, enfolding it and moulding it by love towards his purposes and in conformity with his will, his presence is uniquely focused in the humanity of Jesus Christ. Refining the point somewhat, Pittenger says (*The Word Incarnate*, pp. 194, 196) that the Word of God, the eternal Logos who is the Self-Expression of God, is supremely active and most completely manifested in the humanity of Christ, 'the focal point or concentration of divine activity in terms of humanity' (ibid.).

The variation in terms in this last sentence, faithful as they are to Pittenger's own description of these matters, raises the subject of nomenclature which he regards as important. We recall (above, pp. 202–9, 212ff) the many efforts of Cobb to distinguish the names of Christ and the different purposes to which he put these names. Pittenger is far less hair-splitting and, as he himself admits, is not always entirely consistent. His principal definition of terms is to say that the term 'Logos' or 'Word' should be applied only within the trinitarian reference, to the second person in the Godhead, whereas the term 'Son' is applicable only to the incarnate Lord, though uniquely he would himself prefer to use the term 'God Self-Expressive'. To complete his lexicon, he would use the usual term 'Jesus Christ' for the incarnate Lord.

Pittenger examines two matters concerning the presence of God or the Logos in Jesus Christ, which have been central to christological discussions for at least a century now. First, at p. 196 of *The Word Incarnate*, we are told that the talk of Jesus Christ being the focus of God's Self-Expression in the humanity of Jesus Christ does not imply that the whole of God is incarnate, or that that Self-Expression exhausts the totality of God's revelation. Pittenger allows for the 'mystery' of the operation of the Logos throughout the rest of creation, insisting, however, that God's activity there is consistent and of one piece with the supreme Self-Expression in Jesus Christ. He safeguards his statement in another direction by claiming that God's Self-Expression in Jesus Christ is 'for man, as it is in man that it takes place' (ibid.). It is interesting, too, that despite his reading of H. R. Mackintosh and his agreement with him over the problems of *anhypostasis* and *enhypostasis*, he at no time considers the kenotic theory of the person of Christ which Mackintosh made popular for decades in both England and Scotland. That fullness of the Godhead which the human situation in all its sordidness and glory requires for its salvation and its making whole is affirmed in the incarnation. Indeed, the kenotic position which Mackintosh affirmed would be totally out of place in the model which Pittenger is so carefully constructing.

The second matter relating to the presence of God in Jesus Christ is of considerable importance to Pittenger, for he feels strongly that the case has not been made against him. It is the question whether the difference between the presence of God or the Logos in Jesus Christ, and his presence in ordinary men and women and throughout creation generally, is a difference in degree or a difference of kind. The charge against him, one which he shares with Donald M. Baillie and Nels Ferré, is that he holds a 'degree-christology'. Pittenger had already laid a firm foundation for the refutation of this charge in his application of the emergence notion to the God–man, when he argued, in effect, that the presence of God in Jesus Christ is to be described on the analogy of his presence in mankind and nature generally, and the negative element in this analogy is the unique novelty of God's presence in Jesus Christ. True emergence implies that at the higher level, something, or rather, in this case, Someone, appears who is both continuous with the earlier stages of the emergence and discontinuous. Pittenger is particularly anxious to hold to both these features of the highest emergent. On the one hand, by abandoning the element of continuity he would make too great a concession to Barth and more so the Barthians who, with their theme of Christ coming *senkrecht von oben*, rather than as the Logos working within, would endanger the full humanity of Jesus Christ. On the other hand, by surrendering the discontinuity, he would be making common cause with those liberals and modernists who think of deity as humanity writ large. Though he does not himself make this point, what he is saying about the difference in question is that it is both a difference in *degree* and a difference in *kind*. The closest he comes

to such a summing-up of the controversy is the acknowledgement that in some circumstances a difference in degree is so great
that it becomes a difference in kind – an argument which appears
later in the exchange between John Hick and John Baillie over
the christology of Donald M. Baillie.

So far we have been considering largely the theological case
which Pittenger makes for his claim that he has met the first
element in his analysis of the christological enterprise, by
showing how he upholds what is classically called the deity of
Jesus Christ. But by doing so we have stated less than his full
case, for he has still a pragmatic answer to give (ibid., pp. 190ff)
to the question of our meeting God in the encounter with Jesus
Christ, as he has described him. In the end, there is only the
experiential answer to that question. But the christologist has an
immense responsibility – to facilitate that response by removing
the impediments to its happening. He would argue, for example,
that neo-Chalcedonian, enhypostatic theories of the person of
Jesus Christ have produced inadequate, less than human, and
consequently unattractive, accounts of Jesus Christ, and that his
own fully human, personally and psychologically complete view
of Jesus Christ assists the enquirer on the way to the
understanding which leads to faith. Steps in that same direction
are taken by his portrayal at many points of the essential being of
God as love, and the loving operation of the Logos, seen in Jesus
Christ, indwelling both nature and mankind and reacting with
them prehensively. As he also says, Jesus Christ 'releases into the
world a new stream of divine energy' (ibid., p. 167) through the
quality of his life and teaching and by the love expressed in his
death and resurrection. Such a portrayal is not an academic
exercise, but is in the nature of an invitation to hearers and
readers to test for themselves the authenticity of the claims
which the Church has made for Christ across the centuries, by
participating in communion, fellowship, prayer and worship.
The ultimate response to such an invitation is decision and
commitment by believers and their loving acceptance by the
community which is the Church into the body of the Christ
who still lives. Presenting his case in these terms, Pittenger has

amply fulfilled the demand of his first element in the christological enterprise, in indicating the nature of the encounter that he sees taking place between the believer and Jesus Christ and – perhaps even more importantly – the ways in which that believer may respond to the invitation of Christ to come and follow him. In fact, in both of the books we have been considering, he concludes with what amounts to an evangelical challenge to discipleship. The fact that the books end in this way is a tribute to his overall theological method, which supplements the Anselmic *credo ut intelligam* with its converse, *intelligo ut credam*.

OVERALL ASSESSMENT

Pittenger, it will be recalled, stated what he considered to be three elemental principles to which any christology ought to conform, three criteria by which, in the honouring of them, any proposed christology should stand or fall. It would appear that on the whole his christology meets these requirements. First, for example, he has presented the humanity of Christ as genuinely identical to that shared by all his sisters and brothers, with body, soul and intellect and its own centre of the many experiences to which such humanity is heir. In fact, as we saw, one of his recurrent themes, as well as his motivating complaint, is that the concept of humanity associated with both Chalcedonian and neo-Chalcedonian christology is lacking in a truly human centre, even being called 'impersonal', and he insists on the wholeness of the humanity of Christ. Secondly, he has argued strongly for the full presence in Jesus Christ of Godhead and manhood, their compresence in him being both continuous and, emergently, discontinuous with the presence of the Logos in all humanity and the rest of creation. Avoiding the trap of Nestorianism, he nevertheless holds strongly to the integrated unity of the person of Jesus Christ, claiming that the relation of Godhead and manhood in this unity is not to be understood in logical categories but in terms of the bond of love. Thirdly, in meeting the criterion that the person of Jesus Christ should be supremely the revelation of God, he himself makes an evangelical invitation to those who read, listen and understand to respond by offering themselves in commitment, obedience and love to Jesus Christ. The quality of such a response would ultimately be the only indication as to whether his christology had met this criterion. Since, therefore, it would seem that Pittenger's christology is highly credible and could be assured of a place in the witness of the Church to the person of Jesus Christ, why is it that we are left with a feeling that the full christological enterprise has not been completed? My suspicion is that, detailed and comprehensive as Pittenger's works are, there are nevertheless some questions remaining over from traditional christology, in excess of those dealt with by his three 'elements' fundamental to christology. These call for examination, not least because some of them arise in direct relation to Pittenger's theory. We shall now consider these 'remainders', and return to ask how far that consideration affects the overall assessment of Pittenger's christology.

THE SUBJECT OF THE INCARNATE LORD, AND THE UNITY OF THE PERSON OF JESUS CHRIST

We have just mentioned how strongly worded were Pittenger's criticism of the so-called impersonal character of the humanity of Jesus Christ as portrayed by Chalcedonian and neo-Chalcedonian christology, and his insistence upon the complete humanity of Christ. In fact, so committed was he to that position that he came near to exposing himself to a charge which E. L. Mascall (*Via Media*, Longmans, London, 1956, p. 90), brought against the Nestorians, that they 'were prepared to worship Jesus of Nazareth as divine, while holding that he was indwelt by divinity' – in the case of Pittenger, by the Logos. We have already, as we thought, exculpated Pittenger of the charge of Nestorianism. But, returning to it for a minute, we can see that, if we turned the edge of Mascall's criticism of Nestorians on to

Pittenger, he could be construed as holding that the humanity of Jesus Christ is in-filled with the divinity of the Logos, and for that reason we worship Jesus Christ as divine. In Pittenger's words (*The Word Incarnate*, p. 91), his own view is that 'God the Word . . . became incarnate as a man, the man Jesus Christ'. Or, as he says later (ibid., p. 185), 'God always reveals himself, as he always acts . . . in the terms appropriate to and provided by the vehicle of his self-disclosure and operation'. Relating these quotations to our original problem, we may ask, Who, then, is the subject of the incarnation? Since whatever happens in the event of the incarnation is describable in the first instance in human terms, *ad modum recipientis*, it would appear that the humanity of Jesus Christ, or 'the man that was called Jesus', is the subject of the incarnation. Yet there must be more, and it appears when Pittenger says, '. . . the specific revelation in Jesus Christ is not disclosed as something "added to the creaturely" but is apprehended in faith through the very conditions of the creaturely' (ibid., p. 185). In other words, even if the *grammatical* sentences about Jesus Christ have his humanity as their subject, in fact the sentences are 'about' the whole event of Jesus Christ, which includes what is 'apprehended in faith'. So the word 'revelation', in a few short steps, takes us back to what we said in discussing the revelation model and to the earlier reminder that the revelation model is a second-order model and depends for its content on some of the other first-order models. Or, to state the matter in another way, the *epistemological* subject of the sentences about Jesus Christ, his life and mission, his redemptive death and his resurrection, is the entire revelatory event, with divine and human components, carrying information about men and women, the world and nature, as well as understanding of God and his being, his essential goodness and his goodwill towards us.

But even so, the whole truth has not yet appeared concerning the question of the subject of sentences about Jesus Christ. For in his reaction to a possible charge of Nestorianism, Pittenger had replied rather sharply that, in his theory, given that the humanity of Jesus Christ is the perfect *organon* for the

Self-Expression of the Logos, in the union of the *organon* and the Word they are integrally one (ibid., p. 188) and the union is an '*ontological* union' (ibid., p. 197). So emphatic is Pittenger's language that it would be forgivable to accuse him of mono-physitism, even remembering the four classical Chalcedonian adverbs which he has himself invoked. For the four adverbs apply to the two natures (*physeis*), and their unity is located in the person (*hypostasis*) of Jesus Christ; there is never any question of the Godhead and manhood of Jesus Christ becoming organically united. The meaning of the phrases 'ontological union' and 'organic union' is difficult to fix; but in other theological discussions, for example in ecumenical cases, organic union is taken to entail the total integration of one system with another to create something more comprehensive than either and totally unitary.

It would appear, then, that Pittenger, in his self-defence against the charge of Nestorianism, has gone too far in the opposite direction in his anxiety to secure the unity in Jesus Christ of Godhead and manhood. Now, that may appear to be an unusually harsh and undeserved judgement, for has he not said, either explicitly or implicitly, that the union has grammatical, epistemological and ontological aspects? Truth to tell, I was somewhat disappointed that he did not follow up a view which he expresses from time to time, that the relationship between Godhead and manhood in Jesus Christ is the relationship of love. This account ensures that manhood is not absorbed by Godhead in the unity, thus preserving the truth of the Chalcedonian adverbs. On the other hand, the union of Logos and manhood in Jesus Christ is not jeopardised, for the fact that the relation-ship is one of love entails a high degree of integration, short of absorption of one by the other. It was the view from which we began our account of the relation of Godhead to humanity in Jesus Christ (above, p. 238), but, it will be recalled, that relationship was said to be an analogy. So while the relation closely resembles human love, there is greater interpenetration of spirit, higher identity of purpose, a purer degree of shared love, than is ever possible on the human level or even between the saint and God. My firm conclusion is that it is wrong to try to convert that unity of the Logos and the humanity of Christ into any kind of logical category, for fear of making it, to use Pittenger's own word, 'static'; at that point we must desist from searching for equivalences with Chalcedonian christology, and abandon talk of 'ontological union', 'integrated unity', or the humanity of Christ being an *organon* of the Logos. I feel that this conclusion is inevitable for anyone who, like Pittenger, has opted for a fully contemporary concept of the human person in preference to any theory of *enhypostasis* or *anhypostasis*. In a word, there is no logical bridge between the unity which Pittenger claims for the person of Christ and that degree of distinction which has to be preserved in order to avoid the charge of monophysitism, and which is essential to the love relationship, even at the highest level.

PART IV

NEO-CHALCEDONIAN CHRISTOLOGY

10

JOHN MACQUARRIE

The process theologians whose christological writings we have been discussing have, on the one hand, quite explicitly abandoned the classical metaphysical framework which has provided a scaffold for christology for some 1,600 years; and, on the other hand, they have been equally explicit about the alternative philosophical system which they propose to use. How far they have been successful in their drive for independence from the classical forms has been a subject for inquiry. We turn now to John Macquarrie's *Jesus Christ in Modern Thought* (SCM Press, London, 1990), surely in many ways the true successor of H. R. Mackintosh's *The Doctrine of the Person of Jesus Christ* (T. & T. Clark, Edinburgh, 1912), which straddled the history of British christology for some six decades after its publication. Macquarrie shares two convictions with the process theologians. First, he finds that the metaphysics employed in classical christology used technical philosophical language which no longer has any significance for our contemporaries. He dates the 'tidal wave' which has swept away so much traditional thinking about Christ back to the Enlightenment and the writing of Reimarus, and he traces its course through Kant, Schleiermacher, Hegel, Strauss, Ritschl, Harnack and many others. From the 1930s onwards this 'tidal wave' of doubt of the validity of traditional christology and its metaphysical components gained further impetus from the linguistic analysis which dominated philosophy generally for some forty years and greatly distorted theological discussion for roughly the same period. The main component of this process of philosophical deconstruction was in effect the *reductio ad absurdum* of metaphysical and, by implication, theological language. Secondly, and notwithstanding, Macquarrie affirms that 'Metaphysics or ontology in some form or another is not finally dispensable in any adequate christology' (op. cit., p. 344); he cites, in support, Donald M. Mackinnon, 'The simplest affirmation, for instance, concerning Christ's relation to the Father, must include the use of the sorts of notions of which ontology seeks to give account' ('"Substance" in Christology – A Cross-bench View', in S. W. Sykes and I. P. Clayton (eds), *Christ, Faith and History*, Cambridge University Press, Cambridge, 1972, p. 288). At that point, the similarity with the process theologians seems to end, for whereas they are explicit in their choice, there is a question over what exact metaphysics or ontology it is that Macquarrie has elected to use in his christological statement.

Throughout the book, Macquarrie quotes and illustrates from the history of christology a distinction which is now widely accepted, between christology 'from above' as seen in classical christology and christology 'from below' as expounded by Rahner, Pannenberg and Robinson. When he sets out, therefore, to make his own mark, he adopts the latter, interpreting it to mean that christology must take as its starting-point the humanity of Christ. This humanity is not the reduced version of the Chalcedonian creed or of its post-Chalcedon interpreters, but one which is wholly and fully human as we are. In fact, given the contemporary secular *Zeitgeist*, if we ever hope to communicate with our generation we have to address them, not in terms of some elusive 'God', but where they are and in terms of the humanity which, with all its mystery, they do to some degree understand. However, if christology with such a beginning is in the end to be adequate to its subject – the whole person of Jesus Christ – it still has to deal with the question of the way in which God is especially present in this man, a question which Macquarrie keeps clear in his sights as he develops his position.

MACQUARRIE'S CHRISTOLOGY

THE HUMANITY OF JESUS CHRIST

The subject of what humanity is arises immediately for a christological beginning 'from below', and Macquarrie is not slow to indicate the highs and lows of human self-understanding, and the variety of attempts in the years since the Enlightenment to isolate the peculiar *humanum* from among human characteristics. On occasion, as with Nietzsche and some scientists, humanity is credited with unlimited powers over the rest of the universe and its components, and even over the future. At other times, the bubble is pricked and the human race is given a place within the evolutionary process evident in nature, subject to its laws and dependent upon it for material resources. Macquarrie strikes a mean between these two excesses, arguing that humanity represents the emergence of a new entity in the planet, with limited intelligence, freedom and conscience; but for its proper understanding we shall require distinctive concepts inapplicable to lower forms of existence. Whereas Kant had opted for autonomy in his analysis of the *proprium* of humanity, Macquarrie selects the notion of 'transcendence' for that purpose. Its application to christology, as distinct from its usage in the doctrine of God, is to be found extensively in J. B. Cobb, Jr's *Christ in a Pluralistic Age* (cf. above pp. 201ff). To clarify his understanding of the concept, Macquarrie draws a distinction between the static sense in which the term is used and a dynamic sense. The former is first apparent when the term is applied to God, and is classically regarded as equivalent to that 'infinite qualitative difference', spoken of by Kierkegaard, which enshrines the superiority of God in all respects over mankind. Cultural movements, influenced by scientific thinking in the past two or three centuries, tended to extend that superiority of God over creation to the superiority of humanity over the natural order, even when humanity was still regarded as part of nature. On the other hand, Macquarrie unpacks the concept of dynamic transcendence in a series of carefully thought-out steps (op.

cit., p. 363). First, he begins by using the etymological source of the term, with its idea of going over or beyond the limits of one's own territory into uncharted country, 'moving from one horizon to another' (ibid.), these limits and horizons retreating indefinitely. Secondly, here Macquarrie senses 'the germ of a religious element'. This notion, which turns out to be so central to his presentation of the humanity of Christ, is equated with 'a taste of the infinite', which is the attraction luring – to use the process term – humanity into the process of dynamic transcendence. Thirdly, it is proposed as a 'perhaps' that there is a previously existing 'affinity', later called a 'reciprocity', between this infinite and humanity, which accounts for the attraction. Fourthly, the religious connotation of these terms is now given clear expression, when it is construed in terms of the mythological biblical story of the creation of man and woman in the image of God. This image is not, however, to be understood, as it has so often been in the past, as *dominium*, or reason, but rather as 'spirit'. Spirit may then be regarded as the basis of affinity between God and humanity and the principle of transcendence, of growth towards God and the ability both to receive God and to make him manifest. Fifthly, Macquarrie, continuing with the mode of possibility in the use of the word 'perhaps' in the previous step, considers that there might be a human being in whom that image of God resides, not defaced as it is in the rest of humanity but perfect in all respects and capable of limitless transcendence. If there were, that being would be 'God's existence in the world' (op. cit., p. 371), and could be described as 'God–man' conceived within the conditions of human existence. Sixthly, Macquarrie now switches mode from possibility to actuality, with the acknowledgement that in the biblical–Christian witness the 'possible' God–man outlined in the previous steps was and is actuality. He is, however, emphatic that christology 'from below', as he has outlined it, is the starting-point and requires as its complement christology 'from above', which brings out the prevenient and the pre-eminent part which God plays in the events which constitute the Christ-event. Seventhly, the relation of the humanity of this God–man to ourselves is that of representative human being. In a living experience of him that spans the centuries, in worship, sermon, sacrament and prayer, we too acknowledge that he is the realisation of all our aspirations as human beings, 'an archetype, an ideal, a lure, which draws us on' (op. cit., p. 374). Not least, this attraction is felt in the love to which he gave so much prominence – love to God, love to all mankind, love even to nature.

THE DIVINITY OF JESUS CHRIST

Although the christology from below, or humanistic christology, to which Macquarrie has been referring, has several contemporary exponents, such as Rahner, Pannenberg and Pittenger, it can be traced, he claims, not just to Schleiermacher but even as far back as Irenaeus and, with less certainty, to Maximus the Confessor. Early in that tradition there appeared the term *theopoiesis*, deification of humanity, primarily in relation to the statement of Irenaeus: 'The Word of God became what we are that he might make us what he himself is.' But if we extend it to apply to what happened to humanity in Christ, it gives us the corresponding term *enanthropesis*, 'inhumanisation' or incarnation, the theme of christology from above. The question which immediately arises is how these two processes, the deification of humanity and the inhumanisation of God, are related to one another – probably one of the major problems that any christology has to face. Macquarrie, anxious to silence any premature charges of adoptionism or pelagianism, makes it very plain that it is inhumanisation which conditions deification. 'All this is from God' (2 Cor 5.18). Recalling the notion of transcendence which we noted recently, with the distinction between static and dynamic transcendence, he proposes that the dynamic sense is attributable to God, even in a primary logical sense over its human application. God thus understood in the Christian context, and despite the contrary weight from considerable areas of Old Testament teaching in favour of the idea of the otherness of God, is not wholly wrapped up in himself but rather, by virtue of his nature, goes forth from himself – one would add, in love for the other, the whole of mankind. Inhumanisation is the process in which God goes out beyond all previous boundaries and horizons to be with his people, indwelling a nature one with theirs.

Macquarrie offers another context in which to regard the dynamic transcendence of God which takes the form of the incarnation. The incarnation, he argues, might be less than credible if the presence of God in Christ were an anomaly in a created order from which he was totally absent. On the contrary, not only does God communicate, in whatever different ways, with the whole of creation, but there is in every person the capacity of self-transcendence (the essence of humanity) and openness Godward, supremely in evidence in Jesus Christ. He is that summation of that presence of God in the cosmos, and of consummate openness to God on the human part, which constitutes his especial status as revelation – both of God and humanity. It is as if, in the words of both Pittenger and Macquarrie, God focuses the essence of his Being and the ultimate of his self-communication at this point in human history.

COMPATIBLE WITH CHALCEDON?

At an earlier point we noted Macquarrie's agreement with the present general feeling about the unreality of the terminology of Chalcedon; but before he departs the present discussion he feels constrained to answer the question, 'How does the christology which he has been outlining relate to the Chalcedonian formula?' Because of its continuing use in confessions and liturgies, he now accords it 'a certain normative status' (op. cit., p. 383), so that, whether we are stating a christology in the fourth, the sixteenth or the twentieth century, we have to assess our formulae by their conformity with Chalcedon. But since the words of that creed are time-conditioned, they carry no significance for our contemporaries and cannot, in their original sense, be allowed normative status. Rather, that role is assigned to something called 'governing intention', 'that can never be expressed apart from words, yet may be capable of expression in many verbal formulations' (ibid.). Macquarrie's hope is that the christology he offers, first, remains within the parameters of classical christology and, secondly, says in its own terms exactly what that christology said in the terms of another day. The latter hope is reminiscent of Barth's words as he set out on the enterprise of his *Church Dogmatics*, that 'we must say to our generation in its language what the apostles and prophets said to theirs in their language'.

In order, therefore, to make the necessary assessment, Macquarrie demonstrates how his expressions individually match the classical terms and formulae. For example, he has no great difficulty in claiming that the term *ousia* is more appropriately translated 'being', than the classical 'substance' which has in recent times acquired the association of solidity. In line with the process influence, he would wish to add to being, becoming, as apparent in all transcendent beings. The word *hypostasis* had a fluctuating career from the third to sixth centuries in trinitarian as well as christological debate. However, though there is now general agreement that the appropriate translation for our day remains 'person', new problems have arisen through the variety of connotations of the word, and even of philosophical schools which have arisen around it. Finally, in regard to the term *physis*, usually translated 'nature', we have already in the study of the humanity of Jesus Christ, had an inkling of the way in which Macquarrie is going to treat this term. It is not to be thought of in the static, self-contained sense suggested by the notion of essence, or as it was commonly used in the old logic, which thought of the nature of an entity as definable in a list of its distinguishing characteristics or *per genus et differentiam*. Rather, we return to the notion of transcendence which was the *proprium* of humanity and in the present reference is the clue to regarding human nature as in a sense unfulfilled and incomplete, but reaching beyond itself and, as was said earlier, lured by the infinite. *A fortiori*, the nature of God, who is in so many ways unknowable, will not be confined within a definition. He, too, is transcendent, surpassing his own horizons and reaching out in love to the creatures of his hand. Macquarrie gathers together the accounts of the nature of man and the nature of God within a single rubric when he says, 'we move away from "nature" (*physis*) as a fixed essence to the dynamic or processive understanding of *physis* as "emergence" or "coming into being"'. By offering his 'translations' of these Chalcedonian concepts, Macquarrie would claim that he had fulfilled the norm of communicating the content of Chalcedon to his contemporaries in contemporary terms.

There remains, however, a further element in the Chalcedonian formula which might be considered to be more of a problem for Macquarrie, namely, the relation of the human and the divine natures to one another in the unity of the person of Jesus Christ. Given that both the natures are in the process of emerging or transcending, then they may be said (op. cit., p. 385) to 'concur' in the person of Jesus Christ, to use the word which appears towards the end of the creed of Chalcedon. The one nature, humanity, is seeking its fulfilment in fellowship with, obedience to, and love for, God; while the other nature, God, is transcending himself, to be present in that person who will be the supreme expression of his love for mankind, who will return that love in its fullness and who will be the most complete manifestation of his purpose for his people. Macquarrie has here used the term 'concur' to describe the relationship of the two natures of, or in, Jesus Christ; he expressed a similar view earlier (op. cit., p. 380), that the incarnation is the 'meeting-point at which the transcendence of humanity from below is met by the divine transcendence from above'. An early description (op. cit., p. 375) of the relation of the two natures to one another, which is only understood in the light of the whole chapter on 'The divinity of Jesus Christ', is that they are not mutually contradictory or exclusive, in the sense in which Schleiermacher said that one person could not share two natures. Rather, they are to be regarded as different perspectives on the same event, the idea of 'perspective' appearing later in the chapter (p. 382).

ASSESSMENT

As we have already recorded, Macquarrie himself (op. cit., p. 383) asks the question, 'How far does the christology so far expounded agree with the traditional teaching of the church as expressed in the formula of Chalcedon?' He acknowledges the importance of the question, because on the one hand that creed has acquired normative status within the historical church; and on the other hand, to ignore or abandon it altogether would amount to denying our own Christian identity. What, then, is to be the third way which he is considering, which lies between literal acceptance and outright rejection of Chalcedon? It is a singularly difficult process to define exactly, and has been the source of a great deal of controversy when used in theological discussion, for it is in effect a double process. It involves first the discernment of the so-called 'governing intention', in this case embodied in the Chalcedonian formula; and secondly, the formulation of contemporary words to express it. The 'governing intention', which exists only in verbal form, may therefore mean several things: for example, what the speaker intends to convey to readers or listeners by the words, or the actual meaning of the words which is somehow contained within them. The new form of words is intended to convey that same meaning to a different generation. The exercise is not unlike the activity of translating sentences from one language into another language. Looked at in logical terms, the construction of a contemporary christology proceeds as follows: given a creed with sentences a, b, c . . . which include strictly theological names and concepts as well as elements from the then contemporary culture, metaphysics, moral values and so on, the christologist, after understanding the sentences as far as he can, seeks to formulate sentences A, B, C . . . which again will include theological names and concepts and the above-mentioned elements, this time from present-day contexts. It is then his hope that he will be able to convey to his present-day listeners, in their culture, etc. what the original credal sentences conveyed to the listeners in the far-off days. So our task in assessing Macquarrie's presentation will be to see how far he has succeeded in making that translation and achieved the intention of the formulators of Chalcedon.

A SHORT ANSWER

Clearly, the determination of the authenticity of a modern statement claiming to be a fair transcript of an ancient creed will hinge largely upon the criteria we choose to apply to it. In the case before us we may apply either of two sets of criteria, the one yielding a somewhat brief answer, the other being much more extended. For the first criteria, I wish to go back to what Norman Pittenger called 'three essential elements in the christological enterprise' (*Christology Reconsidered*, pp. 6–14), which we have, of course, considered in relation to his christology. They are, first, 'the firm conviction that in some fashion we meet God in the event of Jesus Christ'. Second, 'the equally firm conviction that God is thus met in a genuine, historically conditioned, and entirely human being'. Third, 'the assurance that God, met in that man, and the man in whom God is met, are in relationship to one another, in a manner or mode which is neither accidental not incidental but the most complete interpenetration' (op. cit., p. 7). These criteria I would say Macquarrie meets. For example, he argues strongly, with a variety of arguments and statements, for the view that in Jesus Christ, believers are aware of being in the presence of God. He speaks of God focusing his presence and activity in Jesus Christ. His analysis of the notion of transcendence, in contradistinction to the idea of God's being *totaliter aliter*, wholly other, favours Hartshorne's view that God 'surpasses himself' to become involved in time and history, and supremely in that man whose life was wholly open to him and his love. Now there may be some residual suspicion that Macquarrie is guilty of a form of gradualism, thinking of God as invading humanity and history stage by stage in a process of emergence, and Jesus as part of such a process, soon to be himself surpassed. But he refutes the very idea with his repeated contention that, while God's focusing his presence in Jesus Christ is different only in degree from his ingression into the world and all humanity, that difference in degree is unique and, as John Baillie often argued, might well be regarded as a difference in kind, though never in any sense absolute. Some readers might want to question the brevity of Macquarrie's account of the *being* of the God who is so uniquely present in Jesus Christ, which is so comprehensively set out in traditional accounts of the classical christologies. Macquarrie has an immediate reply in that, in Part One of his book, he has set out a comprehensive understanding of the being of the God of the incarnation in his account of the biblical views of the person of Christ and the being of God, as well as in the classical and other christologies which have followed. What has been said there may justifiably be pre-supposed when he writes of 'the divinity of Jesus Christ'.

Pittenger's second requirement of a sound christology was that it should present Jesus Christ as 'a genuine, historically-conditioned and entirely human being', and there is no doubt that Macquarrie's account of Christ's humanity meets this desideratum. He shares completely Pittenger's dissatisfaction with the Chalcedonian and neo-Chalcedonian notion of *anhypostasia*, that the human nature of Christ was lacking a *hypostasis*, a human 'person'. On the contrary, Jesus was fully 'consubstantial' with his human brothers and sisters, sharing the fullness of their humanity, particularly in two respects. First, as human, Jesus Christ shares in the capacity for tran-scendence, advancing beyond perceived horizons, attracted by the infinite, responding to the lure of love and perfection. Secondly, as human, he too shares in being in the image of God, construed not as dominion or reason but as spirit, in reciprocity with his fellows and with God. But what of the 'historically-conditioned' element in the humanity of Christ as Macquarrie sees it? He has, in fact, dealt with it comprehensively, both by sketching the changing understanding of the 'historical question' in the history of christology, and by outlining the importance and the content of historical assertions in christology today. In short, Macquarrie has met the second of Pittenger's desiderata in a christology.

The third requirement is more complex. It stipulates that the God met in that man Jesus, and that man in whom God is met, are not related to one another accidentally or incidentally, but in a manner of the most complete interpenetration. Pittenger took great care to demonstrate how he met this requirement (see above, pp. 240ff), and went on to say that it was love which was the bond between humanity and divinity in Jesus Christ, between the man Jesus and God. Once again. I would say, Macquarrie meets the requirement – in fact, by using several concepts. For example, he speaks of Jesus Christ as the meeting-point of the transcendence of humanity and the transcendence of divinity; of the raising of a human life to a capacity for divine revelation made possible only through the descent of God into that life; and of humanity pursuing its fulfilment in its search for God, and concurring with God, in his love for his whole creation, manifesting himself in the one being who has been totally open and receptive to him. It would be fair, also, to say that each of these slightly different concepts implies some level, even a high level, of interpenetration of the two natures, described as they are in process emergent terms. What I miss somewhat from Macquarrie's account of the relationship of the two natures to one another in Jesus Christ is the emphasis upon the love of the one to the other, reciprocated in the person of Jesus Christ, which characterised Pittenger's account, in spite of his strong statements on the integrated, organic unity of the two which raised the question of monophysitism. Macquarrie does mention love of each for the other, but it is such terms as 'meeting' and 'concurring' which carry weight.

THE LONGER ANSWER

The assessment might rest there, and perhaps we shall say in the end that it ought to. But Macquarrie opens up a very interesting range of issues when he asks whether he has abandoned Chalcedon in his account of christology; or whether he has made the only kind of sense of it that is possible in a cultural climate in which the metaphysic used at Chalcedon is no longer intelligible or, if it is, then no longer relevant.

Let us take the matter up at the point where we left it at the end of 'the short answer'. In his introductory comments to his account of the divinity of Jesus Christ, Macquarrie affirms that the 'deification' of humanity and the 'inhumanisation' or incarnation of the Logos are 'complementary' processes; they are 'different perspectives' of the same event. The application of the term 'perspective' to what used to be called 'the two natures' gives me pause on certain grounds. For example, a perspective of an object usually in some way distorts the shape of the object perceived, in a way that a two-dimensional diagram does not. A square tower in the distance may have the appearance of being round; a cube lying on the table will, in perspective, have a top which is diamond shape and two sides which are rhomboids. In other words, the perspectives do not give accurate information about the shape of the object perceived. It is only through experience, by combinations of sight assisted by touch, that rectilinear figures of varying quadrilateral combinations can be known to be surfaces of a cube. In other words, a perspective or group of perspectives require the services of a key before they can be the clue to the true shape of an object. But the actual shape of the object is not any one perspective or combination of perspectives. Besides, the perspectives are no more than views of the exterior and do not introduce us to the inner character of the subject. So when the perspective analogy is used of the 'two natures' of Jesus Christ, it seems to me to be less than informative or adequate. The deification of humanity and the inhumanisation of the Logos are not in any sense distorted appearances of the character of the person of Jesus Christ. They are veridically perceived elements in his person, and they are the substance of his inmost being. The problem probably lies deeper. It may be that to speak of the processes of deification of man and inhumanisation of the Logos as perspectives is to make the category mistake of treating them as static entities, a position against which Macquarrie has argued with great persuasion. The two natures are self-transcendent, emergent, dynamic, whereas perspectives are stationary.

If we stay with the perspectives analogy for the description of the Chalcedonian two natures, we encounter yet another problem, namely, the question of who or what corresponds to the person of Jesus Christ. Here I have to draw attention to a confusion which has caused trouble over the years, between the notion of the person of Jesus Christ as, on the one hand, embracing the entirety of what in Chalcedonian terms comprised the two *physeis* (natures) and the *hypostasis* (person); and, on the other hand, denoting only the *hypostasis* of Jesus Christ, who is the subject of the whole Christ-event. It is with the latter that we are now concerned. Two problems come under the guise of one. The first is that, since the two perspectives appear to exhaust the field, there is no *tertium quid*, third entity, who could function as the person in whom they inhere. The two transcendences meet, the one from above and the other from below, each with a *hypostasis*, a person of its own, but their meeting, their concurring, *is* the Christ-event. Only if these two transcendences *per impossibile* merged into one another would there be one person, that of the divine nature; but then the inhumanisation would have disappeared. So this problem could be put in a second way, Who is the subject of the two perspectives which are the translation for the two natures? Now since there has been so much severe criticism of the anhypostatic (impersonal) character of the humanity of Christ as depicted in Chalcedonian and neo-Chalcedonian christology – criticism accepted by both Macquarrie and previously by Pittenger – it is imperative that the subject of deification/inhumanisation should be at least human, and fully human. Equally, for a genuine inhumanisation/deification, it is necessary that the concurring natures also have divine *hypostasis*. Accordingly, we have reached the matter raised by the charge of Nestorianism against Pittenger, and his reply, which quotes the support of an earlier view of Richardson's (p. 244). In the case of Macquarrie, it is a question whether the processes of deification and inhumanisation can be attributed to one *hypostasis*. Prima facie, in order to secure the integrity of the two natures, or the two transcendences, a *hypostasis* for each has to be affirmed, and Nestorianism becomes a real threat. Yet this possibility never seems to arise for Macquarrie. He speaks often of the event of Jesus Christ as if it were integrated and not dualistic, and of the person of Jesus Christ in single terms; but my understanding is that he may be referring to the entire Christ-event rather than to the *hypostasis* who is the subject of that event. So the question of who is the subject of the two natures remains.

There seem to me to be two ways in which we can resolve this problem. The one is general and to some extent pious. It is to follow the suggestion implicit in the quotation from Alan Richardson which, as we have noted, Pittenger has adopted. In our christological statements concerning Jesus Christ, full justice must be done to his humanness and to his divinity, and to the unity of these two in the person of Christ. I have called this response 'pious' because such an affirmation is sufficient for the proclamation of the Christian faith and the support of personal faith in Jesus Christ, and no assistance is required from the sophistications of academic christology. But it is also 'general' in that it does not prescribe any theory as canonical, nor does it proscribe any of the sophistications we have just mentioned. Having defined what belongs to the *necessaria* of a Christian christology, it enjoins that while a variety of different theories may be extrapolated beyond these *necessaria*, they must not lose sight of them or violate them.

The other way open to us is to employ some of the ideas already within the system. In speaking of the humanity of Christ in the work we are considering, Macquarrie conceives of a human being (op. cit., p. 370) who has so advanced in the process of transcendence and is so closely united with God that he can be described as 'deified'. Then again, thinking of God, he conceives of him as surpassing himself in his outreach of love to his whole creation and focusing himself in the one man, Jesus, who is openly receptive to his presence and fully expressive of his being and intention. It is perhaps tempting to think of these two processes as occurring in parallel – tempting but erroneous. For then we would have a real case of Nestorianism, and we would have ignored the issue we are presently investigating – who is the subject of the unity claimed for the two natures or transcendencies. For a pointer to an answer to that question, let me go back to the text from Galatians (2.20), 'It is no longer I who live but Christ who lives in me', which, when interpreted in terms of the 'paradox of grace', was for D. M. Baillie (*God Was in Christ*, Faber & Faber, London, 1951) the key to the understanding of the person of Christ. Though Paul thinks of Christ as working in us 'both to will and to do what God requires of us', traditional theology has rather spoken, as Baillie did, of the grace of God, or even the Holy Spirit, working in us to those ends; but my argument will develop equally validly with any one of the terms. On such occasions of moral or spiritual achievement, we are aware of three facts: first, that we put every ounce of effort into what we were doing; but, secondly, we have to acknowledge that what was achieved was not of our doing – it was all of God, or of Christ, or the Spirit, or the grace of God; and, thirdly, throughout the whole process, we were not aware of two subjects operating – 'synergising' is the technical word – within us, but rather felt ourselves to be wholly integrated, much more so than when we have been failing miserably. Now that ingression of the Spirit into our innermost selves is the clearest analogy of the double process which Macquarrie was describing with his terms 'deification' and 'inhumanisation'. If it is, then these two processes which are taking place in the person of Christ have the same involvement with one another, though to an infinitely higher degree, as that to which Paul bears such potent witness at Galatians 2.20. What we are examining at the moment, then, is: Who is the subject of the two natures, these being understood in Macquarrie's transcendent terms? Is it the human subject, of Jesus the man, or the divine subject, of the Logos? When faced with this question, Chalcedon and neo-Chalcedonians had answered that it is the *hypostasis* of the Logos who is the person of the incarnate/deified Jesus Christ; which answer, it will be recalled, drew forth the charge of a less than truly *human* Jesus. It is here that the Pauline analogy drawn from human endeavour in the grace of God, or by the power of the Spirit, or simply in Christ, is singularly helpful. I would say, then, in answer to our original question, that the person of Jesus Christ is the integrated unity of the person of the Logos and the person of the human nature of Jesus. In Chalcedonian categories, we can say of the *hypostaseis* of the human and the divine *physeis*, that they are not *asugchutos* (without confusion).

Let me comment upon this answer. First, it is an echo of the view of Ephraim of Antioch discussed above (pp. 101–3), reflected through the writings of Photius of Tyre, that the person of Jesus Christ is a *synthetos he hypostasis*, a fusion of the *hypostasis* of the Logos and that of the man Jesus. Indeed, I have never quite understood why Chalcedonians and neo-Chalcedonians have failed to adopt such a position in answer to the criticisms which they have had to face over questions of *anhypostasia* and *enhypostasia*. So in the christology which we are now considering, it could be said that the subject of the two natures, or ascendencies, is a fused subject in which the *hypostaseis* of the man Jesus and the Logos have so interpenetrated one another that they are in fact and effect one. Secondly, we might, by using this approach, glimpse a way of dealing with some of the questions which are raised concerning certain aspects of the God–man, for example, the nature of his knowledge. Did Jesus know the date of the Battle of Hastings or the second law of thermodynamics? The question may seem frivolous and irreverent, yet no one who has taught a class in christology will have escaped it, or others very like it. Once again, the Pauline notion of 'I, yet not I, but Christ' is helpful. In that human situation, the presence of God, or Christ, or the Spirit, or grace, as we choose to describe it, does not result in the elimination of all human inadequacy through the assumption by God of the entire moral effort. Indeed, the human effort, such as it is, is affirmed. So, remembering that it is analogy that we are employing, we may say that even the compresence of the divine *hypostasis* with the human *hypostasis* in a single person does not entail a human omniscience. Remembering the long-established theological adage, that God's revelation to his creatures and his indwelling of his creation, these activities of God's, are always *ad modum recipientis*, in accordance with the capacity of the recipient. Therefore we shall not be surprised if that revelation of God which is Jesus Christ, this man Jesus, is not omniscient. On the other hand, such divine compresence does not preclude the possibility and the actuality of moral perfection, in one who was wholly obedient to God, wholly receptive of his love and entirely lovingly responsive to a degree far beyond his fellows. Thirdly, by making this distinction, we have stumbled, almost unwittingly, upon a form of the distinction which H. R. Mackintosh adopted from Thomasius of Erlangen, between the 'relative' attributes of God and his 'immanent' attributes. In mentioning them, we are not committing ourselves to the kenotic theory of the person of Christ which they both advocated, or to the strictly logical definitions which they would give of the human and divine natures of Jesus Christ, a subject to which we shall soon return. We are using only their distinction between relative and immanent attributes of God. The former include omniscience, omnipotence and omnipresence, which arise through God's relation to his creatures; and the latter are of the very essence of God's being, for example, holiness, truth and love. So if there is in Jesus Christ one person, one *hypostasis* who is both human and divine, we should expect those attributes which are of the essence of God to be present in their fullness, as it were at the disposal of that integrated person. On the other hand, the relative attributes will be modified through the *hypostasis* according to the needs of the human nature and the purposes of God's plan of salvation. This distinction does certainly seem to answer to the situation of the Christ-event, in which Jesus is seen to be humanly weak, culturally conditioned as to knowledge and limited to one geographical space, but is equally filled with the love, the mercy and the integrity of God himself.

FROM ABOVE OR FROM BELOW?

A distinction of which much has been made in recent years, and of which we have heard, is between christology from above and christology from below. Prima facie it is clear enough. On the one hand there are some christologies which follow the classical creeds and begin from a trinitarian position, proceeding thereafter to trace the movement of the Logos from within the Godhead down to earth, to be incarnate in Jesus Christ, to live among his fellows, to die at their hands and to be raised from the dead, and to return to reign with the Father and the Spirit from eternity to eternity. On the other hand there are christologies which begin from below with the human life of 'a man that was called Jesus', and go on to describe his life, death and resurrection, tracing within the community which he created and subsequently left on earth the dawning revelation of who he really was, the One from above. The distinction has been broadened to show that christology from above tends towards docetism, or towards a less than adequate account of the humanity of Christ. This defect has been shown throughout these recent chapters to appear in christologies which have their roots in Chalcedon and commit themselves to the notion of *anhypostasia* – that the humanity of Christ lacked a human *hypostasis*, variously translated as person or centre of consciousness, and was therefore less than truly human. Christologies from below, contrarily, run the danger of not being able to go further than the humanity of Christ, and may finally have to settle for a human Christ; or if they try to go further, they may say that the divinity in Christ is his humanity 'writ large'. Readily acceptable as the distinction is, surely both approaches are necessary. Christology must be both from above and from below, the two elements corresponding to the fact of the humanity and the divinity of Christ. Also, the impact of Jesus upon the disciples and those others who knew him in the flesh was in human terms to begin with, and only afterwards was the full stature of his being fully appreciated, some scholars arguing that the revelation took place during his earthly life, others that knowledge of his divinity came to them only after the resurrection. But either way, such revelation was always related to the man whom they had known as one of themselves. But as the Church, in the face of enquirers, in the milieu of other cultures, in its own reflection upon its faith, came to rationalise its thought about Jesus Christ, it began to realise that the story from below as they knew it and had been told it was preceded by a vaster story from above. Then the christology of the creeds was born, and it acquired dominant and, as we have heard from Macquarrie, normative status. The neatest way to sum up this part of the history of christology is to say that 'from below' to 'from above' is the *ordo cognoscendi*, the order of knowing or, more precisely, coming to know; while the movement of thought 'from above' to 'from below' is the *ordo essendi*, the order of being described so graphically in the Prologue to the Gospel of St John (1.1–14). This account of the matter is so patently the case that we have to ask why so many of our modern christologists claim to begin their christology from below.

Several answers to this question offer themselves. The first we have already indicated, namely, the dissatisfaction felt with the view of human nature which was apparently endemic to christologies ancient and modern based upon Chalcedon. These views of human nature had been dominated largely by definitions which conformed to logical norms which they had to follow. No wonder both Pittenger and Macquarrie dismissed them as 'static'. What is remarkable is that such a definitional approach to human nature, as well as to divine nature, was being accepted as late as the turn of this century by theologians such as H. R. Mackintosh, and A. B. Bruce, whose theory of kenoticism depended heavily upon it. Secondly, disaffection towards the Aristotelian metaphysic which had formed the scaffolding for much of the christology prior to Chalcedon and for more than a millennium after it, meant that a substitute metaphysic had to be sought and was found in process philosophy. This new structuring for christology provided not just a general ontology but also a fresh anthropology, and a complementary understanding of the being of God. The view of human nature is, as we have noticed in

Pittenger and Macquarrie, that it is dynamic not static, surpassing its own limits and reaching out to infinite horizons. This process model, interpreted from below, is a fitting analogy for the transcendence which characterises God's Being as he too surpasses himself and reaches out in love to focus on the man Jesus, there to be so comprehensively manifest. Thirdly, ever since Martin Buber's *I and Thou* (ET by Ronald Gregor Smith, T. & T. Clark, Edinburgh, 1937) and the writings of John MacMurray and the Existentialists after World War II, human nature has been construed more in terms of personhood and interpersonal relationships than of logical entities. This interest was not confined to christology, for in an appendix to *Statement and Inference*, Cook Wilson argued the case for understanding our knowledge of God on the analogy of our knowledge of other selves rather than on the analogy of our knowledge of the natural world, as had been the case for centuries of philosophy of religion. Such insights were made part of the description of the human nature which Jesus Christ shared with us, and the starting-point for christologies from below. Fourthly, there has been, not just in the Reformed Churches but also in the Roman Catholic Church, a rigorous study of the roots of christology that lie behind the creeds and are to be found in the Scriptures. Having laid bare the way in which the creeds have evolved from these origins, scholars have felt that some of the mystique is removed from them; and the way is open to think of christology developing along other lines. But in such a reworking of basics, much of that christology has been from below, because the Scriptures are predominantly about the man of Nazareth. Fifthly, the theology of revelation, which was so prevalent in the middle two quarters of the twentieth century, might also in a rather interesting way be regarded as an element in the popularising of christology from below. It might initially be thought not to be so, but rather to represent the classical case of christology from above, propositionalising what had come *senkrecht von oben*. Yet the christology associated with revelation theology was solidly founded upon the human historical events of the life, death and resurrection of Jesus Christ. Even

Kierkegaard, who with Lessing must accept much of the responsibility for the historical scepticism which I can only say be-
devilled European theology for a century and a quarter, affirmed
'the scandal of particularity'. That was his acknowledgement
that the truth of revelation, universal in its implications,
was nevertheless indissolubly tied to the particularity of the
historical event of Jesus Christ. The revelation which was given
by God through his Spirit was related to this event and, in
Kierkegaard's language again, could only be reached by the
leap of faith. So, in a very real sense, the christology developed
from this revelation was initially from below, but fulfilled only
from above.

IN THE END – WHAT OF CHALCEDON?

The time has come, I feel, to be more realistic than we have been
up to now about the role which Chalcedon may be said still to
have in a modern christology, judging by the christology which
Macquarrie has offered and his own understanding of his relation
to it. If we may recapitulate, three ways have emerged in which a
modern christology may be said to meet the normative standard
or standards of Chalcedon. The first was used by Pittenger and
came from an early book of Alan Richardson, *Creeds in the
Making* (SCM Press, London, 1951, p. 84), where he holds
that Chalcedon enunciated a principle not a theory. The
principle is that a christology should affirm unequivocally that
'God and man are brought together in the Person of Jesus Christ'.
Macquarrie most adequately meets this norm. Secondly, we have
Macquarrie's own conception of his relation to Chalcedon, which
is that in his christology he fulfils the 'governing intention' of
Chalcedon, which we interpreted in Barth's terms of saying to
our generation in its language what the apostles and prophets –
and the creed makers – said to theirs in their language. Thirdly,
there are 'the three essential elements in a christology' laid down
by Pittenger, which again Macquarrie has been shown to include
in his christology.

It would, I think, be fair to say that these criteria for adjudging the adequacy of a christology, either as such or *vis-à-vis* Chalcedon, however adequate they may be taken separately or together, seem to be fairly general; thus they leave the relationship to Chalcedon of any christology favoured by them still open to discussion. In terms of detail, we have already paid considerable attention to the absence from Macquarrie of any considerations of how the two natures in Jesus Christ 'concur in one person (*prosopon*) and in one *hypostasis*', beyond his view that the person of Jesus Christ is the meeting-point of the transcendence from above with the transcendence from below. But no account is taken of how that meeting happens, or of the problems which have traditionally been occasioned by it in the history of christology. We have also observed how Macquarrie matches his language and understanding of the key Chalcedonian terms and concepts – *ousia*, *hypostasis* and *physis* – with their originals. His account of the modern meaning of these terms and concepts is coherent with what he has already said, and very convincing as a contemporary account of what christology is about; but it is hard to see them as transcripts of Chalcedon. What, also, of the four classical adverbs – *asygchutos*, *atreptos*, *adiairetos*, *achoristos*? They form a central and critical part of the creed, tied in as they are to several controversies which raged up to and after Chalcedon. Macquarrie does not make cross-references between the adverbs and his own statements, perhaps because the former were so rooted in history. Yet Pittenger thought it important enough to fight off the charge of Nestorianism, and it might have been relevant to raise this in relation to Macquarrie, even though the case would not have held.

So we are left with the title-question of this section: in the end, what of Chalcedon? It would seem to me that, though he wishes to make his peace with Chalcedon, Macquarrie does not in fact quite succeed. Not only does he omit to make certain correlations, but where he does he interprets them in what are mainly process terms, close to those of Pittenger. Moreover, he has subscribed to those criticisms of Chalcedon's Aristotelian ontology which have now become common currency in several modern christologies, and to the alternative, now popular, process thinking. So slender have become the bonds holding Macquarrie – and also Pittenger – to Chalcedon, other than in the general sense offered by Alan Richardson, that it is doubtful whether it is any longer necessary to uphold the connection.

If such a conclusion should be felt to be too dramatic or extreme, and if we wish to recall Macquarrie's own words, 'We could hardly reject it [the Chalcedonian formula] without rejecting our own identity as Christians' (*Jesus Christ in Modern Thought*, p. 383), then perhaps there still remain the escape words of H. R. Mackintosh:

> the decisions of Chalcedon may reasonably be viewed as a great utterance of faith, aware of the wrong turnings which theory may take so easily. They have been well compared to buoys anchored along a difficult estuary, on the right and left, to guide the ship of truth. (*The Person of Jesus Christ*, p. 213)

If the escape were adopted, then defence of a christology would take a rather different tack, not simply producing a form of translation of Chalcedon into modern terms so much as demonstrating how the reefs and whirlpools shown on Chalcedon's map have in fact been avoided. At that point, however, the metaphors themselves may have begun to mislead. So to go any further along that line is to begin to realise that perhaps we miscast it if we endow it with a 'normative' quality. Then we fall back on Mackintosh's cryptic words, 'With the religion of the Creed, we have no quarrel', completed in the ominous opening sentence of a new paragraph, 'But with its theology it is otherwise.' That judgement, to my mind, just about sums up the opinions of both Macquarrie and Pittenger; and they might both be said to be offering us an alternative theological account of the unique Person, of whom Chalcedon has given them a very special vision.

11

GERALD O'COLLINS, SJ

Professor Gerald O'Collins, SJ, of the Gregorian University in Rome, opens his work *Christology* (Oxford University Press, London, 1995), by reviewing the challenges encountered by any writer on christology, which come from disciplines which are contiguous with that subject, and all deeply involved in it. These disciplines include history, philosophy, language, and particularly, religious language, and Old and New Testament criticism. He responds to these challenges, together with the ever-changing fashions within christology itself, with a very comprehensive 'biblical foundation of christology', together with a critique of the patristic, medieval and modern writers on the person and work of Jesus Christ. The quality of the scholarship in this book marks it out, with that of Canon Macquarrie which we have just been considering, as among the most eminent and fair-minded of the works in this field for many years. In fact, as we proceed we shall notice how similar their method is, and how profitable it is to consider where they differ. As to similarity, for example, they both agree upon the inappropriateness, verging on irrelevance, of the language of Chalcedon in the context of a modern christology, O'Collins describing it as 'the distance between the idiom of any present-day Christology and older formulations modelled closely on Chalcedon's language' (op. cit., p. 224, n. 1). Nevertheless, they both seek to conserve the basic insights of Chalcedon, that in the man Jesus Christ believers identify one who is divine, so that in this human being was discernible the being of God, God acting and living in an altogether human way. Both have an interest in the distinction between christology 'from below' and christology 'from above', acknowledging that they are complementary to one another but nevertheless giving a very full account of the humanity of Jesus Christ. Each affirms the unity of Jesus Christ, and we have already considered how Macquarrie dealt with it. They differ, however, in that, whereas Macquarrie had opened his account with a study of the humanity of Christ, showing perhaps a sympathy for a 'from below' approach at least as a beginning, O'Collins opens with the question, 'What is it for Christ to be divine?' (op. cit., p. 225). To that matter we now turn.

THE DIVINITY OF JESUS CHRIST

O'Collins answers the leading question with which he thus begins in a series of definable steps. First, the term 'God' has to be given content, which is established in several ways: through Jewish–Christian history as recorded in the Scriptures: through the understanding of God's being diffused throughout that literature and history; and through the worship, teaching and moral experience of the nation and the community across many centuries. The God whose being is thus known through his self-revelation is 'one, all-powerful, eternal, all-good, and so forth' (ibid.). He may be thought of as indefinable, mysterious, supremely wise and holy. Yet at the same time he is indwelling in the hearts of believers, merciful and infinitely compassionate. But conceptualisation of the understanding of this God followed upon the presentation of the Gospel in the Greek philosophical context, yielding dogmatics, apologetics, theodicy, natural theology and philosophy of religion. Each of these contributed to an increasing sophistication in the answer to the question, 'Who is God?' What might appear to be becoming a remote theologoumenon is saved from sterility by the part which God plays through prayer, dedication and religious experience in the lives of ordinary men and women.

Given such a comprehensive view of God as might be recognisably central to Christian theology, there are two ways in which the relation of Jesus Christ to God may be portrayed. On the one hand, we have what O'Collins names the 'soft' account. This claims that God is in Jesus Christ in a manner which is in no way qualitatively different from his gracious presence in all men and women. The revelation which he brings to them, may mediate redemption to them. He may have opened up a new and living way to God in quite unique fashion, succeeding in focusing the minds and hearts of his brothers and sisters upon God. We may even be able to say that he does so to a unique degree, even to the point of being the norm of all revelation, but by a series of rhetorical questions, O'Collins both dismisses the 'soft' view of the relation of Jesus Christ to God and indicates where his own conviction lies. Is Jesus Christ only a window on God, a representative from God, with a message from him? Is he only the embodiment of God's purposes of revelation and redemption? Contrarily, how could he be the supreme revelation of God without himself being equal with God? In Brunner's opening sentence in *The Mediator* (ET by Olive Wyon, Lutterworth Press, London, 1937, p. 13), 'Through God alone can God be known.'

It is this latter view of God which O'Collins claims Christians discern as present in Christ, so that they can say that the very Son of God entered into a human person. For that reason, they have adored him across almost two millennia and given him that worship, obedience and devotion which may appropriately be given to God himself, and they still do. Through this discernment of the divine being of Jesus Christ, who has entered space and time to be part of their human existence, they have come to appreciate the depth and quality of the love which God bears to them. O'Collins then uses the term 'two-directional' to describe how we think about Jesus Christ. His meaning is twofold: on the one hand, Christians, as indeed they must always have done, use previously acquired understanding of the attributes of God in order to recognise and speak of the divinity of Jesus Christ. That has been the point of his exposition of the content of the name 'God'. But on the other hand, there is 'feedback' (op. cit., p. 229). The content of the name 'God' has now vastly increased. I found this part of O'Collins' exposition somewhat of an understatement. Admittedly, he includes in the feedback awareness of the threefoldness of God's being and the interrelatedness of Father, Son and Spirit in the activity of God. But if the term 'feedback' is mentioned at all, its content has surely to be exposed, including the redemptive self-sacrificial love of God for his creatures which was 'in his heart before the foundation of the world', the redemptive activity of Jesus Christ to fulfil that purpose, and the work of the Holy Spirit to bring it to fruition. This was feedback which was revolutionary, even when it was fulfilling so much of what the prophets had dreamt in their vision and communicated to unhearing ears.

THE HUMANITY OF CHRIST

When O'Collins raised his introductory questions, 'What is it for Jesus to be divine?' and 'Who is the God recognised as being present in Jesus Christ?', and subsequently gave his answers, it was not difficult to recognise his sources – the Scriptures, the centuries-long hermeneutic of them down to the present time, the ongoing life and worship of the Christian community, the individual Christian's personal experience of the mercy and compassion of God. What ought also to be said is that for the first disciples and followers of Jesus, behind all these sources and in a sense inspiring them was the impact upon them of the presence of Jesus in their midst – when they gathered in thousands to hear him preach, followed him from village to village, or gathered by the lakeside; or still more significantly, on the road to Emmaus, or when they met behind closed doors in total dispiritment, or were blinded on the Damascus road. When, however, he turns to answer his question, 'What is it to be human?' and to give an account of humanity comparable to that given to divinity, his sources are not quite so clear. They are not so apparently grounded in Scripture and tradition as his treatment of divinity, and initially he gives us a fairly run-of-the-mill, anthropological account of what it is to be human. For example, he lists (op. cit., p. 229) 'five essential characteristics:

organic bodily existence, coupled with rationality, free will, affectivity, and memory'. To these five, he adds being 'dynamic' and 'social', which in fact are very much human activities which involve permutations and combinations of the other five. The attribute of being 'dynamic' is the capacity to discern meanings, achieve set purposes, develop personal abilities and reach self-awareness; while being 'social' involves, by definition, trans-personal relations, as well as sexuality, participation in a culture and acting 'the political animal'. The religious element enters into the account when he first affirms that being human entails a living relationship with God. Later he goes on to say, in the context of the recognition of human finitude, that consequently it is dependent not just upon other humans but also upon God. The religious component enters again, in a form to which we have become accustomed in both Macquarrie and Pittenger, with mention of the human attribute of transcendence, the capacity to reach to the infinite, and again this is considered as one aspect of the *imago Dei*. O'Collins elects to regards it as the human yearning for fullness of 'Life, Meaning and Love'.

Having outlined the attributes of humanity, O'Collins, as was his method when discussing the divinity of Christ, measures the life of Christ against the designated attributes and pronounces that in such terms his life was fully human. Also, as in the case of the divinity of Christ, he adds that there is 'feedback', so that in the humanity of Christ our understanding of what it is to be human is greatly enlarged.

Any one person's assessment of what it is to be human is bound to be fairly subjective; and there is no doubt that O'Collins' selection of identifying characteristics would gain general approval among christologists, especially his highlighting of the notion of transcendence which is enjoying great popularity at present. Nevertheless, I wonder whether he ought not to have made some mention of the fact of Jesus' historicity. In using this term, I have three considerations in mind. The first is to emphasise – against both early docetic attempts to claim that it only appeared to be so, and modern views that the historical mise-en-scène of the Christian message is expendable – and the whole may be converted into timeless truths – the fact that Jesus' actual entry into the human historical process was itself part of the Gospel. My second interest in mentioning the historicity of being human – and I agree that O'Collins himself may mentally be including it in the attribute 'social' (op. cit., pp. 229, 232) – is to enable us to include in historicity such elements as particularity, probability and so on, which caught the interest of theologians from as far back as Lessing and Kierkegaard, to Tillich, Brunner, Barth, Van Harvey, and all their followers, and down to the present day. Thirdly, if we neglect the fact of the historical element in the humanity which we discern in Jesus, we then eliminate one of the major problems which exist for the Christian. How is it that that man who lived there and then can be of significance for us here and now? Put in another way, the problem for Christian faith in every generation is how it can become the faith of what Kierkegaard called 'the contemporary disciple'. The historical is the stage for that scene.

HUMAN AND DIVINE

Continuing with his series of questions in the form, 'What would it be like for someone . . .', O'Collins finishes this question with the words, 'to exist, who would be both divinely infinite and humanly finite?' In order to remove the impediment to considering our theme which was raised by Schleiermacher, that 'one individual cannot share in two different natures' (*The Christian Faith*, ET by H. R. Mackintosh and J. S. Stewart, T. & T. Clark, Edinburgh, 1928, p. 393), O'Collins argues that the several elements in the two sides of the equation are not as incompatible as might appear prima facie. It is an argument which I have to confess is difficult to follow, but it runs thus. Conceptually, terms such as infinite/finite, matter/spirit, time/eternity, transcendent/ immanent and divine/human do seem to be logical contradictories and to exist either side of 'a huge ontological gap'. But, we are told (though I cannot vouch for the evidence), the subjects designated by these opposed terms or entities are not to be considered as finally exclusive of one another. For example, matter must contain an element of the spiritual, for a God who was totally spiritual could not create matter *per se*. Eternity and time contain an element of each other, a fact implied by God's creation of time, which ensures the possibility of the Son of God entering time. The concept of the *imago Dei*, affirmed at Gen 1.26f, presupposes 'something divine about every human being' (*Christology*, p. 233). Finally, the fact that the Word assumes humanity entails the presence of an element of humanity in God.

As I have already indicated, I have to question both the validity and the intention of O'Collins' argument here. First, the question of validity: it would seem that the logical entailment which O'Collins affirms in each of these arguments is simply not the case. There is no necessity to regard matter as in some way spiritual because the Creator is spiritual. Dogmaticians have not, in the history of their subject, felt obliged to do so. Moreover, in what way is matter spiritual? One part matter, one part spirit? Or is matter through and through enspirited? So, too, the subject of time: we all learned early that eternity was not just 'an awful lot of time', and Gifford lecturers spent much energy seeking to show that eternity was a different form of existence from time. In the case of the doctrine of the *imago Dei*, with its supposed implication of divinity in human beings and humanity in God, the proposal is approaching the Stoic notion of the 'divine spark' in each of us. There is a problem, too, for the doctrine of redemption, for the implication would be that less than the whole of our humanity stood in need of salvation, a view rejected in most classical soteriologies. But it is the final argument of O'Collins that I find least acceptable, the conclusion, from the fact of the incarnation, that there must be an element of humanity in God. Dogmatics certainly has from time to time affirmed 'the humanity of God', but it has done so as a consequence of the incarnation, the humanity so assumed remaining in union with the Word. I fear that not one of these arguments, involving in each case words such as 'must', 'can', 'cannot', 'could not' with the logical force of entailment, is at all convincing.

Besides, there is a degree of uncertainty left in each case by the repeated use of the words 'something' or 'something of' to refer to the intrusive element from the other side of what I have called the equation.

So I have to raise the second question – of O'Collins' motivation for drifting into what I am sure is for him unfamiliar territory, in adopting these short logical entailments. The answer to the question lies, of course, in the quotation from Schleiermacher, that 'one individual cannot share two natures'. The purpose of these stated entailments is to show that the two natures of Christ, normally thought to be so incompatible with one another as to be unable to co-exist in one being, are, when examined, not mutually exclusive; and, moreover, each incorporates in itself 'something' of its contradictory. Now, O'Collins hopes, I am sure, to counteract the effect of Schleiermacher's sentence by modifying it with the addendum, 'provided the difference is not total'. The intention is to make the incarnation more credible by eliminating its contradictions. Then it would be possible to say that it is not inconceivable that there should exist a person who has both a human and a divine nature, for every human being is in any case part human and part divine. But I do not see how we should then state what is happening in the incarnation – should we say that in Jesus Christ there is a divine nature which has something human about it, and a human nature that has something divine about it? Not to mention the resultant *reductio ad absurdum* of the problem of how the two divine elements and the two human elements are related to one another. It is all unthinkable and irreverent.

My suspicion is that, having set up this fairly elaborate construction to enable us to understand how it is that one person has two natures, O'Collins senses that it is not advancing the argument. So he reverts to talking again about 'a contradiction in terms' when we consider the 'human' and 'divine' in Jesus Christ, and he chooses to meet the problem head-on. This contradiction is particularly in evidence in the attributes of knowledge and power, 'the same subject being credited simultaneously with pairs of essential characteristics that are simply incompatible' (op. cit., p. 234). To meet this very longstanding christological problem, O'Collins seeks to avoid the above conclusion by observing that the contradiction is dissolved if we recognise that the two sets of incompatible attributes are not ascribed to the same person 'at the same time and under the same aspect' and within the same frame of reference. I am afraid that once again I do not follow the argument, for it seems that one or other of two things is happening. Either, on the one hand, the 'explanation' of the incompatibility in question amounts to a restatement of the problem, namely, that within the divine frame of reference, or in his divine nature as the old language would have it, Jesus Christ is omniscient, and within the human frame of reference, in his human nature, he is limited in knowledge. Certainly, there is no contradiction within each frame of reference, or 'under the same aspect', but since he is both human and divine all the time there must continue to be an overall incompatibility between the two frames of reference and the two aspects, which is the age-old christological problem. Or, on the other hand, if there is not to be constant incompatibility between two such diverse natures, then the other option is that alternation takes place between the two frames of reference. An event, an action, a saying, a judgement, an emotion, or even a prayer would be referred to one frame or the other. Within that frame it would be compatible with others, and there would be no problem of compatibility or otherwise to be solved. If that is what is intended, the idea is certainly original. Yet it is hard to conceive that the events and so on in the life of Jesus could be so precisely compartmentalised as this solution suggests. There is the additional problem that in many cases it would be hard to say to which frame of reference they should individually be attributed. Concerning these two interpretations of how O'Collins is meeting the problem of the contradictions between the two natures of Jesus Christ, I reckon that neither is satisfactory.

But then again, I suspect that O'Collins is equally uneasy about his previous resolution of the problem of the two natures of Jesus Christ. For, before leaving the subject, he offers a further opinion, different from what has gone before. He acknowledges that the very concept of a person with two such contradictory natures as those revealed to us in the life, death and resurrection of Jesus Christ far exceeds our capacity to reduce it to truly descriptive formulae. Let us note that if we take that view seriously, it does two things. First, it seems to retreat from the genuine attempts of the two previous treatments of the subject of the two natures to explain how their relationships are to be seen as less incompatible than prima facie they appear. In a sense it gives up explanation. But secondly, it retreats to a position of pious agnosticism, which pre-empts further ratiocination. Even so, O'Collins' statement of that position falls short of what might have been said to reduce its unsatisfactory conclusiveness. For however difficult christology has found it to come to terms with the affirmed dualism in the person of Christ, the presence of the two natures in Christ has always been the origin, the inspiration and the strength of faith, which finds them to be totally compatible in him, as undivided as his seamless robe.

ONE PERSON

We come now to a matter which has exercised us from time to time in this study, most recently in our reflections on Macquarrie, namely, the question of who is the subject of the two natures of Jesus Christ, to whom the actions and the experiences recorded concerning him are to be referred. Chalcedon has always been taken as quite explicit in its definition that the two natures, as qualified by 'the four adverbs', concur in one person (*prosopon*) and one *hypostasis*, and that one person is widely taken to be the person of the Word. May I make two brief comments at this early stage, partly to confess my own uncertainty and partly to conserve my position? First, as will be recalled, the assumption implicit in this reading is the source of the concept of *anhypostasis*, the theory that Chalcedon denies any personhood to Jesus' humanity, though that interpretation is not conclusive. For, secondly, as I have argued before and hope to do again, since the creed does not specify the person, it is logically possible that the person is the person of both the Word and the human nature. This possibility will arise out of O'Collins' account of the matter.

Once again, as he did with divinity and humanity, O'Collins follows his method of giving us an account of the concept to be discussed (this time, person or personhood) which has been drawn from several sources, philosophical and theological. The account or definition is then applied to the christological material. 'A person', we are told, is *this* rational and free individual, who is the subject and centre of actions and relationships and who enjoys incommunicable identity, inalienable dignity, and inviolable rights' (op. cit., p. 235). It was odd, though we need not pursue the question, that O'Collins did not include the attribute 'moral' along with 'free' and 'rational' to describe the person, and someone like Macquarrie and certain process theologians would also include the term 'religious' in that list. But he does carefully unpack the definition, in order to establish a number of further points. For example, given that the individual exists within relationships, it may well be that they are as important for the establishing of self-identity as the inherent character of the individual itself and, in the case of Jesus Christ, his relation to God as 'Abba'. He adds an additional element when he considers the interrelation of a sense of identity, consciousness and personhood. Here we have to be very careful of our terminology, and I am not sure whether O'Collins intends to be as subtle as his actual phrasing suggests. Rightly, he points out that consciousness and personhood are not the same; next, that personal identity (that is, identity as a person) cannot be a simple function of self-consciousness: our sense of identity is a function of self-awareness, and the latter is the medium of personal identity and an 'I'. Finally, he considers the case for memory being named the condition of personal identity and what he calls 'diachronic identity' and rejects the idea on the ground that such a view would have to say that loss of memory entails loss of personality. He modifies this rejection somewhat (op. cit., p. 237), but a point has to be made by distinguishing between the effect of loss of memory upon personal identity and upon diachronic identity. The effect of the former may not be totally destructive, in that the person may begin again to build up some new sense of identity through using the gifts and skills which have survived the memory loss. On the other hand, the effect of loss of memory upon diachronic identity may well be devastating. It is now a well-known fact that in the time of the so-called 'Cold War' there were techniques, both psychological and medical, designed to destroy personality by deconstructing the memory of the agent. So the part played by memory is of great importance in the analysis of personal identity.

O'Collins uses this analysis to define the personhood of Jesus Christ in the light of his two natures. In so far as Chalcedon is normally taken to regard the person of Jesus Christ as being the person of the Word, O'Collins begins by pursuing this line, and immediately becomes involved with the question of the pre-existence of the person of Jesus Christ. He issues several caveats. For example, he warns against the idea that Christ is thought to pre-exist his incarnation, as if his eternal existence were part of a temporal succession which extended on into earthly events. Rather, the eternity which is a synonym for pre-existence is a different form of existence which transcends space–time, yet in a way that God who is eternal and the person of the Word who is pre-existent are dynamically and really present within space–time. Therefore, when we speak of the pre-existence of the person of Jesus Christ we are referring to the Word who existed before the incarnation, as would seem to be the intention of such passages as Jn 1.1–5, 14, Phil 2.6–8 and Col 1.15–20. This statement cannot be made without implying some degree of temporal succession, and yet to omit it would give us less than the truth.

Another caveat which O'Collins issues leads us to consider what is involved in the identity of the human nature of Jesus. While it is agreed that the personal existence of Jesus Christ as the eternal Son of God is secured in his being within the Godhead, it would be wrong to suggest that Jesus Christ as 'this man that was called Jesus' pre-existed eternally. That man did not exist before his conception by Mary. He is a creature like ourselves, of one substance with us in respect of his humanity.

So we would expect to find in him those activities of self-consciousness and self-identification which minister to the growth of personal being. After a review of several Roman Catholic Commissions in the 1970s and 1980s on the question of whether Jesus Christ was conscious of his personal pre-existence as the Word, O'Collins very cautiously and with balanced effect concludes that there is no Synoptic ground for holding that the earthly Jesus was aware of his eternal pre-existence, even though he was aware that he had been sent as the Son. So while Jesus Christ as the Word does not depend upon his human self-awareness for an understanding of his identity but derives it from his own being within the Godhead, his self-identification as a human being does arise from his own understanding of his relationships with others and, in particular, with God.

This excursion into questions about the meaning of Christ's pre-existence and the reference of the concept seem to have delayed somewhat our address to the subject of 'One Person'. It has served, however, to illustrate the complex context into which the subject has to fit, and the matters of which it has to take careful account. O'Collins outlines in a very concise way the answers that might be given to the interpretation of our theme. I shall not take them in the order in which he propounds them because of a declared interest on my part in one answer which has links with the last of his options. The first we shall consider under our notation (in fact, O'Collins' second, op. cit., pp. 245f) begins from a distinction between person or personhood and personality, for which little evidence would be found in classical christology. The intention is to meet the much-discussed criticism of Chalcedon that, by affirming that the person of Jesus Christ is the person of the Word, it advocates an impersonal human nature in Christ (*anhypostasis*). Under the present proposal, the divine person would have a human personality, formed no doubt of those items which O'Collins had detailed on pp. 229f (op. cit.), but so superbly composed as to be out-standing and quite unique. Here we would have conflict with that strand in Protestant theology which has emphasised the hiddenness of God's self-revelation in Jesus Christ – I am thinking of certain Lutherans and of Barth in particular. The majority of christologists would be on O'Collins' side, I should think. I have at this point to register a doubt. O'Collins is very careful to distinguish person and personhood from personality. But as he advances in the exposition just given of the way the distinction may be used in connection with the problem of the *anhypostasis*, as bequeathed to us by Chalcedon, I begin to wonder whether there is any distinction between personality and nature, especially if we think of nature as the particular human nature of Jesus Christ. If there is a genuine distinction, then where does personality come in the hierarchy – between nature and person? Indeed, it may be the case that, despite his definition of the distinction between person and personality, personality does operate in O'Collins' scheme of things as the person of human nature, thus ensuring both its integrity and its subordinate relation to the person of Jesus Christ, that is, the person of the Word.

This distinction between person or personhood and personality does not seem to assist in dealing with the question of the relation of the two natures in Jesus Christ, and in particular the relation of two minds or two consciousnesses which O'Collins had already discussed at length on p. 234 (op. cit.). The problem has arisen, he now says, because critics of Chalcedon had assumed that the two minds or two consciousnesses were coordinated with each other, two 'subsystems' of the kind thought to exist in multiple-personality cases such as the text-book example of Sally Beauchamp. In fact the two minds or consciousnesses are disparate, the human mind working by a process of propositionalisation and ratiocination, the divine mind, if we can even describe it, in a much more intuitive and immediate way, with the whole subject of knowledge present to it *totum simul*. O'Collins sums up the situation with a certain finality: 'There exists an infinite epistemological gap between the divine mind and any human mind, including that of Christ' (op. cit., p. 246). But, despite the note of finality, that surely cannot be the last word, for it amounts to a reaffirmation of the problem which

O'Collins himself says is for so many a knockdown difficulty with Chalcedon – that it affirms among other things that Jesus Christ is the subject of limited knowledge and of infinite knowledge. If, on the other hand, we were to tie this discussion on to his use of the distinction between person and personality, would he be saying that the human personality, including the human mind, has the word as personal subject? The Word is also the personal subject of the divine mind, on a totally different dimension from the human mind, and the human mind is obedient to the divine mind through the person of the Word.

This discussion of the problem of Christ's two minds turns out to be much less fruitless than may have appeared, for it seems to me to lead to a more satisfactory account of the concept of the 'One Person' which is our present interest. O'Collins now embarks upon a very close-knit argument, and I would not guarantee the accuracy of my own interpretation, for he operates with several concepts we have met before and also some fresh ones. But in advance I may say that my problem is to know which are equivalences. Despite the difficulty and my hesitation, the argument is for me a new one and leads to a conclusion which I would find acceptable. O'Collins begins by acknowledging that each person, being an ontological unity, has a psychological unity, a unity of consciousness, an ego or an 'I' which integrates, in the language of Kant, the 'I think' of theoretical or pure reason, the 'I act' of practical reason, and the 'I should' of moral freedom (op. cit., p. 247). (From now on, we have to translate O'Collins' rhetorical questions, which are on the whole Latin-type questions beginning with *num* and expecting the answer 'no', into affirmative statements.) If we apply the previous analysis to Jesus Christ, then his unity of person requires us to posit a unity of consciousness to which are to be referred the traits, habits and activities of his experience. But to take the matter further, since, as has been argued earlier, Jesus Christ's human nature is complete, with self-consciousness and awareness of self-identity, then his human nature so described has fulfilled the requirements for having a human unity of consciousness, for being a human 'I' or ego with full personhood. But this human ego is not self-dependent as it is in human beings. For not only is it the point of reference of the self-consciousness and the sense of identity of the human nature, but in being so it is also the Word of God or, should we say, the ego, the person of the Word of God incarnate. Now, concludes O'Collins, since the ego of the human consciousness is the Word, the Son of God, the Word 'takes as his own, this human self-consciousness, self-identity, and centre of reference' (ibid., p. 247). In other words, the divine person unites with the human person, as *mia hypostasis*, so that the subject of the incarnation is God–man, Jesus Christ, and in his actions he acts through a divine or a human nature. If this is truly O'Collins' view, then, as I have indicated, I find it acceptable. Once he adopted what has now become the well-worn criticism of the *anhypostasis* imputed to Chalcedon and insisted that the human nature must be total and integrated, then he had to find a way of, first, relating the ego, the person of that nature, with the person of the Word of God in such a way that the primacy of the latter is in no way endangered; and secondly, securing the unity of the two persons in the *mia hypostasis* of Chalcedon. Jesus Christ was/is a person, both human and divine, as his name, with its divine and human components, would suggest. It is, if I may refer to the matter again, a modern form of the position adopted by Ephraim of Antioch (see above, pp. 101–3).

Perhaps the concentration of this argument will be eased if we attempt an analysis of its main components. For example, as I read it, the classical term *hypostasis* appears as 'person', 'ego', 'I', 'subject', in the form of 'personhead' and 'centre of reference'. Next, O'Collins comprehensively attributes to this term the concept of 'ontological unity', a subject to which we shall have to return in a wider connection. For the present its occurrence does not affect the argument. Next, where we might have gone on to discuss *physis*, nature human and divine, we consider a range of psychological terms which are particularly the components of humanity, though they received no prominence in the earlier review of the notion of humanity (op. cit., pp. 229ff). These include unity of consciousness integrating the 'I think', 'I act' and 'I should', integral human consciousness, self-consciousness and sense of identity. Occurring together they constitute the actuality of a human ego or 'I'. The divine person of the Word, through his union with the human ego, thus has at his disposal this whole range of human activities, traits and experiences.

Having established what I consider to be O'Collins' last word on the 'One Person', I must now return, as was promised, to the first of the ways of dealing with the subject which he discussed (op. cit., pp. 244f). He noted that a number of modern christologists, aware of the difficulties of *anhypostasis*, held that Jesus Christ was/is a divine–human person. There are two ways, he says, in which this theorem may be understood. First, some who have used it have meant no more than that Jesus Christ had two natures, human and divine. They elected in this way not to raise the issue of who the 'person' was, and so to avoid the pre-Chalcedonian, Chalcedonian and post-Chalcedonian controversies. We have to acknowledge, before criticising such a view, that it is the position most of us take in the course of our devotional and liturgical life. The question is a very theological one nonetheless, so long as *fides quaerens intellectum* is an accurate statement of what we are about in this discipline and we are not yet looking for a religious escape route. Secondly, it is alternatively suggested that the genuine intention is to ascribe a human–divine personhood to Jesus Christ. Having but stated this position, O'Collins immediately sets off to show how such people commit the theological solecism of thinking of person-hood as something which Jesus Christ 'has'. They commit the category mistake of failing to realise that person is what one 'is', and nature is what one 'has'.

In drawing attention to this confusion, O'Collins takes support from Daniel Helminiak's *The Same Jesus; A Contemporary Christology* (Chicago, Loyola University Press, 1986, p. 292). Helminiak had already said that Jesus Christ is completely human, because he has a human nature and it is through having a human nature that a person is human. The fact that Jesus Christ did not have a human *hypostasis* did not make him any the less human – a sentence in which Helminiak calls the bluff of generations of christologists who have deplored the *anhypostasis*. For 'hypostasis is not something someone has. The hypostasis is the someone who has whatever is had'. But Helminiak, having been drawn into the discussion, albeit involuntarily, leads us off on a false trail with his next statement, namely, that 'if the divine hypostasis, the Word, has all the qualities that constitute someone as human – a human nature – then the Word, a divine hypostasis, is a human being, and fully so, period'. The intrusion of Helminiak leaves me faintly pursuing when I try to reconcile it with the position which O'Collins is gradually building up, because of the crop of difficulties he raises in one short paragraph. For example, when Helminiak says that the Word, as the divine *hypostasis*, has a human nature, he does not indicate whether this 'completely human nature' has a human psychological centre of reference, an ego, an 'I', as most post-Chalcedonians have insisted; or whether he is quite reconciled to accepting the anhypostatic theory of the humanity of Christ and flying in the face of the consensus that personhood is a necessary feature of a complete humanity. If, however, he does agree that personhood is necessary to complete humanity, one of several aspects that constitute a person human, then he is saying that the *hypostasis* of the Word has a human *hypostasis*, which is counter to his claim that *hypostasis* is not something someone has, it is what he or she is. On the other hand, if he had held to this latter rubric, then he could have said that the person of Jesus Christ was/is both human and divine, as is implied by the name God–man. His final sentence is perhaps the most enigmatic of all: 'the Word is a human being'. It could mean either that the Word is also a human person, the centre of reference for the human nature, which tallies with what I have just said; or the elision involved rises almost to the point of error – the Word is not a human being *simpliciter*. I am reminded of H. R. Mackintosh's remark in a related area, that 'to say that "Jesus Christ is God" is not a true way to say a true thing' – nor is this a statement of Helminiak's.

The irony of Helminiak's position appears in the first sentence quoted by O'Collins, 'Current insistence that Christ was a human person does not appreciate the classical meaning of the term, person' (ibid.). In fact, what has not come out in the discussion of the *anhypostasis* so far is another possible reason for uneasiness about its use in christology. Usually this uneasiness is attributed to the development of the understanding of the concept of person and the growing importance of psychology in christology. It has been felt that psychologically Jesus would be less than completely human if his human nature lacked personhood. In fact there is another problem associated with the *anhypostasis*, and it springs from the ontology on which Chalcedon is structured. It has always been a puzzle to me to locate with any precision the source of that ontology. It has been assumed, certainly by myself, that the metaphysical background to Chalcedon is Aristotle's *Categoriae*, c.5, and it certainly seems to fit. But my misgiving arises from the consideration that almost eight centuries separate Aristotle from Chalcedon. So while it is possible to prove continuity across that period, it is somewhat of a stretch of the imagination to believe that changes in Aristotelianism, as well as social, political and cultural upheavals of one kind and another, did not to some degree affect the tradition. Nevertheless, *faute de mieux*, I find myself still relying upon Aristotle's distinction between primary substance and secondary substance as the clue to the distinction between *hypostasis*, person, and *physis*, nature (cf. above, pp. 87ff). The primary substance is not predicated of any entity, whereas the secondary substances consist of categorial predications. The former is the subject of the different attributes of the species or genus to which the subject belongs, even when the subject forms a one-member class. 'Everything except primary substances is either predicable of primary substances or present in them, as subjects' (Aristotle, *Categoriae*, 5.2a). A point which is often ignored, despite its importance, is that there is a close correlation between the primary and the secondary substances, so that the primary substance is a particular instance of the species or genus named as the secondary substance. If, therefore, we intend to retain the Chalcedonian formulae, it is hard to see how the divine Word can be the subject of human nature and its several attributes; rather, in line with Aristotle in the *Categoriae*, it is a human ego, an 'I', who fulfils that role. Thus emerges what I called the irony of Helminiak's criticism of his contemporaries who insist that Christ was a human person. He has himself failed to understand the interrelation of *hypostasis*, person, with nature, in the classical meaning of the terms to which he refers, and commits the solecism of attaching the divine *hypostasis* to a human *physis*. Those he criticises, on the contrary, are rightly aware that if he was truly human, Christ was a human person.

But this excursus into Helminiak, even at the invitation of O'Collins, must not be allowed to obscure our major purpose. That was to consider why O'Collins, in his discussion of the *mia hypostasis* of Chalcedon, should discard so swiftly the notion of a divine–human *hypostasis*, a double personhood. His ground for doing so is that 'those' who adopt this position commit the error of which we have been speaking, and fail to see that personhood is something that one *is*, and nature is something that one *has*. Surely, even if some christologists have done so, their error does not in itself prove that the view itself is wrong. What is more interesting is that O'Collins himself in the end adopts a view which is substantially that which he here misrepresents by equating it with an erroneous interpretation of it. Moreover, even Helminiak with a little persuasion might well have found himself in support of this same position of the united *hypostasis*, because the premises leading to such a conclusion are all there in that short paragraph quoted on p. 245 of G. O'Collins' *Christology*.

That O'Collins in fact has accepted the fused two-person theory, if I may so call it, is seen in one of the 'further issues' which he tackles in the wake of the discussion of 'One Person', namely, what degree of knowledge the human ego has of his relation to the divine person. He sets out to answer this question with an analysis of the nature of our knowledge of finite and temporal entities. He claims that in experiencing the limited and the temporal, we at the same time experience the infinite and the eternal 'that lies within them' (ibid., pp. 247f). Further, we could not experience the limited and the temporal without *eo ipso* experiencing the infinite and the eternal. When this analysis is applied to the human Jesus and his self-awareness, then we say that in the consciousness of his own finite and temporal existence, he had experience of One who was not only infinite and eternal but was also his Father, and he was related to him by the love each bore for the other. This acknowledgement of the love of the Father and the Son as the integrating bond of the two persons is a theme which we encountered in Pittenger, but which is not heard frequently in christological exposition. Yet in this context it is the most natural and convincing way of describing this relationship, replacing the metaphysical with the moral and the religious at the heart of the person of Christ.

JESUS' KNOWLEDGE OF THE DIVINE SUBJECT

If, however, we continue the discussion of the description just given of the relation of the human nature to the divine nature in Jesus Christ somewhat more critically, we begin to encounter difficulty. Let us refresh our memories as to the question which O'Collins is setting out to answer: 'Does, and how does, Jesus' human ego know that he is a divine subject, God the Son?' (op. cit., p. 247). O'Collins, as we have just seen, began by speaking of the way in which every human being, as conscious of the finite, intuits in that perception the infinite and, in the same way, the eternal with the temporal. In the case of Jesus Christ, the infinite so intuited in the finite and the temporal is God the Father. On reflection, I sense a two-sided problem here. On the one hand, as we have said, the human ego, 'Jesus' as O'Collins names him (ibid., p. 248), intuits the Father whom he calls 'Abba'. Yet it was the incarnate Lord Jesus Christ, rather than the human ego of Jesus, who was the recorded subject of the events in the New Testament and could therefore utter the word 'Abba'. Nor can this statement be an answer to the generating problem of this paragraph, how the human ego of Jesus knew he was the Son of God. The human ego *per se* was not the Son of God. On the other hand, the infinite whom Jesus intuited in the finite entities and happenings of his life could be regarded, not as the

Father, but as God the Son. In the intimacy of the union of the persons which I have here been advocating, there would be the possibility of Jesus or his human ego learning that the incarnate Lord and, by implication, he himself through the union, was the Son of God. If I might summarise my problem: O'Collins uses the argument that Jesus, in being aware of the finite and the temporal, also intuits the infinite and the eternal, to demonstrate Jesus' awareness of God the Father and, presumably, his mission in relation to him. Yet what we expect is that the argument should lead to the presentation of Jesus' awareness of the Son of God, and so of his union with him, his mission shared with him, and their shared love for one another. Then the love which bonds Jesus and the Son of God is not the eternal love wherewith the Father loves the Son and the Son the Father, of which Augustine wrote, but the intimate relation between the two natures of Jesus Christ, which are preferably described in this way rather than in metaphysical terms.

PSYCHOLOGY OR ONTOLOGY

Reference was made above (p. 297) to O'Collins' application of the term 'ontological' to the unity of the person of Christ, which in his judgement 'required some psychological unity or one self-aware centre of reference for his actions and experiences' (op. cit., p. 247). It was truly a *hapax legomenon*, and nothing was made of it by him in the subsequent argument, nor was there explicit anticipation of it in the previous argument. Yet perhaps there should have been, for the language of 'I think', 'I act' and 'I should' is all reminiscent of Kant's first two *Critiques*, which the commentators have agreed were studies in ontology or epistemology rather than psychology. Kant apart, the very use of the word 'ontological' reminds us of a question which arose at the end of the examination of the 'psychological model' (above, pp. 140ff), and to which we shall return in our final chapter, for it is central to the assessment of the role to be assigned to Chalcedon in contemporary christology. Let me introduce it by recalling a statement by E. L. Mascall already quoted on p. 141): 'Christological doctrine is not primarily psychological but ontological. No amount of discussion of our Lord's psychology can have any *direct* bearing on the Catholic creeds and the Chalcedonian definition.' True or false?

12

WHAT, THEN, OF CHALCEDON?

While our main intention has been to trace the different configurations which christology has assumed at different times and under different external pressures, there has been running concurrently a sub-plot. It concerns the understanding of the role which the Chalcedonian model has played in relation to the other models, and even at times how it is composed. Two somewhat contradictory accounts of it have emerged, and this fact has been the trigger of this final investigation. On the one hand there has been a widespread complaint – judgement, even – that not only is the Greek philosophy which seems to appear so often in the creed irrelevant to the way folk think nowadays, it is even unintelligible to the mass of our contemporaries. So, we are told, though they may on rare occasions repeat it, they are literally mouthing words bereft of meaning. We have encountered such sentiments on several occasions in our previous studies. On the other hand, these christologists, sometimes even the same ones, have maintained a lingering respect for the creed, attempting to demonstrate that their novel views actually conform to Chalcedonian standards or could be used as a hermeneutic device to modernise Chalcedon.

E. L. MASCALL AND CHALCEDON

The question of Chalcedon has been considered by most christologists over the past century and a half, but one who has been particularly articulate and sympathetic has been E. L. Mascall, whose *Whatever Happened to the Human Mind?* (SPCK,

London, 1980) has interesting answers to the question, 'Is Chalcedon relevant today?' His answers to certain objections (op. cit., pp. 28ff) which are thought by their supporters to eliminate Chalcedon as a live contemporary option, amount in effect to his vote of confidence for the continuing validity of the creed, allowing for certain qualifications which he would admit. The first of three such objections which he considers is that the creed presupposes and employs a fifth-century metaphysic which is no longer acceptable to modern philosophers, a comment that we have now recorded almost *ad nauseam*. Mascall points out in reply, however, that the creed assumes no philosophical doctrines, with the exception of what he calls 'personal identity'. In addition, there are certain central terms which have a clearly philosophical flavour, such as *ousia* ('being'), *physis* ('nature') and *prosopon* and *hypostasis* (both meaning 'person'), but these are all words which have a place in ordinary speech. Also, far from the Greek origin of such terms dominating usage in the credal context, the reverse occurs and the meaning of the borrowed terms is prescribed by their theological connections. Secondly, he counters the accusation that the creed is 'formal and static' by pointing out that it does not stand on its own but must be read along with the creeds of Nicaea and Constantinople. They present a picture of the incarnation which is 'thoroughly dynamic'. Finally, the judgement of no less a figure than William Temple, that Chalcedon 'is in fact a confession of the bankruptcy of Greek Patristic Theology' ('Seven Oxford Men', *Foundations*, Macmillan, London, 1912, p. 230), elicits from Mascall the criticism that Temple has here fallen victim to the 'Syllabus Error'. This error, the delusion that somehow christology wound up in AD 451, was fostered by the examination schools who limited their courses and examination prescriptions to that *terminus ad quem*. In the event, Chalcedon had a long and healthy life after 451, not only through the Middle Ages but also in very recent times as we have just seen.

Mascall goes on to mention two other characteristics of Chalcedon which impart to it a contemporary validity and which he finds commendable *vis-à-vis* the 'New Christologies'. One is its wholehearted commitment to the total and complete humanity of Jesus Christ, and the other is its affirmation of the immediate involvement of God with the events of the life and death of Jesus Christ. As against kenotic theories with their acceptance of a diminished divine nature of Jesus Christ, it holds to the full deity of Jesus Christ. It also maintains this stand against some 'New Christologies' which, while emphasising the complete humanity of Christ, regard his 'divinity' as different only in degree from the rest of humanity.

At this point we find emerging in Mascall an interpretative pattern of analysis of Chalcedon encountered in some other writers such as Alan Richardson, Norman Pittenger, John Macquarrie and Gerald O'Collins. Having discussed the divinity and the humanity of Jesus Christ, they concentrated, it will be recalled, on the problem of how these two natures, by definition so contradictory of one another, can concur in the same person. Now, while Mascall by his argument reaches a conclusion similar to theirs in terms, his starting-point is somewhat different. He begins from the premise that the terms *hypostasis* and *prosopon* ('person') which appear in the creed are to be understood as 'subject'. If the Second Person of the Trinity, through the incarnation, becomes the subject of created human nature, thereby imparting to that nature actual existence, individual identity and, particularly, openness to God, then there can be no ultimate incompatibility between God and manhood. Human nature is assumable because it has been assumed in the incarnation. It is an argument *ab esse ad posse valet consecutio*. The difference between Mascall and most of the others mentioned, who reach a similar conclusion, is that their argument for the ultimate compatibility of humanity and divinity derives from an anthropological theory about the openness of humanity to divinity, while Mascall derives his, as we have noted, from the incarnational situation itself. For Mascall as for the others, the notion of the orientation of humanity towards God and its openness towards him constitutes a basic ontological fact about humanity. But for Mascall it is from the hindsight of incarnation that we perceive what could never have been conjectured from the other side of incarnation, that there is a certain appropriateness about the incarnation of the Eternal Son in humanity so described.

Mascall, however, in his treatment of the unity of the two natures in Jesus Christ, in fact addresses himself more comprehensively than the others (op. cit., pp. 35ff) to the matter of the concurrence of the two natures into one person (*eis mian hypostasin*), as we discovered in our study of, for example, Macquarrie and O'Collins. He made a significant point which we have already met in Helminiak, that 'person' and 'nature' are not logical co-ordinates, 'not on the same level of being' (op. cit., p. 33), but are rather disparate, much as Aristotle's primary and secondary substances were and for similar reasons. In this context we shall return now to a matter discussed in earlier chapters (see above, e.g., pp. 101ff, 292f), namely, who exactly is the 'person' referred to as the person of Jesus Christ, or who is the *mia hypostasis* spoken of in the creed as the one in whom the two natures 'concur'. The position which Mascall himself ultimately favours is the traditional enhypostatic interpretation of Chalcedon (though for some reason he never uses the term), namely, that the person of the Word, the 'one, Christ, Son, Lord, only-begotten' is the person or the subject of the two natures; he alone was pre-existent, as the creeds say. Mascall, in a *hapax legomenon*, describes the person of the divine nature as the 'metaphysical subject', the divine subject, of the human nature. But short of that eventual statement of his own position, Mascall raises some subtle points which lead up to it. He poses the problem whether the one person, in whom the two natures of Jesus Christ concur at the incarnation and who is their common subject, pre-existed this event; or whether it was the concurring of the two natures which occasioned the existence of that person. The problem, he explains, derives from the fact that the creed does not state in so many words that the subject of the two natures pre-existed the incarnation as a person. Far from being simply a theological poser, this matter exercised the christologists for a whole century after Chalcedon.

So let us look at the two options relating to the *mia hypostasis* which Mascall says are left open by Chalcedon to be argued over by future interpreters. The view which Mascall himself accepts eventually, as we have noted, is that the subject of the two natures is the person of the Word. He would rest his case on the fact that the Fifth Ecumenical Council of Constantinople II, in AD 553, declared unreservedly that the *hypostasis* or *prosopon* of the eternal and pre-existent Son or Word was the person or subject of the two natures of Jesus Christ. This position, even with the authority of the Fifth Ecumenical Council behind it, I find to be inadequate on three counts. First, Mascall expands it less than accurately when he says (op. cit., pp. 33ff) that it was God who was born at Bethlehem, walked in Galilee, was crucified on the cross, and rose on Easter Day – *God*, not the man Jesus. We are reminded again of the oft-quoted words of H. R. Mackintosh that 'this is not a true way to say a true thing'; for surely it was the *God–man* who was born in Bethlehem, lived in Palestine, was crucified and rose again. Or, to put the point another way, it was the God–man, designated by his double name Jesus Christ, who was and is the subject of the two natures. Secondly, this position favoured by Mascall disregards the connection between Aristotle's primary and secondary substances and the *hypostasis* and *physis* of the christological controversies of the third to the sixth centuries. Once this connection is accepted – and I have not come across another to replace it – then it implies that there is a consonance between any *hypostasis* and the *physis* to which it relates – human to human, and divine to divine. Consequently, thirdly, Mascall also seems to have disregarded the long-running complaint that Chalcedon does not allow a human *hypostasis* to the humanity of Jesus Christ, affirming instead what has been called (rather inaccurately because of a misinterpretation of the notion 'persona') an 'impersonal nature', so that, although the human nature is not without a *hypostasis*, because it is enhypostasised, it still does not have a human *hypostasis*.

This false step, as I would regard it, on Mascall's part directs attention to the position which he refuses to accept, namely, that the person of Jesus Christ was and is what he named 'a composite hypostasis'. Unlike some of the writers previously examined, Mascall does not offer any reason for rejecting out of hand this view of the subject or person of the two natures of Jesus Christ. Consequently, he fails to notice the considerable advantages which it offers in solving certain christological difficulties which have already been itemised (see above, pp. 103ff) and need not now be rehearsed. Additionally, however – for these issues had not been raised then – we can now see that the disjunctive question put by Mascall, with its two options – did the one person in whom the two natures concurred at the incarnation exist before the two natures concurred, or did the one person come to being only when the two natures concurred? – did not exhaust the logical field. The further possibility is that the two natures concurred in one person who was from conception a fusion of human subject and divine. The use of the word 'concurrence' deceptively suggests a time-scale (as if there were any separation between the concurrence of the two natures into the one person or subject) and the fusion or composition of the two persons into one divine–human subject. In fact, the whole complex happened at once. I simply repeat that perhaps this issue of the person in whom the two natures concur is best resolved by using the device which Mascall has mentioned and frequently uses, namely, equating 'person' with 'subject'; and say, as we have done above, applying the substitution, that the subject of the two natures, of the events in Palestine two thousand years ago, was both human and divine, the God–man, Jesus Christ.

THE CASE FOR CHALCEDON

Our concluding task now must be to concentrate our thought upon the role that might still remain for Chalcedon in the field of christology. It has come up for assessment in most of the models we have considered, and has persisted, as an ever-changing model, into the late twentieth century. No alternative seems to have successfully challenged its place, and even when one has been offered, it has been a derivative of it, or an attempted translation, or even a negation of it which in itself is an admission of dependency. Let us then consider the possible roles that Chalcedon may still have in christology.

NORMATIVE

The role of norm is one which arises in regard to any creed we consider, for that surely was the initial intention behind their promulgation; but none more so than in the case of Chalcedon, partly because of its central place in the history of christology, partly because of its use as a point of reference for christologists and their critics in that history. But as we have learned in churches which over the years and centuries have had to deal with a supreme standard as well as a subordinate standard, a standard or a norm which consists of a document, however long, never operates or is applicable *in toto*. At a very early stage, a norm within the norm begins to appear. The Church of Scotland has found that in its supreme standard, the Bible, there are many texts and passages which cannot be considered as norms for morals or doctrine; even its subordinate standard, *The Westminster Confession*, is criterially imperfect. This consideration has led, in the case of Chalcedon, to the attempt to distil the essence of its main contentions. We have encountered several such distillations, one notable example being a combination of Alan Richardson and Norman Pittenger:

> God and man are truly brought together in Christ . . . [so] that there is in the total person of Jesus Christ that which is truly human, that which is truly divine, and that which truly establishes the union of the two in one incarnate life. (Alan Richardson, *Creeds in the Making*, pp. 84f and N. Pittenger, *The Word Incarnate*, p. 96)

Forty years ago, when writing these words, Pittenger felt that perhaps such 'a traditional evaluation of Jesus Christ as the

Incarnation of God in Man' allowed too much licence to err, and that constraints of some form would need to be placed on the christological imagination if the creed were to retain its normative validity. There were constraints aplenty in the original Definition, but they were thought to be so intertwined with the vicissitudes of theological warfare that it became increasingly difficult and unsafe to secure what might be authentic modern forms to match them. Besides, in the history of theology since Chalcedon, shadows of these ancient heresies have found their way into accounts of the person of Christ which at the time were regarded as wholly orthodox. But the atmosphere has changed in the forty years since Pittenger wrote, and, given the range and variety of alternative christologies, some of which were included in what Mascall was calling 'New Christologies', Chalcedon in the quint-essentially distilled form referred to might appear unduly general, generous and all-embracing.

Accordingly, I am persuaded that more is required for normative purposes than the rather minimal Richardson/ Pittenger combination; and I would like to extend it in two respects. First, I think it necessary to affirm the unity of the person of Jesus Christ as a divine–human unity, as I have recently maintained. The almost unanimous claim made by most christologists since the days of nineteenth- and early twentieth-century kenoticism, for the total integrity and completeness of the humanity of Christ, entails the fused personhood of Jesus Christ. The adoption of the enhypostatic position in any of its forms is exposed to the criticism of endangering that integrity and completeness. So let us see how this norm would work if applied to two examples, the first being the strange statement recorded from Mascall (*Whatever Happened to the Human Mind?*, pp. 33ff) that it was God that was born in Bethlehem and not the God–man as a baby. The other example of how we might apply the norm is the account of the identity of the person of Jesus Christ given by Daniel Helminiak (*The Same Jesus: A Contemporary Christology*, p. 292, discussed by Gerald O'Collins, *Christology*, p. 245, and further examined above – pp. 299ff. Here the interest is in whether Helminiak's christology is tenable in the light of Chalcedon). Helminiak is seeking to refute the claim that Jesus Christ is not fully human because (on the anhypostatic position) he lacks a human person, by arguing that it is by possession of a human nature that someone is human. *That*, says Helminiak, Jesus has completely. But surely, what his opponents are saying is that someone who has a human nature is a human person. He further claims that to argue the lack of full humanity in Christ from his non-possession of a human *hypostasis* is to fail to realise that a *hypostasis* is something one 'is', not something one 'has'. Again there is misunderstanding: agreed, *hypostasis* is something that one 'is', rather than 'has'; but what Helminiak's opponents are saying is that a person who has a human nature and a divine nature *is* a human–divine person. To rephrase his own words: if Jesus Christ has all the qualities of the divine nature and all the qualities that constitute a human nature, then the *hypostasis*, the person who is Jesus Christ, is both human and divine. In a word, Helminiak's position is such a reduction of Chalcedon that the question has to be asked whether or not it is genuinely valid.

The second extension that I would like to make to the rather minimalist Richardson/Pittenger extraction of the essence of Chalcedon is to reinstate the 'four adverbs', which state, with a comprehensive covering of the field of logical possibilities, the negative ways in which the relationship of the two natures of Jesus Christ to each other are to be regarded. The four adverbs are: *asugchutos* (ἀσυγχύτως), without confusion, or mingling together; *atreptos* (ἀτρέπτως), without changing into one another; *adiairetos* (ἀδιαιρέτως), without being divided; and *achoristos* (ἀχωρίστως), without separation. By retaining the four adverbs, whose significance is not ossified through any relation to a metaphysical system, because they are intelligible in ordinary terms, we shall ensure the integrity of the two natures together with their indissoluble relatedness to one another. These requirements are as necessary today as they were in 451; for example, we have noticed a danger for some process theologians of confusing the upthrust of perfect humanity with the downward transcendence of divinity, as if they were no more than two sides of the same action; or, nearer home, some christologists are in danger of treating the difference between humanity and divinity as one of degree rather than one of kind. On the other hand, some christologies of the revelation model may drift in the other direction and present the picture of Jesus Christ in strictly human terms, arguing that that person is the medium of divine revelation, with the result that humanity and divinity are dangerously divided. We saw, too, how strenuously Pittenger had to argue to fend off the criticism of Nestorianism, but it is always an open risk for any christology which makes much of the humanity of Christ, as so many have done of late, and does not have a strong argument in defence of the fused person of Jesus Christ.

NON-PRESCRIPTIVE

Application of the concept of 'norm' to a creed must immediately convey the impression that its function is to exercise control, limit extravagant constructions, and suppress originality. To deny that there is an element of control in the concept would be dishonest, if not also self-defeating. Therefore it is immediately necessary to press on to our second characterisation, namely, that in being normative Chalcedon is *not* also being *prescriptive*. A prescriptive creed would outlaw ('anathematise' is the ugly word that would be used) all variants of the canonical terminology and cultural changes intended to clarify meanings. Such possibilities are not unheard of, for there are denominations of the Christian Church which have adopted such a prescriptive and literalistic view of their creeds and confessions. Whether such a view is altogether tenable without some degree of self-contradiction is a thought to be mentioned but not at this point to be pursued. What is perhaps an apocryphal reflection attributed to Dean Inge, the 'Gloomy Dean' of the earlier part of this century, is pertinent here as a comment on the notion of non-prescription. He said that as a young man he protested against what he considered the narrowly confining character of the Christian creeds, inhibiting all independent thought. As an older man, he continued, he had come to regard these creeds as rather more like an umbrella under which a whole wide-ranging variety of thought might be accommodated. It is a similar point that I am making: because it is normative in character, Chalcedon does not *eo ipso* exercise prescriptive rights over changes of expression and cultural style. This is also a judgement that emerges, not a priori, but very much a posteriori, consequent upon the protracted study of several christologists. It can be illustrated from a series of instances.

A case that springs immediately to mind is that of the Aristotelian metaphysics in which Chalcedon has been thought to be embedded. Several positions are here determinable, all of them, I would say, beneath the one umbrella. Despite Mascall's dissociation of Chalcedon from what he calls 'a fifth-century Greek philosophy' (*Whatever Happened to the Human Mind?*, p. 29), it is still arguable that Chalcedon is most readily understood when its principal terms, for example, the connection between *physis* and *hypostasis*, are related to Aristotle. A second position would be that of Mascall, just mentioned: that terms which have been considered philosophical turn out to be essentially Christian in content and remarkably free of philosophical technicality. Certainly, Mascall would consider himself well within Chalcedon with such views. A third position appears when theologians who do not share Mascall's view of the role – or rather the non-role – of Greek philosophy propose to introduce into christology an alternative metaphysic in the form of process of the Whitehead, Hartshorne or Teilhard variety. They might resent being categorised with Chalcedon, but that would most probably be due to their assumption that Chalcedon was prescriptive and not inclusive in the sense presently argued or permitted by Mascall's view of the metaphysics involved (or rather, not involved) in Chalcedon. What might be regarded as a fourth category, although those appearing in it would also be included in one of the others, would be those christologies which introduce non-Chalcedonian terms, such as 'perspective' (Macquarrie) or 'presence' (O'Collins), to help a modern reader understand the Chalcedonian verbiage. The fact that these different approaches to the philosophical component in Chalcedon can all be justifiably thought by their proponents to fall within the aegis of the creed is witness to the claim I have been making for the non-prescriptive character of Chalcedon.

Another of the elements in the Chalcedonian formula which has been paid very great attention across the centuries is the term *hypostasis/prosopon*, *persona*, person. It had a very shaky beginning in both its bilingual contexts. Because *hypostasis* is etymologically very close kin to *ousia*, it was long understood as equivalent to what we would name as 'substance'. *Prosopon* and *persona*, with overtones of their original meaning as a 'mask', suffered guilt by association through appearing in Sabellian writers. With Chalcedon there came a stabilising of connotation, while Boethius half a century after Chalcedon impressed upon the Latin mind then and for centuries thereafter the definition of *persona* as 'an individual substance of a rational nature'. But it was in the twentieth century particularly, with the rapid development of psychology, that changes came in the understanding of the nature of personhood. Added to that, there emerged several philosophies of the 'person' which had considerable consequences for both theology and christology. In theology the doctrine of the Trinity came to have new interpretations in line with the new awareness of the human person, which, helped by the doctrine of analogy, produced what came to be called the 'social doctrine of the Trinity'. In christology, on the other hand, it was the human nature of Jesus Christ which received fresh interpretation, which emphasised, as we ourselves have seen, the completeness of his humanity over against what had been considered the impersonal nature of Christ's humanity. That fuller and completer view of Christ's human nature seems to be almost generally accepted in today's christology. Once again we have an instance of the way in which, across the centuries, Chalcedon has been able to accommodate within its breadth a wealth of interpretations of one of its central affirmations.

Would the same affirmation be applicable to the four adverbs which we have earlier included within the normative core of Chalcedon? At a first glance it would seem that, by their negative quality and their overtones of 'thou shalt not', they are by definition prescriptive. They certainly seem to have been so originally, for the history of the run-up to Chalcedon yields identifiable christological positions which are effectively ruled out, proscribed, by the adverbs. But as we have already discovered, the adverbs, while forbidding this and that, do not specify what may be positively said; christologists have stepped in all along the way to supply such positives to replace the negatives of Chalcedon. How, then, is this original intention to be prescriptive to be reconciled with the actual history of the way christology has treated the adverbs? At the risk of repetition we may find the answer in H. R. Mackintosh's comment on Chalcedon – and he was quoting an unnamed source – that 'the decisions of Chalcedon ... have been well compared to buoys anchored along a dangerous estuary, on the right and left, to guide the ship of truth' (*The Person of Jesus Christ*, p. 213). The comparison is especially apt when applied to the four adverbs, differentiating, as Barth said in a different connection, between 'what must be said under all circumstances and what may be said under none'.

THEOLOGICALLY DEFINITIVE

It would be a commonplace to repeat that it was the event of Jesus Christ which created the Christian understanding of God, especially after St John (3.16) had expressed it with such perception and compactness: 'For God so loved the world that he gave his only begotten Son, that whosoever believeth in him shall not perish but have everlasting life.' As it was in the beginning, so it was in the event: the doctrine of God and the doctrine of Jesus Christ were mutually influential both in the first three formative centuries and equally thereafter in the years and centuries of theological and christological definition. For example, while the Chalcedonian Creed was cradled in the Nicaeo-Constantinopolitan Creed, some of its great affirmations having already been secured there, nevertheless the former not only expanded the understanding of the whole person of Jesus Christ, but also interactively greatly deepened the awareness of the character and the reality of God. It could be said that the Nicaeo-Constantinopolitan Creed secured the Church's commitment to the deity of Christ and his humanity (in fact with a sense of the historical reality of the incarnation which is lacking in the later creed), while within that hard-won context, Chalcedon portrayed the way and the terms in which God effected the incarnation. The case could be pursued further to take in the way in which reflection on the incarnation led to ever continuing definition of the doctrine of the Trinity, throwing light upon the doctrine of creation and the doctrine of the Holy Spirit. Just because of the dominant role of the Chalcedonian formula across the centuries, it tended to impose its form upon the structure of these doctrines. For example, christology centring on the 'cosmic Christ' introduced otherwise ignored facets of creation, while the part played by the Spirit in the work of redemption, in earthing and effecting the work of Christ in the hearts and lives of men and women, became a main element in the doctrine of the Spirit. We have just seen how, in modern times, the profound understanding of human nature and of person and personality, enhanced by its incorporation in christology, has had profound implications for the interpretation of the doctrine of the Trinity. But it was, I would claim, because of the unique character and structure of the Chalcedonian christology employed in each of these cases that these influences were achieved.

CHALCEDON AND THE CHURCH

Such has been the general influence of Chalcedon upon theological definition. There have been instances of a more specific kind in recent times, which have been of considerable importance for contemporary theological debate. I shall consider certain areas in which the application of the Chalcedonian model has been particularly illuminating. The first of these is the Church. Let us begin with Paul's statement to the Corinthians (1 Cor 12.29), 'Ye are the body of Christ', which has in the history of theology been taken as a statement about the Church, even about the nature of the Church. I do not find it particularly helpful to take this Pauline statement literally. Confusion would arise between the body which is the Church and the incarnate body of Christ, and problems about the relation of the two. On the other hand, if we considered that Christ's original body was replaced by this body which is the Church, we might be tempted to think of the Church as the extension of the incarnation. In fact we would be wrong, for the incarnation involves a whole human nature and not only a human body. Since, however, we have here an instance of the compresence of Christ and humanity in a single reality, even though in this case the humanity is a vast group of human beings, it may be possible to apply the Chalcedonian model. If we do, then reminders are due. The first is that we are dealing with an analogy, a modular analogy; and the second, that certain of the elements in the original remain obligatory even in the *analogatum*.

In the divine–human reality which is the Church, we are confronted at once with the fact that the humanity in this case is sinful and sinning humanity, whereas the humanity of Christ was, and is, not sinning. Now it may be recalled that, for example, both Barth and before him Edward Irving held the view that it was *fallen* human nature that the Word assumed, but neither of them went so far as to say that in his human nature Jesus Christ ever actually sinned. What we can say, however, is that the human component in the Church is not only *peccator*, but, through the merciful redemption of God wrought through Jesus Christ, is also *iustus*. The Church will always be a mixture of both until the end of time – a point which we shall need to remember as the discussion proceeds. Next, coming to the question of the divine component in the divine–human reality which is the Church, I find a certain difficulty, which has not been solved for me in the studies of the subject. It is the matter of who this divine component is. The position which I am inclined to support is that the divine component is Jesus Christ the incarnate Lord, and that the humanity which is the human members of the Church is related to Christ analogically to the relationship of human nature to the Word in the original Chalcedonian model. That is, the community which is the human side of the Church is 'enhypostatised' in the person of Jesus Christ. It does not find its unity in some social cohesion or ideological commitment, but in its rootedness in the person of Christ. It is at this point that the Chalcedonian adverbs become importantly relevant. For, on the one hand, the adverbs *asygchutos* and *atreptos*, warn us to avoid that fusion or confusion of the humanity of the Church with the very being of Jesus Christ, lest that sinful humanity be transformed into his perfection. In a word, if we wish to call the Church the *ecclesia una, sancta atque apostolica*, we have to remind ourselves that we speak of the Church as it shall be in God's good time; at present, in view of the human elements within it, it is still fragmented, less than perfect and all too often unfaithful to the apostolic tradition entrusted to it. Yet because of the union with Christ *kath hypostasin*, such a judgement on the Church cannot be pessimistic and certainly not final, for in that union lies the redemption promised and fulfilled in Jesus Christ. On the other hand, we dare not fall foul of the other adverbs – *adiairetos* and *achoristos* – which warn us against separating the human and the divine in the Church so that the Church reverts to being thought of as a social gathering, entirely human in origin and nature and doomed to perpetuate its failings to the end of time.

CHALCEDON AND THE BIBLE

The second area of theology outside christology in which the influence of Chalcedon may be illuminative is the Bible. It has always been agreed that there is a human element as well as a divine element in the Scriptures, but how these two are related has been a subject of discussion and very often of controversy, never more so than throughout the world today. For my own part I have found the Chalcedonian adverbs, which we have just been discussing in relation to the Church, to be instructive also in this connection. Once again the two extremes are ruled out. With *asugchutos* and *atreptos* we are warned against regarding the human writings of the Scriptures as identical ('fused', 'confused') with, or transformed into, the actual words of God. This position may be variously described as the dictation of the Scriptures by God, or as the inspiration of the Scripture-writers in such a way that they committed no errors, an assertion that is called in question by what are said to be errors, contradictions, inadequate moral views, male chauvinism and dominance, misrepresentations of God's character – the evidences of human involvement. The warning against a monophysite view of the Scriptures would therefore be well taken. The other two adverbs – *adairetos* and *achoristos* – give an opposite signal, because they rule out any attempt to regard the human and the divine elements in the Scriptures as wholly separate ('divided' and 'isolated') from one another. The Scriptures are unthinkable if they are regarded as the religious intuitions of their authors, or as the heavenly aspirations of humankind; while if God is considered not to have spoken or revealed himself through the Scriptures, then it is inconceivable where else he has done so. Yet provided we keep to the channel marked by the two pairs of buoys which are the Chalcedonian adverbs, no attempt is made to chart a single specific course. But a further step remains if we are to follow the Chalcedonian model; this involves departing from Mackintosh's metaphor of the buoys, in order to show how these two 'natures' in the Bible are to be considered one. The answer is, as in Chalcedon, *henosis kath hypostasin*, unity as regards *hypostasis*, a *hypostasis* which incorporates both the divine and the human. The presence of the divine justifies the description of the Bible as the Word of God, and the presence of the human writers secures that this Word is heard in human accents, even if at times they falter.

CHALCEDON AND THE
SACRAMENT OF THE LORD'S SUPPER

The presence of the creaturely – the bread and the wine – along with the Lord Jesus Christ in this sacrament has been central to Christian theology throughout its whole existence, and we are enquiring whether the Chalcedonian model still has any light to throw upon the subject – despite the fact that in this case the human element will be replaced by the creatures of bread and wine. At a first approach, it would seem that the four adverbs play the same significant part in this area that they did in the previous examination of the Bible and Chalcedon. They issue a clear warning about fusing and confusing the Divine and the creaturely, and about transforming the latter into the former. To ignore this warning would eventually lead to imbuing the creaturely with the attributes of the divine, Jesus Christ. It would also draw close, if by another way, to the Roman Catholic doctrine of transubstantiation, and would certainly entail a process of *communicatio idiomatum*. The adverbs that reject complete separation and division of the Divine from the creaturely seem explicitly to ban the views of this sacrament which separate the bread and wine from Jesus Christ, and allow the connection to be only one of remembering an event in the past, the death of Christ, by re-enacting a token of it here and now. I would also support the suggestion made in relation to the Bible, which accepts as applicable the interpretation of Chalcedon (as in Ephraim of Antioch) which allows the *hypostaseis* of both natures to be conjoined. In this way, while the bread and wine would physically remain bread and wine, yet because of their special union *kath hypostasin*, when received they would in faith be to communicants the very body and blood of Jesus Christ, or in liturgical terms, 'we receiving them, may, by faith, be made partakers of his body and blood, and all his benefits'.

CHALCEDON: WORSHIP, LITURGY AND DEVOTION

It would be extremely surprising if Chalcedon had achieved its accepted place within the *theoria*, the theology of the Church, the Bible and the sacrament of the Lord's Supper, without at the same time coming to hold an equally central place in the *praxis*, the worship, liturgy, prayer, Bible reading and devotion of the Church and its members. Perhaps even that is the reverse of what actually happened, and the survival of Chalcedon in the theology of the Church was due to the pivotal place which it sustained for many centuries in these other areas of the life of the worshipping and devotional Church. Let us now consider some of these areas.

The relation of doctrine to Scripture has been a focal topic of theological inquiry from the earliest days of the Christian Church, one to which a satisfactory answer has perhaps never been given, despite the vast studies in hermeneutics in this century. At its simplest it is the question of the nature of the process of interpretation which leads from the biblical statement in Jn 10.30 that 'I and my Father are one' to the trinitarian account of the relationship of Father and Son within the Trinity, using the classical terms; or from Jn 1.1 and 14, that 'the Word was with God and the Word was God' and that 'the Word was made flesh, and dwelt among us', to the statements of the divine and human natures of Jesus Christ and their unity in his person. It is not a transition which has the character of a logical inference. Nor is it altogether satisfactory to argue that the theological statements are themselves also the result of divine revelation on a footing with the Scriptures themselves, for it would be very hard to substantiate the claim that the very heterogeneous contents of what the Church has called 'tradition' share the same qualities and characteristics as Scripture. For my own part, I have been moved to describe the interpretative process we are considering as one of imaginative intuition controlled by the Holy Spirit. I would be the first to acknowledge that I may have resolved one problem at the price of introducing at least two others. But as I have argued elsewhere (*Faith, Theology and Imagination*, Handsel

Press, Edinburgh, 1987), imagination is endemic to theological activity, and when its creativity is absent, theology may degenerate into the aridity for which it sometimes earns itself a bad name. But such imagination is itself neither fantasy nor self-delusion, but is both inspired and harnessed by the Holy Spirit who is the Spirit of the Son and the fulfiller of his work. How that should take place cannot be spelt out step by step, but to speak of it in these terms, even with that degree of agnosticism, is to set the theological interpretative process within a more appropriate setting than analogies drawn from social, economic or even political models.

But the ultimate justification for the account given of biblical interpretation will not be its theological standing in creeds or tradition, or the case of Chalcedon which we are considering, so much as its efficacy in throwing light upon the Scriptures for those for whom the reading of them is the very substance of their spiritual life. The basic elements of Chalcedon – the human nature and the divine nature of Jesus Christ, held together in the unity of his person – provided the schema, the framework within which to deploy an understanding of the theme of the Word made flesh. The whole human story, of the child born in the manger, the boy in the Temple, the Teacher among the people, the healer of broken bodies and spirits, the accused and condemned reject being led to Calvary and crucifixion, was woven into the unity of the person who was himself the Word, sent by the Father, endorsed by his Father, himself forgiving as only God can, himself bearing in that human body the sins of the whole world, the single person both human and divine being raised by the power of Spirit to live for evermore. So the human story was never simply the story of the man who was called Jesus, though it was that; it was also and ever the story of the presence in that human being of the eternal Word, the Son of the Father. Into that framework were both placed and worked the many ways in which our human nature was shaped and behaved when it was the human nature of Jesus Christ; while the divine nature was spoken of and understood as bearing our transgressions and sharing the brokenness of our human existence. The synopsis of the incarnation provided by Chalcedon has for centuries proved to be the substance of Christian devotion, dedication and commitment.

What has been said of biblical understanding and devotion is true by extension of the Christian liturgy. The very core of that liturgy – the Eucharist – is the Chalcedonian affirmation of the incarnation, around which is built the whole progression from the Offertory Prayer, the Prayer of the Veil and the Great Anaphora to the Communion itself and the final Thanksgiving. By implication, as these components of the Eucharist are replicated in the daily and weekly liturgy, so Chalcedon carries its form through the continuing prayer, praise and worship of the Church. Nowhere is this fact more demonstrable than in the *Private Devotions* of Bishop Lancelot Andrewes (Alexander Whyte, *Bishop Lancelot Andrewes and His Private Devotions*, Oliphant Anderson and Ferrier, Edinburgh, 1896). As Dr Whyte shows in his Introduction to the *Devotions*, Bishop Andrewes structures prayers of adoration, confession, thanksgiving and intercession, expressed in carefully selected sentences and passages from Scripture, around the central schema of the incarnation as expressed in the essentials of Chalcedon.

CHALCEDON AND TRADITION

Now that the term 'pluralism' has found its way from religious studies and sociology into theology, a new regime seems to have begun in the latter discipline. Alternative styles of theological definition, with a great variety of contexts and contacts, have emerged; each is regarded as being just as valid as the others. The essence of pluralism is to be non-judgemental, but the price could be too high. It is a sad sequel, in a way, to the decades which followed A. J. Ayer's *Language, Truth and Logic* in 1933, when some critics accused theology of going on a linguistic trip. Maybe to a degree the criticism was fair, and the monumental effort of those decades has now lost all impetus. But we dare not deceive ourselves into thinking that it was all wasted effort, for the inspiration of those decades was to affirm and to demonstrate the *truth-claims* of religious and theological statements. The non-judgemental tolerance of pluralism is in danger now of undoing the achievements of these years, and forms of theism are replacing the structures of traditional theology. For my own part, I have no quarrel with theism; I was reared on it, especially in its heyday. A. E. Taylor's *The Faith of a Moralist* (Macmillan, London, 1937) and the earlier *The Idea of God* by A. S. Pringle-Pattison (Oxford University Press, London, 1917), were but two in that first third of the century who propounded a strongly Christian theism which was not dogmatic.

If, however, the threat to the truth-claims of the Christian religion and theology represented by pluralism is to be best met, it will be by full acknowledgement of the central components of that faith. These, I would say, consist of the Trinity and its inclusion of creation, incarnation and redemption, and sanctification. But the key to that construction is the person and the work of Jesus Christ, with its implications for the nature and intent of creation and the person and work of the Spirit. It is at this point, I believe, that the claims of Chalcedon are most worthy of consideration, for they have been shown *both* to be regulative of the thought of the christologists we have considered, even when they have on occasion attempted to translate it into other concepts and metaphysics, *and* to be a bench-mark for the assessment of the alternatives suggested to it. In serving these purposes and doing so, as we have seen, across many centuries, Chalcedon has shown itself to be the core of the Christian tradition. The times, they say, they are a-changing, and with them many of what were once thought to be structural parts of the edifice of faith are not so much crumbling away as being actively dismantled. Accordingly it is all the more important to identify and commit ourselves and our christology, as well as our theology, to that statement of the person of Christ which has been the major force in sustaining the integrity of the Christian faith.

CHALCEDON AND APOLOGETICS

As has been mentioned, pluralism found its way into theology on a second wave, after it had established itself in religious studies. It arrived there many years after Christian workers in the mission field and the discipline of religious studies had been affirming that uniqueness of moral perfection, absolute truth and the only medium of salvation were to be found in Jesus Christ, offered solely in the Christian Gospel and expressed supremely in the Bible and Christian theology and christology. The converse was the condemnation and rejection of other faiths and, at times, even the proclamation of the damnation of their many practitioners. What cracked the hard shell of such prejudice was the emergence, as has been said, of the phenomenon of pluralism. The reasons for this emergence are manifold. For example, since the end of World War II, two to three million members of other faiths have arrived in the United Kingdom; daily social encounters with them diminish condemnatory assessment of their religions. It has been said that if Karl Barth had lived for some time in Japan, meeting daily some of the thirteen million inhabitants of Tokyo, he would not perhaps have been as uncompromising as he was, particularly at one stage of his career, towards people of other faiths. By contrast, Brunner, who taught for a period in Japan, was much less unyielding in his theological judgements on non-Christians. The increasing secularisation of Western society in the last half-century, coupled with the alleged reduction of the influence of the churches upon society, has contributed to the increase of liberal tolerance towards others of different allegiances. Mention of tolerance takes us to zero tolerance of any injustice – physical, verbal, attitudinal, racial, ethnic, gender or sexual – to minority groups and, in our case, religious minorities. In such a society, with so many forces for liberalism and tolerance at work, it is understandable that different faiths and alien communities cannot come under one single monolithic structure, but achieve cohabitation only through mutual acknowledgement of beliefs and practices. The term 'pluralism' sums up its entire ethos.

But a contraflow has begun to operate in this otherwise harmonious scene. Instead of creating a series of syncretisms, as one might have imagined, the close proximity to one another of the components of the plurality has tended to sharpen and acutely define the differences. Suddenly, both in Britain and throughout the globe, especially in the last two decades and across widely differing faiths, the phenomenon of fundamentalism has emerged. It evinces characteristics common to most of the brands: literalist commitment to an infallible literature, both intellectually to doctrinal content and morally to an inflexible code of behaviour and attitude; severe judgementalism towards co-religionists who do not share the commitment; on occasion willingness to take violent action, either mental or physical, towards them or adherents of other faiths; and a level of self-righteousness which cannot countenance the possibility of being wrong. Fundamentalism exists abrasively alongside the pluralism already mentioned, and such co-existence appears to fuel and excite them both, sometimes to cruel, offensive and unforgiving excess.

What roles can Chalcedon play in such a distressed situation? Several, I would reckon. First, in a time notable for the proximity of faiths to one another and increased movement towards religious definition, Chalcedon has a central part to play in the formulating of a Christian position. We have already mentioned the ways in which Chalcedon constitutes a firm centre from which the other principal elements in the faith can be extended. When these are fitted together, with Chalcedon and all that it stands for as the head corner-stone, the faith which it enshrines is not likely to be drowned out by strident contemporary noises or muffled sounds from alternative 'new' christologies. For I have to confess that no statement of the centre-piece of Christian belief has been brought forward which will yield the dogmatic definition which contemporary apologetic needs, in any way as comprehensively and convincingly as Chalcedon has been shown to do. Secondly, in the religiously and socially pluralistic contemporary situation, this very pluralism can be shown to be shot through with a great deal of ill-concealed exclusivism.

Christianity is not alone in proclaiming, 'There is no other name under heaven whereby we must be saved.' But, thirdly, with the message of salvation and reconciliation at its heart, Chalcedon has ways of meeting such exclusivism. For example, it might speak of a universal exclusivism, if such an oxymoron may be allowed, which is based on the fact that the purpose of the incarnation was 'for our salvation' and that consequently the offer was open to all. Again, it might concentrate upon the humanity of Christ and affirm, with what Robert Bruce, according to Bishop Lancelot Andrewes, once called 'the Orient Kirks', that all mankind is included in the humanity of Jesus Christ, and that what he took he redeemed. Some supporters of Chalcedon have adopted another tack and spoken of 'anonymous Christians' who are known by other names and yet appear to show forth the spirit of Christ. When, however, such inclusivist moves prove unacceptable to the practitioners of other faiths, as understandably they often do, there remains at the heart of the faith the reconciling love which was the essence and prime motivation of Jesus Christ. That still obtains, all the more so when the bonds of religion are replaced by barriers of mistrust and rejection.

CHALCEDON – STILL A LIVE OPTION?

Martha Kneale summarises one of the chief problems in Aristotelian interpretation when she asks (William and Martha Kneale, *The Development of Logic*, Oxford University Press, Oxford, 1964, p. 26) concerning Aristotle's distinction between primary substance and secondary substance: 'Is Aristotle here classifying linguistic expressions or what they symbolise?' She gives as her own answer: 'Aristotle would certainly have answered that he was dealing with things and not with words . . . He uses the differences between rules for different linguistic expressions as a clue to the differences between types of being.' It would seem to be possible, therefore, to take up a position midway between two extremes. Extreme one would be the view that

Aristotle simply elevated a linguistic device into a rigid logical structure, and that it is possible for us now to retain the linguistic analysis and reject the ontological structure altogether. In that case we would be trying to reduce ontological or metaphysical questions to purely linguistic questions. In that connection it has been a matter of interest to me that the linguistic concerns which dominated much British theology in the wake of A. J Ayer's *Language, Truth and Logic*, already referred to, were not nearly so evident in christology as they certainly were in general theology and epistemology. Extreme two would be to maintain an absolute correlation between sentence structure and the structure of reality, in which case we would be approaching very close to the idea that language presents pictorial representations of reality. As I have said we are endeavouring here to adopt a mediating position – in fact echoing the view we argued somewhat earlier in relation to the ontological status of models. The subject–predicate form, closely allied as it is with the primary substance/secondary substance ontological distinction, may not stand in a relation of one-to-one correspondence to the latter, but it is nevertheless rightly understood as one of the ways in which we may legitimately speak about reality. I would not press for all the detail of Aristotelian metaphysics, but unless our language is completely misleading we may fairly say that we expect reality to be not unlike how we describe it.

This short apologia for Aristotelianism is not altogether so heroic or irrelevant as may at first appear. For as we have seen, there has been a strong current of thinking in modern christology against the involvement of Chalcedon with Aristotelianism in general and, with the support of divers philosophers from several centuries, against the doctrine of substance in particular. This current has been so strong at times that those affected by it have in the end abandoned Chalcedon completely. In parenthesis here I would note with a certain ironic interest that some conservative theologians would be extremely critical of the Aristotelianism involved in the Roman Catholic doctrine of the sacraments, with its theory of transubstantiation, while at the same time embodying that same metaphysic in their own christology. Nor should we assume unthinkingly that christology has turned its back totally on the Chalcedonian Definition. Indeed, I would venture that it remains the staple diet in christology courses in all mainline seminaries of whatever denomination; that it is rarely eclipsed by any of the alternative 'New Christologies', which in any case require a knowledge of Chalcedon as that from which they are deviating; and that because of its involvement in Scripture, sacrament, liturgy and devotion, it tends to be the system which remains uppermost in the minds of students, and therefore is that which they most consciously take away with them.

In conclusion, however, I would like to illustrate from our previous discussions the thesis that although Chalcedon in its variant interpretations, particularly in the fifth and sixth centuries, drew heavily upon the reserves of Aristotelian logic and metaphysics, we may still use it without any similarly deep commitment to its origins. We have already examined the first example to come to mind, but it has to be related to our present purpose. E. L. Mascall, it will be recalled, not only rejects any great involvement of Chalcedon with a Greek philosophy, but adds that those words which have a long philosophical history have quite ordinary, everyday usage and can be taken in that sense in christology. When that happens, the christological concepts are in no way dominated by any philosophical usage, but themselves tend to adapt it to the christological intention. Now I would be a little reluctant myself to cut Chalcedon's connection with the original philosophical ambience as radically as Mascall does – and I think that in fact he himself is not as extreme as he seems to suggest. Still, the image which Mascall draws of the autonomy of the central christological concepts strongly suggests that it still has what he called a 'fertile and flexible' future away from the philosophy of its sources. In fact, Mascall states in general what we shall now turn to in the particular.

The second example of the fertility and flexibility of Chalcedon we have discovered for ourselves in the way in which those who chose to substitute a process metaphysics for Aristotelianism

nevertheless employed the Chalcedonian schema of the two
natures (one fully human, the other fully divine), together with
the emphasis upon their unity in the one person, Jesus Christ.
Even when they described the divine nature of Jesus Christ in
terms of a new understanding of his being, away from static
and towards dynamic concepts, and the human nature in un-
biblically-sounding notions such as openness and transcendence, they nevertheless tended to home back eventually to talk
that was conformable to Chalcedon, and to proving that their
theories did not do violence to Chalcedon. Even when some
process concepts, as distinct from the central process ontology,
had entered into the christology of such theologians as Gerald
O'Collins and John Macquarrie, both committed to forms of
Chalcedon, they still had no doubt about their allegiance to
Chalcedon.

A third example of the continuing flexibility of Chalcedon
arises out of the question of how compatible logic and
psychology are in the interpretation of its structure and content.
The problem has a case-history almost of its own. For example,
in the present century H. R. Mackintosh's criticism that
Chalcedon affirms the human nature of Jesus Christ as being
'impersonal' sparked off a long line of christologists who in
protest insisted that his human nature was completely human.
It, too, had a *hypostasis*, which came to be translated as 'ego',
'centre of consciousness', the 'I' and even 'person' – all psychological terms. This psychologising tendency, if I may so call it,
was reinforced by the flourishing personal philosophy associated,
as we have mentioned before, with the names of Martin Buber
and John Macmurray, and with Brown in America. Then we
heard a great deal about 'the fully human person', Jesus Christ.
This insistence became at times so strong that the christologists
affected by it began to modify the divine nature of Jesus Christ,
the so-called kenoticists being classically very outspoken on this
subject. Even the term *ousia*, 'substance', did not escape this
tendency, and came to be translated as 'being', to bring it, in line
as it were, with the mood of the times. We have already traversed
the ground of the logic/psychology controversy, and I closed

by entering a plea (above, p. 143) for the extension of the psychological model. What has become clear is that the psychological model seems to have established itself, certainly in relation to the human nature of Jesus Christ and apparently without giving logical offence. If there had ever been any doubt on this score, the fact that E. L. Mascall, with all his known commitment to Chalcedon, could seriously entertain the question, *Whatever Happened to the Human Mind?*, and, what is more, attempt to answer it, instates the psychological element as a valid component of the Chalcedonian hermeneutic.

Consideration of a fourth example of the versatility of Chalcedon will take us back to Martha Kneale's contention (W. and M. Kneale, *The Development of Logic*, p. 26) that when discussing 'substance', Aristotle 'was dealing with things and not with words'. I wonder if the dichotomy which Kneale here poses is not an over-simplification of the issue. Is it not arguable that Aristotle is dealing with the words that we use to 'deal with', or rather talk about, things? Each seems to imply the other. We illustrated in the previous paragraph the range of translations given in a single language, English, to the key terms in the Chalcedonian model. Sometimes the 'things' described in any given christology have been characterised differently from their treatment in the original Chalcedon, and the 'words' have accordingly been adapted. But the Chalcedonian model has controlled the proliferation of the words and sentences in what they say about the person of Jesus Christ, the God–man, the incarnate Son of the Father.

This fact came home to me at two points. One was when, I think almost by a slip of the tongue, E. L. Mascall spoke about the person of Jesus Christ as the 'metaphysical subject' of the two natures. I would take the term 'subject' to have either a logical or a grammatical connotation, implying a specific relation either to the other elements in a logical proposition or in the other case to the parts of a sentence; and the term 'metaphysical' to denote that the subject in both cases referred to a genuinely existing entity (or 'thing' in Kneale's sense). Therefore Mascall's meaning was that the person of Jesus Christ is in reality the subject upon whom the two natures are predicated; and this predication is not merely either logical or grammatical, though it is so, but also states what is the case. I have already referred to the other circumstance which alerted me to the linguistic part which Chalcedon can play in the explicating of christology (see above, p. 104). If we allow that there is a correlation between the way we speak of them and the way things are, I have contended that the former is a clue to the latter just as much as the latter can be said to prescribe the former. So when we find that in our references to the person whom the Gospels are 'about' we speak of him as Jesus Christ or the God–man or even the Word incarnate, we can conclude that the person so spoken of is not only possessed of two natures but is in his own person both human and divine.

So, in conclusion, we must ask why it should be that Chalcedon has this chameleon-like quality of merging into the models with their varying concepts, structures and even methods, while still retaining a discernible presence. The answer follows from what has just been said in comment upon Martha Kneale on 'words and things', conjoined with what was said in response to Locke's rejection of 'depraved Aristotelianism' (see above, pp. 103ff). It seems as if there is an inescapable link between the way we speak of things and the way they exist. Therefore, though we develop metaphysical theories which reject Aristotelianism, there comes a point in their development when we find ourselves – perhaps even involuntarily – using the logical/grammatical structures initially so closely associated with it. That would in itself account for the normative and prescriptive role which it, almost hauntingly, continues to play in the other christologies which we have been considering. Whether we would expect to find this same influence which Chalcedon exerts upon Western christology if we embarked upon a Japanese christology, with a different metaphysic related to a different structure of concepts, syntax and logic, is quite another matter.

INDEX OF NAMES AND SUBJECTS

Abraham, 72f, 172
Acts, Declaratory, 66
Acts of the Apostles, 69
Adoration, 40
Adverbs, four Chalcedonian, 281, 315, 319
Agnosticism, 116
Alcoholics Anonymous, 131
Amos, 73
Analogy, 59ff
  human, 179
  application of, 180ff
Analysis, sociological, 39f
Anhypostasia, anhypostasis, 102, 269, 275, 277, 299
Anselm, 113, 199
Antioch, School of, 44, 91f
Apokalyptein, 153f
Apollinarianism, 97, 99ff
Apollinaris, 97f, 134, 136
Apprehension, 62f
Arians, 141
Aristotelianism, 169
Aristotle, 87ff, 96, 236, 301f, 317
  Categoriae, c.5, 87ff, 301f
Art, Byzantine, 197f
  Romanesque, 197f
Articles, Declaratory, 66
Articles, Thirty-nine, 68
Assumptions, 28f
Atonement, theories of, 168
Attitudes, 12ff, 25
Augustine, 235

Austen, Jane, 138
Australia, 13
Ayer, A. J., 27

Baillie, D. M., 122, 125–7, 134, 249f, 274
Baillie, John, 250, 269
Baptism, 117f
Barth, K., 20, 22, 31, 35, 74, 79, 99ff, 109–12, 145, 152, 158–62, 166, 170, 321
Barton, B., 45
Beauchamp, Sally, 296
Being Itself, 62
Berkeley, Bishop, 103
Bible, 36, 67
  unity of, 70
Biography, 119
Birch, C., 230
Birth, Virgin, 34
Black, Max, 50
Boethius, 318
Bornkamm, G., 45, 115f, 127–9, 236
Broad, C. D., 237
Brunner, E., 20, 49, 122f, 145, 156–8, 167, 168, 285
Buber, M., 24, 26, 132
Bulgakof, S., 126
Bultmann, R., 22, 35, 43, 106, 117ff, 123, 145, 236
Bush, burning, 146f

Calvin, J., 22

Calvinism, 152

Carrington, Archbishop, 42

Chalcedon, what of?, chap. 12 *passim*, 307–36
  contemporary roles
    normative, 312ff
    non-prescriptive, 316ff
    theologically definitive, 319
  relations to
    apologetics, 329ff
    Bible, 322
    Church, 32
    theology of the Lord's Supper, 324
    tradition, 327
    devotion, liturgy, worship, 325–7
    the case for, 313–36

Chalcedonian Definition, 194ff

Checks, dogmatic, 34ff

Christ *passim*
  and Logos, 201
  body of, 321
  dividing Christ, 198
  divinity of, 263ff
  encountering God in, 247ff
  here-and-now, 21f
  human and divine (Schleiermacher), 286ff
  humanisation of Christ-figure, 197
  his humanity as organon of divine self-expression, 242ff
  'in Christ' 204
  in western art, 196ff
  Jesus *passim*
  his knowledge of the divine subject, 303ff
  incarnation of the Logos, 202
  ontological unity of his person, 303ff
  sinlessness, 220
  unity of the person of, 252ff
  personhood, 295f
  pre-existence of, 294ff

  two minds, 296ff
  work of, 193

Christocentricism, 3–5

Christology *passim*

Church, 20, 39, 65
  Reformed, 22
  'closed circle', 195

Church of Scotland, General Assembly, 66
  Panel on Doctrine, 109

Cobb, John B. Jr, chap. 8 *passim*, 195–224
  and classical christology, 219ff

Coconstitution, 205

Collingwood, R. G., 24, 26f, 37

Commitment, 58f, 77

Compatibility, with Chalcedon (Macquarrie), 264–7

Conception, virginal, 24

Confession, Westminster, 5, 66
  Scots, 66

Conscientisation, 218

Consciousness, of Christ, 139–40

Covenant, 4

Creed, Apostles', 69
  Nicaeo-Constantinopolitan, 49

Creeds, 66

Criteria, models as, 74ff

Criticism, literary, 34f

Cuba, 29

Culture, western, 13

Cullmann, O., 35, 85

Cyprus, 29

Cyril of Alexandria, 95

Davenport, S. F., 246f

Davey, F. N., 86

David the Psalmist, 147

Davis, Stephen, 194

Degree-christology, 249

Dehn, G., 162f

Deification of humanity, inhumanisation of the Logos, complementary, 271

Description, 31, 58f
Devil, 141
Dibelius, M., 45
Disciples, contemporary, 203
Disclosure, 53ff
Divinity and humanity, unity of (Pittenger), 240
Docetism, 39, 101
Dorner, J. A., 134
Downing, F. Gerald, 145f, 152f, 163–7, 172
Dunkirk, 147

Ebeling, G., 22, 236
Efficacy, causal, 202
Ego, the Pure, 237
El Greco, 197
Elements essential to the christological enterprise, 228f
Emergence, 249
Enanthroposis, 263f
Enhypostasia, 96ff, 136–8, 246, 275
  Barth on, 99ff
  Cobb on, 220–3
  Pittenger on, 228–8
Ephraim of Antioch, 89, 101–3, 275
Epistemology, 10
  gap between human and divine mind, 296
  historical, 120–4
  religious, 119f
Ethics, 42ff, 77
Eutycheanism, 92ff, 141
Eutyches, 92ff
Evans, D. D., 164
Everest, 38
Evidence, 29f
Evolution, emergent, 230
Exegesis, typographical, 3, 74
Existentialism, 24, 39, 108, 120
Exodus, 74

Fairweather, A. A. M., 154–6, 161
Faith, 47, 80

Farmer, H. H., 148
Father, 41, 85, 94, 126, 152, 197, 203
Feminism, 211ff
Ferré, N., 249
Forsyth, P. T., 42, 133
Fosdick, H. E., 130
'From above and from below', 238ff, 260ff, 270ff
Frost, David, 36
Fuchs, E., 236
Fulfilment, 4

Geometry, Euclidean, 7
Gilkey, L., 178
Given, the, chap. 1 *passim*, 3–24
God, 20, 26, 30ff, 67
  abstract defining essence, 179, 186ff
  and his kingdom, 182f
  and man in Jesus Christ, 238
  attributes of, 31, 186
    relative and absolute, 274
  becoming, 231
  eternal reality, 230f
  image of, 111f, 235, 262, 287, 289
  'special acts', 181
  special presence in Jesus, 184ff, 192, 248
    and in the rest of creation, 248
  supreme act of self-expression, 183f, 190
  the love of 167, 186, 232
    and forgiveness, 194
Good Friday, 72
Gospel, 29, 39, 42, 46, 78
Graham, Dr Billy, 36
Gregory of Nazianzus, 99, 226f
Griffin, D. R., chap. 7 *passim*, 177–94
Guilt, 168

Harnack, A., 97, 226
Hartshorne, C., 177, 230, 269
Hastings, Battle of, 135, 275

Heidegger, J. H., 24, 99, 106
Heim, K., 132
Helminiak, D., 299ff, 314f
Hendry, G. S., 142
Hick, John, 195, 200
Hiddenness, 31, 162f
Hippolytus, 89
Historiography, 119ff
History, centre of, 3
Hodgson, L., 130, 138
Hollaz, D., 99
Holy Spirit, 5, 47, 78, 85, 128, 131,
    138, 145, 150–3, 157f, 191, 240,
    274
Hoskyns, E., 86
Humanity, five essential characteristics
    of, 286f
Hume, D., 103
    parallels with D. R. Griffin, 187ff
Hymnary, Revised Church, 61, 75
Hypostasis, chap. 4 passim, 83–114,
    276, 318
    mia 298, 302ff
    synthetos he, 275

Idiomata aphoristica, 96
Image of God, 109ff
    express, 239
Imagination, models and, 77–80
India, 166
Indifferentism, 200ff
Inge, W., 'the gloomy Dean', 316f
Inquisition, 80
Internalisation, 200ff
Irving, E., 321
Isaac, 172
Isaiah, 71, 73, 91
Isomorphism, 51, 75
I–Thou, 24, 112, 132

Jacob, 69
James, 73
John, 42, 54, 86, 278
Jones, Tom, 87

Kant, I., Second Critique, person as
    means to an end, 242
    First and Second Critiques, 304
Käsemann, E., 124f, 256
Kelvin, Lord, 31, 52
Keynes, J. M., 60
Kierkegaard, S., 35, 39, 43, 107, 119ff,
    203
Kneale, Walter and Martha, 87f, 331,
    335f

Lamont, D., 132
Land, Holy, 39
Langmead-Casserley, J. V., 38
Language-games, 27
Leo, Tome of, 89
Leontius of Byzantium, 96ff, 136, 224,
    246
Liberalism, 19
Lloyd-Morgan, Conwy, 230
Locke, J., 103, 188
Logic, 26f, 142
    Aristotelian, 26
    peculiar, 27f
Lord, incarnate, subject of, 252ff
Logos, 76, 95, 98, 134, 136, 201f, 218
    and primordial nature of God, 201
    and humanity of Christ, 208
Love, between Godhead and humanity
    in Jesus Christ, 256
Luke, 54f, 60, 85, 153
Luther, 22

Mackintosh, H. R., 92, 95, 133–5,
    138, 143, 162, 319
Macmurray, J., 132
Macquarrie, J., chap. 10 passim,
    259–82
Malraux, Andre, 196ff
Man-and-woman, 110–12
Marcion, 3
Mark, 42
Marsh, John, 69
Mary, 85, 140, 161, 234

Mascall, E. L., 30, 138–41
  and Chalcedon, 307–12, 314, 317, 333, 335
Matthew, 153
Maxentius, John, 89
Mediation, 37f
Mediterranean, 39
Messiah, 65, 71, 117, 123, 163, 234, 240
Metaphor, 52f, 56f,
Method, chap. 2 *passim*, 26–48
  geographical elements, 39
  historical, 35ff
  literary, textual, critical, 32ff
  liturgical, 40ff
  uniqueness, 32
Mind, human, of Jesus, 138ff
  self-constituting, 179
Models, chap. 3 *passim*, 49–80
  first and second order, 169f
  Ian T. Ramsey's views, 50ff
  normative role, 65ff
  psychological, chap. 5 *passim*, 115–44
  two-nature, chap. 4 *passim*, 83–114
  revelation, chap. 6 *passim*, 145–74
  unitive role, 70ff
Moltmann, J., 186
Moses, 73
Mystery, 51ff, 64
Myth, 118

Namatjira, Albert, 13f
Names, in Cobb, 212–17
  in Pittenger, 248
Nature, according to J.-P. Sartre, 112f
  according to K. Barth, 109f
  as the human situation, 112f
  fallen, 321
  human, 105–13
Nestorianism, 90ff
  in Pittenger?, 243
Nestorius, 90, 92, 161
Newton, John, 9, 75

Niebuhr, Reinhold, 132
Nineham, Dennis, 236

Obedience, 40, 77
O'Collins, Gerald, SJ, chap. 11
  passim, 283–306
Odium theologicum, 67f
Ogden, S., 189
Ontology, 179f, 260
  or psychology?, 364f
Orthodoxy, 15
Ousia, prote, 87–9, 98ff, 301
  deutera, 87–9, 98ff, 30

Parables, 76
Paul, 55, 73, 75
Pentz, Rebecca, 195
Performatives, 166f
Person, 229
  integrated or fused, of God–man, 275f
  one, 292ff, 302, 310–12
Persons-in-relation, 233
Personality, 124f
Perspectives, two natures as, 271–3
Peter, 73, 173
  confession of, 117f
Pharisees, 163
Philoxenus, 89
Photius of Tyre, 89, 101
Physis, chap. 4 *passim*, 83ff
  anhypostatos, 75ff, 89ff, 95ff, 136
Pittenger, W. N., chap. 12 *passim*, 225–55, 313
Plato, 46f, 88, 105
Plerosis, 134
Pluralisation, 200ff
Pneuma, 219
Polanus, A., 99
Preaching, expository, 129f
Pringle-Pattison, A. S., 328
Process christology, Part III *passim*, 175–255
Promise, 4

Prosopon, 93, 100
Protestantism, 72
  liberal, 125
Psalms, 153
Psyche, 115
Psychology, 31, 364ff

QED, 7
Qualities, secondary, 6

Rahner, K., 200
Ramsey, I. T., 30f, 50ff
Reformers, 16
Relton, H. M., 136–8, 141, 246
Rembrandt, 197
Revelation, 145–74
Richardson, Alan, 122, 313

Sartre, Jean-Paul, 105–8, 113
Scepticism, historical, 119–24, 171
Schizophrenia, 80
Sciences, natural, 38
Sea, the Red, 146f
Self, 132f
  human, and the Incarnate Logos,
    205
  according to Pittenger, 20
Self-consciousness, 13
Self-revelation, 18
Sellers, R. V., 44, 89ff, 96
Sex, 111f, 166
Siberia, 29
Smith, Norman Kemp, 8f, 11, 62f
Smuts, Jan, 230
Society, Aristotelian, 13, 142
Solipsism, 164
Son of Man, 76f, 81
Sophia, 218
Stebbing, S., 60, 105
Stewardship, 77
Stewart, J. S., 129
Subject-matter, 11f, 17, 25
Substance, doctrine of, 103–5
  primary, 86ff, 98, 301, 311
  secondary, 86ff, 98, 301, 311

Substantialism 189, 204, 220f,
  228ff
Symbebekota chorista, 96
  achorista, 96
Symbol, 149
Synthetos he hypostasis, 101f

Taylor, A. E., 328
Temple W., 134, 230, 308
Testimonium internum Spiritus Sancti,
  16, 65
Theodore of Mopsuesta, 44, 91
Theodoret, 91
Theology, 20, 27, 32, 36
  liberal, 126f
  natural and revealed, 169
  liberation, 209–11
Thomas, 84
Thomas Aquinas, 148f, 154
Thomasius, 134
Thornton, L. S., 66, 230
Tillich, P., 62, 64, 122
Timothy, Bishop of Alexandria, 89, 93
Titles, 49
Tradition, Chalcedon and, 327
  Synoptic, 124
Transcendence, dynamic, 262f
Transformation, creative, 196ff
Tribe, Arunta, 13
Trust, 40, 58
Typology, 70

Unity, 70ff

Verification, 29f
Vischer, W., 22

Wesley, C., 68
Whitehead, A. N., 24, 66, 177, 230
Wilson, Cook, 105, 279
Word, 20, 86,
  of God, 235, 289, 300
Worship, 40

Yahweh, 71